*American Places* calls for campuses to be designed, not only to heighten the quality of the learning experience, but also as working demonstrations of ways in which places everywhere can be transformed into more healthy, humane, civic environments.

For the college campus, "place" should mean much more than geography and physical setting. It represents the sum of the experiences, activities, events, and memories that occur within the campus boundaries. Today, American institutions of higher education are devoting renewed attention to the question of how the quality and character of place can support their goals. In doing so, campus communities are seeking to reclaim psychological ground that was lost in the decades after World War II, when the traditional virtues of campus coherence, human scale, and place distinction were overtaken by explosive growth in attendance and the growing prevalence of automobiles.

The quest to make better places of college campuses has a critical practical dimension, Chapman maintains: it bolsters student and faculty recruitment, and it improves donor support in an increasingly competitive environment. But behind the pragmatic concerns lies the recognition of place as the all-important

*(continued on back flap)*

# American Places

# American Places
*In Search of the Twenty-first Century Campus*

M. Perry Chapman
*Foreword by Richard Freeland*

AMERICAN COUNCIL ON EDUCATION
PRAEGER
Series on Higher Education

Library of Congress Cataloging-in-Publication Data

Chapman, M. Perry.
    American places : in search of the twenty-first century campus / M. Perry Chapman ; foreword by Richard Freeland.
        p. cm. — (ACE/Praeger series on higher education)
    Includes bibliographical references and index.
    ISBN 0–275–98523–7
    1. Campus planning—United States—Sociological aspects. 2. School sites—United States—Sociological aspects. 3. Universities and colleges—United States—Sociological aspects. I. Title. II. American Council on Education/Praeger series on higher education.
    LB3223.3.C53   2006
    378'.196--dc22        2005036538

British Library Cataloguing in Publication Data is available.

Library of Congress Catalog Card Number: 2005036538
ISBN: 0–275–98523–7

First published in 2006

Praeger Publishers, 88 Post Road West, Westport, CT 06881
An imprint of Greenwood Publishing Group, Inc.
www.praeger.com

Printed in the United States of America

The paper used in this book complies with the Permanent Paper Standard issued by the National Information Standards Organization (Z39.48–1984).

10  9  8  7  6  5  4  3  2  1

**Copyright Acknowledgments**

The author and publisher gratefully acknowledge permission for use of the following material:

Citing J.S. Daniel (1996), *Mega Universities and Knowledge Media: Technology Strategies for Higher Education.* London: Kogan Page.

Excerpts from Paul V. Turner, *Campus: An American Planning Tradition* (1987).

Dedicated to the memory of Roy Viklund, colleague and friend, whose architectural ideas have made livelier, more humane places out of many an American campus.

# Contents

*Foreword*

College and university campuses occupy a unique place in the history of American architecture. As Perry Chapman notes, at their best campuses express in physical form important aspects of institutional culture. They reflect, for example, a university's mission, history and traditions, and they evoke the kind of learning and character of scholarship an institution seeks to foster. Campuses also express a university's relationship to its surrounding community and to the world beyond. And, since campuses are growing, organic entities, they reflect changes over time in the ways that individual universities think about all these matters.

Traditional notions of campus design have evoked the monastic roots of universities as places apart from mainstream society. Academic architecture and space planning thus have typically defined sharp boundaries between the world of the campus and the nonacademic world "outside the walls" to achieve what Richard Dober has described as "removal from the stress of the general conditions of modern society."[1] In recent times, however, and particularly since the 1960s, interactions between campuses and surrounding communities have greatly intensified, raising interesting questions about how the evolving character of campus-community relations should be expressed in architectural terms.

One force driving change has been the democratization of higher education. During the second half of the twentieth century, fostered by public policy at both the state and federal levels, there occurred a steady increase in the percentage of young Americans attending college. With this change came increased pressures on academic institutions to provide young people with practical skills for work after graduation. In the latter years of the twentieth century and continuing today, the pressure on colleges and universities to supplement traditional academic concerns with preparation for productive careers has become increasingly prominent. These two forces together have lead to a dramatic increase in the role that off-campus experiences of many kinds—internships, cooperative education, service learning—play in undergraduate education, and this change has inevitably eroded the traditional psychic barrier between the world of the campus and the world outside.

A parallel pattern of change can be observed in the scholarly work of academic faculties. Contemporary universities, responding to both public policy and economic pressure, are placing heightened emphasis on applied work with direct applications in arenas ranging from national defense to public policy to commercial development to public health. This kind of work draws academics into intensified interactions with colleagues in nonacademic institutions and further contributes to a breakdown of the separation between campus and community. Such interactions have become particularly intense and important among urban universities, where faculties often work closely with nonacademic institutions ranging from public schools to health care providers to city planners to local corporations. Indeed, in many ways academic life at a contemporary urban university draws equally on the resources of the campus and the resources of the host city.

My own institution, Northeastern University, provides a pertinent example of the intensified character of campus-community interactions that Chapman identifies and of the challenge—and opportunity—that these changes bring in the arena of campus design. Northeastern is a large, private university located in the heart of Boston. We are committed to a special pedagogy called cooperative education, in which students alternate between periods of full-time study and full-time employment in work settings related to their major. Our emphasis on applied research—in partnership with corporations, governments, and community organizations—contributes to social and economic progress through the fostering of local and regional growth. Building strong connections with the surrounding community and nonacademic world is therefore an important part of our institutional culture as we strive to provide a richer learning experience for our students and scholarly atmosphere for our faculty.

For the past ten years we have been engaged in a major building program fostered by both our academic development and our shift from a primarily commuter to a primarily residential campus. The program has involved the construction of 18 residential, academic, and research facilities and the development of a large, previously undeveloped part of the campus that for years had been devoted to parking lots. Among the values we have most wanted to express, both in the spatial organization of undeveloped land and in the design of specific buildings, has been our commitment to interaction with the community around us as well as our desire to be a good neighbor to those with whom we share space. We are acutely aware that development on the scale we have pursued has a major impact on the surrounding community and would not be possible without extensive interaction and cooperation among the university, our neighbors, and the city.

Our basic design goal has been to put in place structures that simultaneously enhance our academic work and underscore our commitment to community outreach. In our thinking, this has implied not a complete abandonment of the tradition of campus as oasis but rather a blending of that tradition with physical forms that also connect the inside of the campus with the city streets and neighborhoods that surround us. For example, a new residential quadrangle was designed as a marvelous semi-enclosed space that suggests safety and quiet but also includes openings between the buildings as well as two giant three-story portals passing through the buildings to underscore Northeastern's connection to the broader community. The glass façade of a classroom building opens onto a major city thoroughfare inviting the community to observe the work of the university and reminding our students of the nonacademic life around them. Another theme in our design has been facilities that involve both university and community uses. One project provides apartment-style living for nearly 600 students and 75 new units of affordable housing that have been sold to members of the community. A building we acquired in the 1990s is now home to a community health center and a pharmacy, as well as university functions. The first floor of our new recreation center contains retail functions utilized by both students and the community.

We hope, as we pursue our building program at Northeastern, that we are being faithful to Perry Chapman's observation that campus architecture should evolve in parallel with campus character. In this connection, perhaps the greatest contribution of Chapman's book is the way in which it identifies the large forces that are likely to change higher education in the period ahead and then thinks through the architectural implications of these changes. The changing character of campus-community relations is one such force, but by no means the only one. This is a fascinating, important topic, well worth the attention both of academic facilities planners and institutional leaders. As Chapman repeatedly notes, physical place has an immense impact on the quality of institutional life on a daily basis, potentially reinforcing or undermining important institutional goals and values. Getting it right in architectural terms is an important part of getting it right in educational terms. Perry Chapman has done an important service in directing our attention to this complex topic.

Richard Freeland
*President, Northeastern University*

# *Acknowledgments*

I started this book with the ambitious goal of bringing together three complex themes—a discourse on the intrinsic qualities of America's place-based campuses, how societal forces will reshape campuses in the new century, and how the changing campuses will themselves influence the world around them—all in a single, compact volume. In this act of hubris, I came to depend very heavily on the wisdom, guidance, and support of many individuals.

I am profoundly grateful to the five people who consented to be on my review board, scrutinizing the many drafts I put in front of them and patiently pointing out ways to make them better: author/essayist Melanie Simo; Osmund Overby, Professor Emeritus of Art History and Archeology at the University of Missouri–Columbia; Jeff Aper, Provost of Blackburn College in Illinois; Philip Parsons, my colleague at Sasaki Associates; and David Neuman, University Architect at the University of Virginia.

I am thankful for the generous time and ideas given to me in interview conversations by people whose contributions to academe I have long admired: Frank Rhodes, President Emeritus of Cornell University; William Mitchell, head of the program in Media Arts and Sciences at MIT; President Richard Freeland and Senior Vice President for Administration and Finance Larry Mucciolo at Northeastern University; and George Boggs, President of the American Association of Community Colleges. My thanks to Judith Steinkamp, formerly of the University of Massachusetts–Amherst, for sharing the knowledge that she has accumulated as a superb chronicler of town/gown initiatives around the United States.

I am indebted to former clients and other kindred spirits whose insights and guidance were essential in helping me craft the case stories about their campuses at the beginning of the chapters: Mina Amundsen at Cornell; Julia Monteith at Virginia and formerly at Berkeley; Steve Finacom at Berkeley; Scott Hurst, Bill Sanders, and Tom Head at Virginia Tech; Michael Sestric, Jane Atkinson, Greg Caldwell, and Larry Meyers at Lewis & Clark College; Dan Adams (with President Freeland and Vice President Mucciolo) at Northeastern; Clare Heidler and President Joe Grunewald at Clarion University of Pennsylvania; Rana Altenburg, Ron Ripley, and Carol Winkel at Marquette; Bob Wolfe at the Princeton Forrestal Center; and Barbara Donerly at the University of South Florida. Those who went above and beyond to find the right campus image for each chapter include Cornell's Anitra Wilson; Andrew Greene at Virginia; Jane Talbot at Virginia Tech; Lewis & Clarke's Tania Thompson and Shannon Smith; Linda Pedroley at the University of Missouri–Columbia; and my colleague at Sasaki Associates, Terri Gray-Pearce.

It would not have been possible to begin this endeavor without the support and collegiality of my fellow professionals at Sasaki Associates, whose creative minds I raided for ideas without remorse. My thanks to Jim Sukeforth, our firm's chief executive officer, for championing the idea of this book, and to my partners Ricardo Dumont and Dan Kenney, who, with Ginger Kenney, blazed the trail with their superb book *Mission and Place.* I have nothing but praise for Allyson Solorzano, Matt Brownell, and my administrative assistant, Maurine Hulslander, for the essential parts they played in research and preparation, and undying gratitude to Roberta Doocey for her diligence in typing and editing endless manuscripts and helping this first-time author navigate the technical shoals of book writing.

It was my good fortune to find in Susan Slesinger, executive editor of Praeger's Greenwood Publishing Group, someone for whom the themes of this book reso-nated, and who provided gentle encouragement from the very first conversations about those themes.

I am grateful to my wife, Dawn, in so many ways for her forbearance during my self-imposed exiles and for her unfailing encouragement during the times that I struggled to make sense of the complexities of the subject.

Finally, I owe a great debt to Paul V. Turner, whose 1984 book, *Campus: An American Planning Tradition,* is the seminal history of the American campus. Turner's work stands as the benchmark for all who regard the college campus as a singularly American place—a robust blend of institutional aspiration and civic engagement, open in an affirming way to the larger environment of which it is a part. My thanks to Paul Turner for permitting me to draw so extensively from his classic work and for his generosity in critiquing early drafts of the chapters in Part One of this book, summarizing the history of American campuses. As he graciously pointed out ways to improve my material, I was reminded of the concluding passage in his book stating that, in this country, colleges almost always look confidently outward to the world, and thus:

> The result is that uniquely American place, the campus. As a kind of city in microcosm, it has been shaped by the desire to create an ideal community, and has often been a vehicle for expressing the utopian social visions of the American imagination. Above all, the campus reveals the power that a physical environment can possess as the embodiment of an institution's character.[1]

The chapters that follow represent my attempt to build on the spirit of Turner's concluding passage, to take the dialogue about the campus as place and community into the future tense. What becomes of college and university campuses in the twenty-first century will say much about what is to become of all American places.

The McGraw Library Tower at Cornell University. (Cornell University Photography.)

*Introduction*

## An American Place

The campus of Cornell University lies at the western edge of a broad plateau above the valley of Cayuga Lake. Three of the university's original Victorian-era stone buildings—White, McGraw, and Morrill Halls—stand in a soldier row at the rim of the hill, gazing at the lake and the city of Ithaca in the valley below, and at the distant fields and woodlots and subdivisions dotting the hills across the valley. At the feet of the gray stone soldiers, the Libe Slope descends in a grassy apron animated by the trudging procession of students who live in the residence halls, theme houses, sororities, fraternities, and apartments on the hillside below the campus proper.

The buildings at the top of the hill frame the west edge of the Arts Quadrangle, Cornell's historic collegiate space. The east side of the "Quad" is dominated by the classic portico of Goldwyn Smith Hall, the limestone citadel of the College of Arts and Sciences where untold legions of Cornellians have been schooled in English and the humanities. The bell tower of the Uris Library punctuates the southwest corner of the Quad, a visible marker for miles in every direction, and the source of melodious accompaniment to the hourly movement of students from class to class. Footprints painted on the Quad's central sidewalk denote the legend in which the statues of founder Ezra Cornell and his first president, Andrew Dixon White, step off their pedestals to meet and shake hands in the middle of the Quad when they observe the rare spectacle of a chaste coed crossing the space between them. Tradition is not always politically correct.

The Quad is a theatrical transaction in which people, space, and architecture are the players. Most of Cornell's undergraduates pass through the Quad every day, making the space a perpetual parade ground. The schools with addresses on the Quad house an eclectic population, from the sociable lit majors and cerebral history majors in Arts and Sciences to the nocturnal mavericks of the Architecture School in Sibley Hall. The engineers, aggies, and scientists decamped long ago to their sprawling enclaves elsewhere on campus, but they still come back for required and elective adventures in the arts and humanities. The shady lawn invites reading under the trees and playing Frisbee with Cornell's legendary corps of dogs. The capacious building steps provide bleachers for watching, flirting, and conversation. The sense of theater is amplified by the stately façades that contain the space and frame the vistas to the campus and the countryside beyond.

Upslope from the Quad, the campus is an uneasy negotiation between landform and architecture. Buildings of every era, style, and scale are nestled in the vales and perched on the terraces that make up the terrain at the top of the hill. The disparate architectural languages that evolved in twentieth-century Cornell are brought into a semblance of order by the street grid that traverses the campus. Wee Stinky Creek meanders a wooded course through mid-campus, emerging from no apparent source and disappearing into a culverted nowhere in a brief, picturesque fancy that works wonders to knit the campus together.

Farther east, past the heart of the academic campus, past the newest generation of science laboratories and sports buildings, Cornell reconnects with its larger environment in sweeping views across the open plain of Alumni Field toward the surrounding hills. Still farther east, past the tight islands of buildings housing Veterinary Medicine and Agriculture, the land opens wide to the farm plots, pastures, and orchards that signal Cornell's role as the land grant college of the Empire State.

The whole ensemble, from the residence halls on the hillside below the Libe Slope to the upland farm fields, is flanked on the north and south by two precipitous gorges that are etched into the terrain by a series of cascades down to the valley below. The chasms are nature's unambiguous way of defining the heart of Cornell. Few campuses in America can offer a more emphatic sense of arrival than the one a person feels by glimpsing into a 120-foot ravine while crossing one of the high bridges into Cornell. The power of place at Cornell cannot be ignored. It is a power dominated by nature and terrain, for the most part gracefully captured by human intervention. Where the intervention has been less than graceful, nature has been forgiving. So far.

Ezra Cornell clearly understood the power of the place in 1865 when he located his new "institution where any person can find instruction in any study" on the farm that he had worked for years overlooking the canal town of Ithaca. He was a "shrewd, hard-headed farmer and businessman with a practical outlook and a Quaker conscience."[1] He knew the land well, and he comprehended that his college would spring from the majesty of the land. There could not have been a more commanding place in which to have founded the "first American university"[2] than this perch above the Finger Lakes of upstate New York, looking toward the western horizon, and its mythical inference of the American frontier.

Cornell was a seminal experience in my life. Or, more to the point, a running series of undergraduate experiences and discoveries and encounters that accumulated into a changed view of the world. I migrated to Cornell on a rainy September day in the mid-1950s from a small, upstate town in the northern Appalachian foothills 100 miles east of Ithaca. The first thing that captivated me was the natural setting, the unequivocal knowing of where I was on the face of the earth. When I was a freshman architecture student at Cornell, I would look out on the lake and the town below from a window of the drafting room on the top floor of White Hall. I had grown up in a valley town by a lake. I liked seeing things from above for a change. It was one of the first things I learned from being on a college campus. I learned, as well, about the intricate negotiations that are made between people and place every minute of every day as part of the collegial experience.

It took the better part of those undergraduate years at Cornell for me to comprehend that place and experience are inextricably linked in the endeavor that we call higher learning. Each day, I was imperceptibly changed because of the discoveries, exchanges, events, rituals, friendships, routines, and anxieties that were occurring in the place, and because the place enabled those things to happen. There was the professor who unlocked ideas about aesthetics and society that made my mind soar. I have only a dim image of the space where he delivered his energizing ideas, but I can still hear the sound of the recorded jazz riffs he played to demonstrate how the rhythms of modern architecture and music tracked one another. There was the breathtakingly monotone lecturer that I relied on to induce a much-needed nap after pulling all-nighters on projects. I can't remember the lecturer or his subject, but I can still picture the airless room where he droned on. There were the four weeks in the spring of 1959 when we gathered each afternoon in an attentive cluster on the Quad lawn, listening to Buckminster Fuller download the bounty of his prodigious mind. I remember Bucky. I remember the passersby who were drawn into the circle. I remember that it was better that we heard him in springtime on the Quad when the air was damp-sweet with the aroma of maple blossoms and new grass in moist earth. And I know that if we had heard him indoors in a February when the steely gray cloud cover over the Finger Lakes is only occasionally violated by bright sun and blue sky, we still would have remembered all that he said because we would have connected with Bucky by the spontaneity of our collective presence. We would still have been in a place invested with meaning by the quality of the experience.

More than four decades later, this alumnus is struck by how much the campus has changed, and yet how immutable its basic character remains. Cornell's enrollment has doubled from 10,000 to 20,000 since 1960. Building space has doubled as well, filling interstitial spots in the heart of the campus and open fields in what was once the periphery. The campus has become both denser and more sprawling. The automobile is more ubiquitous campuswide, but less so in sacred spaces like the Quad and the area fronting Willard Straight Hall, where streets have been removed in deference to pedestrian safety and tranquility. The white monolith of the Johnson Art Museum now sits as a modernist bookend to the stone soldiers at the brow of the hill. Cornell has expanded its presence in the adjacent Collegetown commercial district with a performing arts center, spurring a revitalization of the area while not diminishing its beloved eccentricity. At other community borders, neighbors have forbidden campus expansion.

As I contemplate how different and yet how much the same Cornell feels after 40-odd years, it causes me to wonder how the place would be perceived by people who were there at different times during those 40 years.

For those of us students attending Cornell in the 1950s, the campus was beginning to fill in at the near edges with the new generation of modern postwar buildings; but still, the campus felt open and rural in its outlying areas, as it must have felt for the generations attending Cornell before World War II. For first-generation college goers, like me, campus life was especially exhilarating, nourished as it was by the postwar sense of limitless material promise, and tempered only by the growing background noise of the nascent cold war. In spite of growing apprehensions about nuclear annihilation, this was not a period notable for campus social activism. The social critics of the 1950s were roundly lamenting apathy and conformity in America. At Cornell, the supreme act of social rebellion was the panty raid. The personal meanings of the Cornell experience would have been different for my classmates from Brooklyn, Bombay, and Bogotá. Their life experiences in the subsequent years would have conflated the memories of Cornell in different ways from mine. But I knew we would always be linked by memories of the immutable character of the place.

The Cornell student of the early 1970s would surely have noticed that the spaces between buildings were being filled with even bigger buildings. He would have seen the graceful skyline of the hill penetrated by multistory dormitories and laboratory towers. The broad lawn of Lower Alumni Field was beginning to be subsumed by new indoor sports buildings. If the pace of campus change didn't contribute to a sense of impermanence for that baby boomer student, the events of that time would have signaled how much the world was changing. Civil rights, antiwar activism, and environmentalism had stirred the baby-boom-generation students into a social rebellion that was reaching a mature phase by the early 1970s. In that heady era of student unrest, the experience of place was sharpened by the very intensity of the events that occurred there. Students of that era are forever linked by those memories in ways that other generations cannot comprehend. The 1970s student and his classmates from San Diego, Milan, and Osaka would definitely draw different meanings from their Cornell experiences in those tumultuous days, but still they would be bonded by their memories of the place.

The Cornellian of the 1990s would observe yet another phalanx of science labs and sports structures closing in campus open spaces. She would see several Victorian-era buildings such as Sage Hall and Lincoln Hall expanded and refurbished for a new generation of users, bringing renewed vitality to some of Cornell's oldest structures. Streets in the heart of the campus were reclaimed for pedestrian use. The new feature in the student's daily life was her desktop computer, broadening and quickening her reach for information in ways unimagined by her predecessors in the 1950s and 1970s. Cornell, like many research universities across the country, was launching into a significant research and teaching initiative in the life sciences. The scientific disciplines were morphing at a level that would have been inconceivable in the 1950s. The atmosphere in the 1990s was charged by the dizzying pace of global change at every level—economic, political, technological, environmental. She was among the first wave of post–cold war collegians, no doubt aware that in spite of the promise of the wall coming down, their lives would be framed by new forms of world conflict. She and her classmates from Charlotte, Kuala Lumpur, and Riyadh would each embark on measurably different life experiences, but they would forever be joined by memories of the powerful, eloquent place where they learned together.

The experiences of Cornellians in the 1950s, 1970s, and 1990s were, of course, very different. Our backgrounds and outlooks were different. Our relationships were different. Our notions of campus community were different, self-crafted to fit our individual comfort zones. Some of us grabbed for the full breadth and depth of the Cornell experience. Some of us found our community in a sorority or sports team or with our fellows in an academic pursuit. Some of us were content with the solitary pursuit of our personal muses. Some of us mixed and matched our community spheres as we went along. The connection among us, as individuals and as generations, was the place in which we converged to pursue one of the most important endeavors of our lives, a place made sacred by those intentions.

The Cornell story, conveyed as a personal memoir, illustrates the individuality and the timeless, yet ever-changing nature of America's place-based campuses. It is a personal affirmation that what is learned and felt in a campus setting is given more meaning by the setting. It is a declaration that the campus is a place that is alive for each individual and every generation. The campus, as I will explain throughout this book, is always the teacher.

## What Is It about a Campus That Makes It a Special Place?

What we call the *sense of place* is a personal phenomenon, having as much to do with our own experiences and cognitions as with the physicality of the environment. The sense of place can strike us more personally or less, whether it is our home, our neighborhood, our community, our country, or a place that we visit. The sense of place associated with a college campus has a particular meaning because it is typically experienced at a time and in a way that is poignant in the lives of those who attend the institution, a time of intense personal exploration. Campus is not a casual encounter for those who go there with a purpose.

Telling the story of the campus as a place from one's own experience is the easy way to embrace a concept whose outlines are not easily revealed by standard definitions. Take the definition of the word *campus*, which is usually described as something like the grounds of a college or school, sometimes including the buildings. What is actually more revealing is the word's Latin derivation, which is a field, or a lawn. As creatures of the primordial savanna, we have a visceral link with that idea. Still, we look for something more descriptive to navigate the journey that I am inviting you to take. Moving to the more elusive idea of *place,* we find that some dictionaries contain more than 30 definitions of the word as a noun. Among those that will have literal translations in this book are:

- A particular portion of space of definite or indefinite extent
- A regional locality, village, town, or city
- An open space or court or square in a city or town (curiously, some dictionaries of the 1950s and 1960s consider this definition as now rare, but newer ones do not give it that caveat)
- A building or space set aside for a certain purpose

- An abode where one lives ("Visit me at my *place*.")
- Position or situation with reference to its occupation or occupant

These definitions have the virtue of simplicity, but they fall short in conveying the meaning of place as an integral part of the collegiate experience. Place, in the sense that this book is meant to convey, is not a physical abstraction. It has more to do with a chemistry that blends the character of the setting, its meaning to those who inhabit the setting, and the interactions that occur between the setting and its inhabitants. I came upon a rather elegant (and economical) description of place in a 2001 book review by Richard Cole, who said, "a place is a location of character and individual significance."[3] He acknowledges the character and singularity of a place, imputing a meaning that goes beyond the merely physical. The description resonated with me an extra measure, perhaps, because of the title of the book that Cole was reviewing: *The Seduction of Place*.

Definitions are, at best, only foundation blocks for the more vivid, more personal idea of place that needs to be captured in thinking about the American campus. It must be understood by the qualities that make it an integral part of the learning experience. A coworker of mine uses the delightful term *emotional resonance* in describing how a campus, a building, or any designed environment can ignite deeper feelings that magnify the purpose of that environment. For him, the campus is differentiated by the feelings that it evokes and the endeavors that it is meant to cultivate. Place (in particular, the campus as a place) is tangible and intangible, real and perceived, actual and felt. Place becomes the sum of the people, experiences, activities, events, and memories that come alive within and because of the exceptional arrangement that we call the campus. I like to think of the campus as five metaphors.

### The Campus as Narrative

Every college and university has a story to tell about itself—about its mission, its history, its traditions, its aspirations. The institutional story is told through the campus: where the campus is located, what has been built there, and what happens there. The campus is an unalloyed account of what the institution is all about.

The location is a message about how the founding goals of the institution were wedded to an idea about the nature of place: how a religious-based institution of the eighteenth or nineteenth century sought the tranquility of a small community; how a land grant university settled in a place where a diverse agriculture could be practiced and demonstrated; or how a twentieth-century community college set up a multitude of places with good parking to serve its widely scattered student body. The geographic boundary between a campus and a community is a graphic story of how separate or how connected with its community an institution has chosen to be.

The character of the architecture and landscape of the campus says, with uncanny accuracy, what the institution's values and circumstances have been over time. The architectural narrative of an elite residential college is likely to be one of the intimately scaled and lovingly preserved buildings in a gracious landscape setting; for a flagship public university, architecture and place have been transmuted several times over to express the successive economic and social priorities of its public constituencies.

Places and artifacts of the campus take on iconic, even ritual, standing in the institutional narrative: the bronze statue whose nose or foot has been rubbed to a golden hue by 10,000 passersby; the garden where declarations of love are made; or the steps of Old Main, where the daily theater of campus is observed and participated in. The sacred places are narratives of handed-down tradition. A practical account of the institution's work, pace, and social life is found in the day-to-day movement and activities of its inhabitants, each of whom contributes a personal narrative to the larger story of the institution.

### The Campus as Experience

The campus is a tapestry of sensory, cognitive, and intellectual experiences that are meaningful in and of themselves, and that can profoundly reinforce one another. Experience is intentional in the design and organization of the place, in the offerings and activities that make up campus life and as means of energizing the learning process. People attend college with the intention of having new, life-defining experiences.

The sensory nature of the campus—visual, aural, olfactory, and tactile—is the foundation of experience and memory that lasts long past being in the place. Every campus offers its particular set of sensory experiences: the panorama of Pikes Peak from Colorado College and of Lower Manhattan from Pratt Institute in Brooklyn; the warm, corky aroma of southern pines at Auburn and the crisp pungency of drying autumn leaves at Hartwick College in upstate New York; the afternoon serenades emanating from the Western Michigan University bell tower and the roar of the Saturday football crowd at the Ohio State stadium; the mellow sea breezes off the Pacific at UC–Santa Barbara and the brisk winds off Lake Michigan that bathe Northwestern University in the spring. These kinds of sensory experiences differentiate campuses from one another.

Campus experience is galvanized by defining events such as winning a national championship or losing a landmark building to a tragic fire; by personal epiphanies like falling in love, receiving or rejecting religion, or changing political ideologies. The experiential nature of campus life is most powerful, of course, in its capacity to nurture intellectual discovery and cultural awareness; that is, when it fulfills the intentions of the institution and the learner.

## The Campus as Intentional Community

Higher education institutions are among the most intentional of communities. Their mission, individually and collectively, is to be communities of learning, places that cultivate an informed, engaged, responsible citizenry. Community is a method and a behavioral system that the campus is organized to facilitate by providing the places that foster discourse, debate, collaboration, and social interaction. The intentional community is more than just a functional idea. As Paul V. Turner concludes in his book about American campus history, the campus "has been shaped by the desire to create an ideal community."[4]

The campus forms the context for the human interaction that lies at the heart of the collegiate endeavor. People arrive on campus as individual learners. They leave with memories of the relationships they made with teachers and other learners in the pursuit of their common intentions. In *Creation of the Future,* former Cornell President Frank Rhodes makes the case that community is a basic function of the campus:

> The great untapped resource of the American university is the campus community. Here the disciplines reinforce one another; here professional practice both draws on and contributes to basic knowledge; here students encounter those of other backgrounds and other convictions; here they learn to respect and understand those who think otherwise. It is here that responsible citizenship is developed, here that leadership is encouraged, here that teamwork is required.[5]

For small colleges and highly specialized institutions, the whole of campus community life is a mirror of institutional values and traditions. In a conversation with me, Dr. Rhodes observed that, in today's larger, more complex institutions, the sense of community is most likely to be found in *nucleations,* where community identity is cultivated in individual colleges, departments, dorm groups, sports teams, social organizations, and interest groups where shared purposes, outlooks, and experiences can flourish. Most of those nucleations are place-centered. They occur in environments that offer proximity, contact at a human scale, and, most certainly, the functions that draw people with common interests together in the first place.[6]

### The Campus as a Work of Art

The campus is a designed place, deliberately conceived by its builders to impart a distinct aesthetic effect. Few constructed environments are as meticulously composed to achieve beauty and order as are campuses. That is not to say that all campuses have been designed at the highest level of aesthetic quality or that any given campus has been consistently well designed over time. Nonetheless, the campus is meant to be seen and experienced as something pleasing, as a work of art. It is a remarkable fact of the American campus that such an idea persists—is so honored and protected—through decades, even centuries, of generational change.

Exceptional attention is lavished on the design of campus buildings, at least those buildings that are regarded as important to the image of the institution. The detailing, proportions, and position in the landscape accorded to campus architecture are unique characteristics of the genre. The leading architects and site planners in every American era have been commissioned to express their art in campus design. Campus landscape is invariably addressed as a form of art, either formal or natural, an intuitive acknowledgement that the land is the aesthetic foundation of the campus experience. There is no aesthetic rule that fits all campuses. The campus may be designed as a unified whole, with each element of site and architecture playing a highly crafted role in the larger order, or it may be conceived as a simple ground for a collection of individual architectural statements. Place as art is a fundamental part of the culture of most place-based institutions in the United States. It resonates in the experience and memory of those who are associated with the institutions.[7]

### The Campus as Pilgrimage

The college campus is a place that is distinguished by the quests of those who journey there, searching for knowledge, seeking intellectual, cultural, and social enlightenment, aspiring to a change in the tenor of their lives. It is distinguished by the time when, in the lives of its constituents, the journey is undertaken—mostly during the passage to young adulthood, but increasingly, in periods of adult life transition. Jeff Aper, provost at Blackburn College in Illinois, elevates the analogy by suggesting that the campus is a place of pilgrimage. He points out that pilgrimage, historically a journey to a place that is sacred, was both a profound learning and developmental experience and a "kind of allegorical experience of the journey through life from immaturity to maturity, from ignorance to knowledge, from foolishness to wisdom, from doubt to faith." The experiences were heightened by encountering the commonalities and differences of all the places along the way. He goes on to say that

> higher education has always seemed to me intended to embody both aspects of pilgrimage—the earliest universities evolved a sense of place (e.g., the aula, or center, of the old universities, where degrees were conferred and there was a sense of the profound meaning of that central space) so that students and scholars might literally journey from the profane space of their home village to the sacred space of the university.[8]

Aper's pilgrimage metaphor is apt because it underscores the role that the campus experience can play in fostering the inward journey of serious learning, the empirical and psychological arrival at a place of greater knowledge.[9] The campus is a place that transforms the inwardness of learning to yet another, more outward, pilgrimage into the larger world beyond the campus.

### No Two Campuses Are Alike, Nor Would We Want Them to Be

When we look at campuses around the country to find tangible expressions of what it is that makes the American campus a special place, we are confronted with a staggering range of campus forms and settings. The archetypal images that people associate with the *traditional* American campus—broad green quadrangles, Gothic archways, bell towers, grand library reading rooms—can be found in abundance in all parts of the country. The images reflect ideals of collegiate form and order that are embedded in the history of American campus design. However, the physical forms of the country's 4,000 college campuses follow no single formula. The *genius loci* of the U.S. campus is embodied in the enormous variety of geographic, cultural, and climatic circumstances in which campuses have evolved. Institutions in New England, the Gulf Coast, the northern plains, and the intermountain West might have superficial similarities in the way that they are laid out, or in generic architectural styles that are too often oblivious to regional differences. But the landscape, the quality of sky and horizon, the seasonal variations, and the rhythm of campus life will give the region or locality away every time. Distinctions in campus character are also tied to the locations of campuses: urban, suburban, and rural settings make for vast differences in the density of building development, the open space patterns around and within which the campus is organized, and in the boundary relationships between the campus and its abutting neighbors. Flat terrain and hilly terrain have markedly different effects on the geometric layout of the campus, on its views and vistas, on the spatial experience that it imparts to its occupants. No two campuses are alike, nor would we want them to be.

As measurable as location and site conditions are in differentiating the feel and form of campuses, the most important distinctions arise from the varying kinds of higher education institutions that abound in the United States. The Carnegie Classification System lists degree-granting institutions, representing a wide range of educational missions, degree levels conferred, student body profiles, local or national (or global) spheres of influence, and scales of operation. With apologies to the official classifiers, I herewith submit my list, condensed to five, emphasizing their typical campus characteristics and the factors that influence campus form.

*Independent liberal arts colleges* typically convey an intimate, domestically scaled place image. They are the collegiate residential "villages" whose enrollments range from less than 1,000 students to rarely more than 5,000. Personal interaction among students and between students and faculty is declared to be paramount. Academic, residential, and social lives are of a whole piece, expressed in the scale and fabric of the campus setting. The dominant, unifying feature is most likely a parklike landscape, in which stately individual buildings are arranged sometimes formally, sometimes informally. A sense of tradition and purpose, even among the newest, most experimental colleges, is embedded in the environment of liberal arts colleges. Examples of such institutions includes Amherst, Colby, Vassar, Gettysburg, Davidson, Salem, Sweet Briar, Kenyon, Carleton, St. Olaf, Reed, Pomona, and Mills.

There are several hundred undergraduate colleges built on the liberal arts model, of which between 100 and 120 are considered elite by virtue of their endowments, selectivity, and academic reputations. Liberal arts colleges vary from traditional to experimental in the delivery of their curricula, but they are together in their emphasis on the quality of the educational experience at the individual level. As fewer than 10 percent of the country's postsecondary students earn baccalaureate degrees at resident liberal arts colleges, such schools will always have a limited, albeit important, demographic niche in the higher education system. Changes in the physical character of such institutions will largely be determined by the extent to which they branch out from their liberal arts roots in order to compete with other institutions.

*Independent research universities* share certain of the place characteristics of the liberal arts college in that most are grounded in a resident undergraduate core mission. Many of the older private universities started out as liberal arts colleges. They differ, however, in the range and complexity of the functions that they have taken on as universities. The student populations at independent universities typically range from 5,000 to 20,000, with a few as large as 30,000 to 40,000. As a group, they are so varied as to transcend a common characterization, as evidenced in a random selection made up of, say, Harvard, MIT, Duke, Lehigh, Chicago, Carnegie Mellon, Vanderbilt, Rice, Southern California, NYU, and Notre Dame. But one can discern in each an air of robustness, cosmopolitan spirit, and tradition that lends coherence to their diverse functions. And functionally diverse they are, with an impressive array of colleges, professional schools, and research institutes drawing students from all over the country and the world. They are providers of regionwide and often world-class facilities for art, culture, sports, and entertainment. Many operate premier academic medical centers. America's 110 to 120 research universities are, in the words of education scholar George Keller, "becoming primarily research factories, the chief source of new ideas, scientific data, and discoveries for society."[10] They are constantly growing, changing, and affecting the communities around them simply to maintain their positions as engines of scientific discovery.

*Public flagship and land grant universities* are similar to independent research universities in having a large undergraduate resident population at the core of a large constellation of graduate, professional, and research functions. On average, the public flagship institutions are among the largest in the country, with enrollments ranging from 15,000 to 50,000. Their characteristically extensive land holdings can add up to 1,000 or 2,000 acres, sometimes more for the land grant universities with their vast agricultural fields and experiment stations. Beyond the traditional greens surrounded by historic buildings, their campuses sprawl outward with large-scale dormitories, athletic buildings, parking lots, and research facilities. As the premier public higher education institutions in their states, they maintain a vigorous civic and economic engagement with their localities by helping to cultivate the human resources, enterprises, and community services that support the quality of life in their home states. Many of the large public universities, such as California–Berkeley, Texas–Austin, Ohio State, Illinois, Michigan, North Carolina–Chapel Hill, and Minnesota–Twin Cities, are as global in the scope of their activities as the premier independent universities, lending a cosmopolitan vitality to their localities.

*Regional public colleges and universities* are predominantly oriented to undergraduate instruction. Graduate and professional programs, although robust at some regional campuses, are modest compared to the research universities.

Enrollments, ranging from 3,000 to 10,000 students, are drawn in large measure from the nearby parts of their states. These are the institutions that concentrate on preparing students to participate in the working world of their states and regions. Their academic missions and operations must have enough currency to keep up with the economic and demographic challenges faced by their homes states. Regional institutions serve a large segment of America's part-time and commuting student enrollment. They sometimes struggle to maintain a unified campus social environment for those who live there and those who come for a few hours a day. Many regional public institutions started out as *normal schools,* specializing in teacher education, later broadening their missions to serve the changing post–World War II socioeconomic needs of their regions. The original college green or *Old Main* has usually endured, giving the campus its iconic imagery. Chances are, though, that later phases of campus growth, built with sporadic state appropriations on land that became available in random pattern, lack the gracious pedestrian-oriented coherence of the original setting. Still, the educational, cultural, and social services that regional institutions provide make them lively centers of civic life in their localities. They are often asked to fulfill these missions with limited public financial support.

*Community colleges* occupy the most eclectic array of collegiate settings of any of the types of American higher education institutions. Their enrollments can vary from 1,000 students in small cities and rural counties up to 20,000 or more in sprawling urban and suburban districts. There is a community college within commuting distance of 90 percent of the population in the lower 48 states. Serving such disparate local circumstances, they are found in equally disparate venues—from old factories, office buildings, and department stores to expansive campuses at the edge of town. Except in urban locations well served by public transportation, parking is the principal feature on most campuses. Nearly half of the country's postsecondary students attend community colleges, most of them on part-time, commuting schedules. America's 1,200 community colleges, 80 percent of which are public, serve the educational and socioeconomic needs of their immediate localities, mainly offering two-year associate degree programs. The student pool served by community colleges is not only the largest and fastest-growing in the country, it is also the most diverse by ethnicity, economic circumstance, age, preparedness, and most every other demographic variable in higher education.

They are attended by college-age students right out of high school and by older learners upgrading technical and professional skills, seeking education later in life, changing careers, or simply pursuing personal educational interests. Because most students attend part-time, traditional collegiate life is modest compared to that of full-time residential institutions. Connections with the community are strong, causing community colleges to constantly recraft the public services they have to provide as local needs change.

There are other specialized types of institutions, such as tribal colleges, service academies, theological seminaries, medical schools, and other freestanding professional and technical schools. Their characteristics are likely to be variants of the smaller-sized campuses described above.

## Why Does Place Matter in the Higher Education Endeavor?

In the introduction to *The Experience of Place,* Tony Hiss eloquently frames the role that place has in shaping our lives and our views of life:

> We all react, consciously and unconsciously, to the places where we live and work, in ways we scarcely notice or that are only now becoming known to us. Ever-accelerating changes in most people's day-to-day circumstances are helping us and prodding us, sometimes forcing us, to learn that our ordinary surroundings, built and natural alike, have an immediate and a continuing affect on the way that we feel and act, and on our health and intelligence. These places have an impact on our sense of self, our sense of safety, the kind of work we get done, the ways we interact with other people, even our ability to function as citizens in a democracy. In short, the places where we spend our time affect the people we are and can become.[11]

Place matters because it is the tangible expression of institutional identity. It is the way that the campus speaks to the personal and civic expectations of its constituents, as much as does a city or town or any institution. In a splendid examination of the great Italian Renaissance cities, David Mayernik makes a telling analogy that is applicable to campuses in his observation about America's "meager aspirations" for urban places when he says, "We never really expect our cities to *say* something important about who we are and what we collectively value."[12] A higher education institution, more than any city, is intrinsically about collective values and the importance of those values in fulfilling the aspirations of its individual inhabitants. The character of the place must say something to its constituents about institutional values and why those constituents are joined in both the personal and the civic pursuit of those values in that place. It matters that the campus clearly expresses the identity of the institution to the community around it and to the world beyond it.

Place matters because it reinforces our sense of institutional pride. Colleges and universities impute great value in institutional pride as a force that galvanizes the interests of their many constituents. Pride in the quality of the campus environment, in the character of the place, has both symbolic and practical implications. Pride of place has an effect on the satisfaction of those who work, live, and learn on the campus. It affects recruitment and retention. It affects alumni loyalty. Frank Rhodes suggests that pride of place is strongly influenced by how well the campus and its facilities are kept, by how much the institution itself cares about its environment and the environment around it.[13] Taken further, pride in the quality of the campus can be affected by the care with which the institution plans its future growth, designs its buildings, and preserves its sacred spaces. If pride of place is compromised, institutional pride is the lesser for it.

Place matters as a reflection of the societal force that higher education has become. It matters in how it enables institutions to engage their learning communities. It matters by providing a multitude of venues and encounters that amplify the learning experience through inquiry, direct observation, debate, action, and social exchange from the playful to the very serious. Being there is learning the choices and challenges of a complex society every day of the week. In the most practical sense, place matters because it is the incubator of the processes that make up the multiple kinds of learning that occur within and beyond campus borders, the intellectual inquiry, the social interaction, the civic engagement, and the cultural enrichment that attends to those experiences. It matters most certainly to students and scholars, who are there to learn and discover; to staff, trustees, and benefactors, who are its stewards; to faculty, for whom it supports the exchange of knowledge; to neighbors, whose daily lives are affected by the presence of the campus; to the community that relies upon it as a civic resource; to alumni and alumnae, for whom it is a compass in their lives.

Place matters because the quality and character of a campus can raise the expectations of people who will enter a world in which the quality of the built environment is under siege. *Sense of place* is a term that has taken on a wistful, even defensive meaning as the regimes of technology, globalization, and migration shift the metaphorical ground under our feet. Some reasonably argue that the new, enhanced conception of place is cyberspace, which is not a place at all, but a pervasive force that shatters the confines of physical space. A growing footloose segment of our population is losing the practical, emotional, and intellectual bonds that have held people and place together for generations. Life in a civil, vital, beautiful, humanly scaled campus can elevate our expectations for all of the settings in which we conduct our lives.

## The Civic Connection: Raising Our Expectations of Place

The inestimable value of the campus as a civic resource can be drawn from the words of the political philosopher Michel Sandel, postulating the need for such resources in an era ever more dominated by ubiquitous market forces:

> The global media and markets that share our lives beckon us to a world beyond borders and belonging. But the civic resources we need to master these forces, or at least to contend with them, are still to be found in the places and stories, memories and meanings, incidents and identities that situate us in the world and give our lives their moral particularity.[14]

Of the many themes that I endeavor to thread through this book, there are two that keep repeating themselves in various guises. In one such theme, I emphasize the *civic relationship* that U.S. campuses have with their communities, regions, and states, indeed with the nation and the world. I will maintain that those relationships will grow stronger in the future because U.S. higher education is a societal force, a *civic* force that will continue to shape and respond to other societal forces, as it has throughout its history. Despite popular notions (and the insistence of many academics) that the campus should be an intellectual ivory tower, the American version has always been a working part of the world around it. It is in the academy's self-interest to be integrated with society.

Colleges were already key pieces of the civic realm in the main towns of the colonial era where revolutionary ferment first stirred, as I describe in Part One. They were defined as civic resources in the Civil War era with the advent of the Morrill Land Grant Act, and went on to help in spurring the economies and social structures of the states as the country settled from coast to coast. Colleges were integrated into the civic fabric of America's growing industrial cities. The civic roles of U.S. campuses burgeoned after World War II, when institutions answered the call to educate a larger, more diverse workforce, to have a hand in urban development, and to be the cultural resources for their host communities.

Understanding the civic relationship is important in revealing the character of the American campus in the broad sense that this book is meant to do. That understanding is paramount in assessing the effects that the next generation of societal changes will have on college campuses, and, in turn, the effects that campus change will have on society. Most of those changes (what I euphemistically call *seismic forces* in Part Two) are magnifications of the civic metaphor. Sometimes they are disruptions of the metaphor. They will affect the ways that campuses cultivate community structure within their borders and the ways that campuses and the communities outside their borders connect with one another. Significantly, institutions are already becoming the centers of vastly enlarged and more complex learning communities that embrace towns, cities, and regions— in fact—the globe. As we contemplate how the sense of place on the campus may change in the future, we need to recognize that the sense of place that is changing goes far beyond the campus gate.

That leads to the other recurrent theme of the book. The college campus, in all its myriad forms, is a distinctive human place that can and should offer society powerful lessons on how the character of the built environment can be made better in the twenty-first century. American campuses have, from the beginning, been designed to impart certain ideals as places in which learning communities can thrive. When those ideals are fully realized, a college campus stands apart from most organized places because it blends the qualities of the natural world with the evocative order of the designed environment such as to foster human interaction, meaning, and memory of the noblest sort. The American campus is a cultural landscape imbued with deep social purpose, more so because it is a landscape in which what is done and experienced ultimately affects society as a whole.

In Part Two, I explain that the place characteristics of many, probably most, campuses will be modified in the future, in turn affecting the environments around them. Those changes are already in motion. Because the campuses in this country have a collective power of place directly and indirectly influencing all of society, academia has a responsibility to nurture an *ethic of place* that can stand as a model to which all of society can aspire. In Part Three, I make the case that whether campuses take new forms in the future or lovingly preserve the qualities they possess today, they must demonstrate to society their mutual adherence to a twenty-first-century ethic of place—one that adopts principles of sustainability, community, and regional authenticity.

The pages that follow show that American campuses are poised to grapple yet again with daunting but necessary tensions between tradition and transformation. These tensions will invariably have an impact on the qualities of place that we revere on college campuses, and validate why those qualities will—must—endure.

## Part One

# A Brief History of the American Campus

## The Legacy of Nature and Urbanity

The American campus today is a manifestation of its own unique and very American history. To be sure, it has roots in the cloistered character of medieval colleges in England. Its architecture and spatial organization were heavily influenced by European historical idioms until well into the twentieth century. Those Old World precedents were modified and adapted to the American landscape from the beginning. American colonial colleges of the seventeenth and eighteenth centuries took shape in the rough-hewn surroundings of small towns and rural countrysides. They were laid out to be open to nature and town. When campuses began to be planned as whole compositions around the turn of the nineteenth century, the connections with the land were still very powerful. The United States was, after all, an open and expansive place, in form and spirit. And so it would remain until the late decades of the nineteenth century, as the country became industrial and urbanized. Even then, the country's campuses, large and small, possessed a spaciousness and transparency relative to their surroundings that bespoke America's continent-spanning optimism. Campuses opened to ever-broadening segments of the U.S. population throughout the nineteenth and twentieth centuries, infusing their generous physical forms with a democratic spirit that transcended their Old World academic traditions. Although many colleges started out as elite, exclusive places, and a few remained that way, the American campus became a remarkably inclusive civic environment by the second half of the twentieth century.

Throughout the nineteenth and early twentieth centuries, there were profound institutional advancements that realigned the contours of American campuses, but the second half of the twentieth century was unmatched in the magnitude of growth and physical change. Until World War II, the typical American campus had a spatial clarity reflecting its classical heritage. It was easy to comprehend and easy to get around; it was in harmony with its surroundings and in scale with its occupants. In the postwar twentieth century, higher education enrollments ballooned in numbers and in the diversity of needs and circumstances of those attending college. Institutions added a prodigious set of functions. They became the basic research arms for national defense and science policy, economic and cultural resources for their localities, purveyors of ever more student educational and social services, and partners in wide-ranging enterprises. Vehicle demand reshaped many colleges from pedestrian-scaled places to minicities laced with roads and vast parking areas. Campuses themselves grew larger and more complex; buildings became more massive and taller; and neighborhoods were often bulldozed for campus expansion. Growth-driven changes in scale, order, and character often eclipsed the gentler settings and the nature of the campus experience that had prevailed for 300 years. On the other hand, the variety of new campus forms and organizational patterns was often refreshingly different from the conventions of prewar campus design. The advancement of university research and expanded access to part-time and lifelong learning contributed, in the 25 years after the war, to what some called the "golden age" of academia.

In the late twentieth century, there was a renewed appreciation for the attributes of human scale, collegial vitality, and quality of the campus experience. There was also a pragmatic recognition that those very qualities were critical in the competitive drive to attract and retain students, faculty, and alumni support. Higher education institutions were moved by those practical demands to renew the stewardship of their environments and their communities. The central ideas that had long distinguished the American campus—connection with nature, openness to the surrounding community, a sense of civic and democratic vitality—were affirmed as values that most institutions were determined to maintain. Those values would prove to be an essential foundation for grappling with the seismic forces of the twenty-first century. Chapter 1 describes the progression of place-making ideas for American campuses from the seventeenth century until the period prior to World War II. Chapter 2 discusses the momentous reshaping of the American campus that took place in the 55-year period between the end of World War II and the millennium.

# one

# The Academical Village and the Power of Place

## Jefferson's Exquisite Diagram

Near the end of his remarkable life, Thomas Jefferson famously sought to be remembered by the inscription that he wrote for his own grave monument. In the inscription, he cited three achievements: "Author of the Declaration of American Independence, of the Statute of Virginia for religious freedom and Father of the University of Virginia." He made no mention of being governor of Virginia, secretary of state or the U.S. president who presided, among other things, over the young republic's greatest single geographic expansion. Jefferson's most profound desire, according to biographer Nathan Schachner, was to be remembered for "those points in his career when he performed some service in the unending struggle for the human mind."[1] In his quest to build a regional public academy in central Virginia, Jefferson would play a seminal role in shaping the American campus as we know it today. He called it the "academical village," implying an intimacy of scale that would nurture the exchange of ideas between professors and students. Still, he relentlessly pressed for his school to attain the status of a great university during the nine years (1817–1826) that he was involved in its construction.

The university occupied most of Jefferson's attention in his last years. Few individuals would play such an all-encompassing role in the birth of an American educational institution, from being the architect of its physical form to framing its pedagogical structure, all the while fighting for its very survival. Jefferson struggled with the Virginia legislature to have the institution located in Charlottesville, on a site in view of his beloved Monticello manor house. He constantly cajoled the legislators for the appropriations needed for its construction

The lawn at the University of Virginia. (UVA, Office of the Architect.)

and operations. He labored to recruit faculty. He nearly despaired of seeing its construction completed enough to matriculate the first handful of students in 1825, barely a year before his death on the 50th anniversary of the signing of the Declaration of Independence that he authored. In the last months of his life, too feeble to venture from the heights of Monticello, Jefferson would send urgent messages to legislators pleading to keep his nascent institution from languishing for lack of funds.

The academical village did not languish. As one of the last great acts of the Jeffersonian will, it has endured as the most powerful original idea of place in the American educational landscape. It was named in a 1976 poll of the American Institute of Architects as the "proudest achievement in American architecture."[2] Jefferson's design has been rhapsodized and analyzed in the circles of architecture, planning, and landscape design to the point of being a cliché. And yet, the eloquence of the place cannot be denied. The eminent architectural writer Paul Goldberger captured the singular American character of the Jefferson grounds in a 1989 article:

> There are few buildings anywhere that manage to wear powerful symbolism as lightly as the Academical Village, few places in which symbolism is so strong and yet so unintrusive. For at the end of the day, it is the physical form of this place that is its truly sublime aspect—the perfection of the proportions, the exquisite way the campus sits poised between civilization and wilderness. The University of Virginia is, in the end, an essay about balance. It is open, yet enclosed; rhythmic, yet serene; a model village, yet a set of discrete buildings. And it is at once an homage to Western civilization, and a celebration of all that is new and profoundly American.[3]

Jefferson's architectural plans for the academical village were superb in their diagrammatic clarity. They expressed the practical notion that communication among students and professors can be fostered by the arrangement of the setting that they inhabit together. The collegial ideal sought by Jefferson was not, by itself, revolutionary. It drew from the Socratic circles of ancient Greece and the medieval European universities wherein scholarly exchange and individual contemplation were nurtured in the intimacy of an intellectual household. Jefferson's originality was in his emphasis on the larger experience of place as a central feature of the educational endeavor.

Jefferson's basic design principles for the university fused his inclinations as an architect with his sense of how scholarly interaction should take place. Those principles were burnished by his agrarian predilections, as evidenced in this passage in an 1810 letter describing his developing ideas for the Virginia campus:

> I consider the common plan followed in this country, but not in others, . . . of making one large and expensive building, as unfortunately erroneous. It is infinitely better to erect a small and separate lodge for each separate professorship, with only a hall below for his class, and two chambers above for himself; joining these lodges by barracks for certain portions of the students, opening into a covered [passage]way to give a dry communication between all the schools. The whole of these arranged around an open square of grass and trees would make it what it should be in fact, an academical village.[4]

The ensemble is all about proportions and scale of place that promote communal vitality. It is about regional expression in its use of the timeless building materials of central Virginia: red brick with limestone trim, white-painted wood porches and window frames, and slate roofing. It is about its natural environment, with the shaded lawn and the colonnade walks acting as inviting passages during the humid Virginia summers.

Jefferson's idyllic campus green is scaled so that one can recognize the faces of people on the other side, less than 200 feet away. The colonnaded pavilions that flank the lawn offer dozens of front doors, making frequent human encounters an everyday certainty. The noble Rotunda at the high end of the lawn declares itself as the functional and symbolic nexus of the institution. For all of its intended intimacy as a place for human connection, Jefferson made sure that the campus embraced the broad landscape of the Virginia piedmont. He laid out the diagram on a hilltop that afforded a stunning visual grasp of the surrounding countryside. This was no medieval Oxford, cloistered from the unseemly outside. Jefferson reached for the tapestry of the American land, and many campus builders would follow him for the next 150 years. In this, he fulfilled an aspiration of the new nation to create a university shaped to America—"one that would negotiate a new relationship with nature in the New World."[5]

Even in their zeal to adapt the new American campus to the rural environment, Jefferson and the founders of other early nineteenth-century colleges applied civic design ideals to their campuses—ideals that embodied an implicit sense of urbanity in a natural setting. It is well known that Jefferson was no advocate of urban life. His declaration that the "mobs of great cities add just so much to the support of pure government as sores do to the human body"[6] left little doubt that he regarded cities as corrupting influences on the minds of men. Still, it is difficult to imagine that the civic organization of the academical village was not informed at some fundamental level by his immersion in the rich cultural crosscurrents of Paris during his earlier years as a diplomat. The rural/urban tension would stand as a defining factor in the creation of the American campus, arranged, improvised, and adapted to this very day. Paradoxical themes abound in the academical village. In *Mr. Jefferson's University,* Garry Wills enumerates the contradictory values that Jefferson placed in artful balance—regimentation and individual expression, hierarchical order and relaxed improvisation, a mix of the prescriptive and the self-determining—concluding that "it is the reconciliation of these apparent irreconcilables that is the genius of the system."[7] The academical village stands as a metaphor for the American experience.

It is fascinating to speculate on whether Jefferson ever conceived that his original grounds for the University of Virginia would be a national icon nearly two centuries after the university's founding. He certainly aspired for the university to persevere as a fountainhead of intellectual liberation, as a place that would cultivate future leaders of the republic. As an architect, he clearly saw the academical village as a model for the American collegiate place. It became just such a model, replicated in every region and climate in the United States, at small liberal arts colleges, great flagship universities, and everything in between. Though not often executed as exquisitely as on the Charlottesville hilltop, the offspring of the Jefferson diagram express a compelling need to create an iconic campus space that, by its own power, holds the whole of the institution together. Perhaps the most profound lesson of the Jeffersonian model for a campus is that the campus itself gives strength and meaning to the learning experience.

## Campuses for the Colonies: 1636–1769

The American campus narrative did not begin with the academical village. The beginning preceded America in the medieval European universities that grew out of the monastic tradition in which teacher and learner lived and studied in a cloistered setting. It was not the monastic setting itself that eventually migrated to the Americas, but the English notion of how a scholarly community can be shaped by the character of its setting.

The primary European influence on early colonial American educational institutions was the English and Scottish collegiate system. The early colleges in America were chartered by the English monarch and formulated in the minds of people whose only experience of a university came from England. As distinct from the universities on the European continent, where students were largely on their own in making their social and living arrangements, the English universities had evolved by the sixteenth century into complex communities that brought housing, dining, and social life into the learning endeavor. Oxford and Cambridge had become centers of liberal inquiry and were, for that time, remarkably accessible to large segments of the English population. Education was a popular and important movement in seventeenth-century England, one that was enthusiastically received in the new British colonies in North America. Oxford and Cambridge were the collegiate models that were followed in the colonies, reinterpreted to fit the rough-hewn setting and religious culture of British North America. Russell Edgerton puts it succinctly in an essay summarizing the history of American higher education:

> In the beginning there was Harvard. After erecting shelter, a house of worship and a framework for government, one of the first things the Massachusetts colonists did (in 1636) was found a college modeled on Cambridge and Oxford, where many of the colonists had studied. Their aims were twofold: to pass on their religious values and to recreate a bit of old England in the new land.[8]

Harvard College was founded a mere six years after the establishment of the Massachusetts colony, a reflection of the standing that the Puritan settlers gave to education from the very beginning. It was also a harbinger of the American idea of higher education that took form in the colonial period, wherein colleges were created to fulfill the particular needs and circumstances of the widely scattered settlements. Although Harvard was meant to embody the educational and moral ideas coming out of Oxford and Cambridge, the colonists, in laying out the new college, avoided the cloistered physical forms of the ancient British colleges. Whereas Oxford and Cambridge each developed over centuries as intricate, ever-evolving networks of enclosed courtyards and quadrangles in crowded town settings, Harvard's first buildings were organized to form a three-sided space thrown open to the surrounding town. This, as Turner points out, was a conscious move to connect with the new colonial village of Cambridge, not an accidental or incomplete version of old Cambridge.[9]

Nine campuses were built in the colonial period, all adhering to some expression of spatial and visual linkage between the college and its larger environment. The colonial colleges were made up of separate buildings set in the landscape, a further departure from the tight monastic character of their British forebears. Nevertheless, each college expressed itself in its own local way. William and Mary (1693) stood prominently at the end of Williamsburg's main street, with its three buildings forming a great space facing back to the town. Yale (1701) was laid out so that its first buildings stood in a row overlooking the New Haven Green. Princeton, originally the College of New Jersey (1746), consisted of one large building, Nassau Hall, sited in the midst of a broad field. Princeton's grounds were the first in America to be called "the campus."[10]

The importance of education in the American colonial period was conveyed by the size and prominence of the buildings created for that purpose. The main buildings at Harvard, William and Mary, and Princeton were attributed as being the largest yet built in their locales (with Princeton's Nassau Hall acclaimed as the largest in North America at the time). The importance of education was manifested, as well, in the distribution of colleges throughout each of the colonies as far south as Virginia. In proportion to the population, there were more colleges in America than in England.[11]

## The Campus of Post-Revolutionary America

By the time that the University of Virginia was founded in the second decade of the nineteenth century, there were 45 degree-granting colleges in the United States. Nearly three dozen institutions were created in the half century after American independence was declared, some as public colleges and most of the rest with sectarian affiliations. By that time, schools could be found in every region of the nascent republic. Education's seminal role in the American experiment continued apace.

Southern states pioneered the development of public colleges. In 1792, North Carolina established its university in rural Chapel Hill, a location central in the state but deliberately removed from the capital city of Raleigh. The plan for the campus was tied to the plan for a new village adjacent to the campus. The University of South Carolina (then called South Carolina College) was, on the other hand, founded in 1801 on a site in the new capital city of Columbia.[12] Both colleges were designed around iconic central spaces. The broad mall configuration of South Carolina's central space, open at one end to the town beyond, proved to be the progenitor of a campus form that would be replicated throughout America. Jefferson would later adapt the form at Virginia.

Meanwhile, the former colonial colleges were expanding, taking advantage of American architectural talent that was beginning to attain stature in the young nation. Architecture was increasingly approached with as much attention to contextual site planning as it was with building form. Charles Bullfinch's design for Harvard's new hall in 1812 resulted not just in the creation of a multipurpose building, but an advancement of the idea that Harvard should develop around a system of quadrangles. Benjamin Latrobe was retained by the University of Pennsylvania in 1800 and Princeton in 1802 to design the renovation and expansion of buildings on those campuses. His assignment at Princeton was to rebuild fire-damaged Nassau Hall and to design new buildings to be composed around it. He was later to design the buildings for Dickinson College in Pennsylvania. Latrobe's signature contribution to the evolution of American campus design emanated from a proposal that was never built—a new national university on the Mall in Washington. For that 1816 scheme, he conceived of a main building with perpendicular wings forming a courtyard open to the Mall (and facing the Capitol) on the east. The main building would have accommodated the common academic and social functions of the prospective university, whereas the flanking wings would have housed the residential quarters of students and professors. In the next year, Thomas Jefferson asked for Latrobe's advice on the early formulation of ideas for the University of Virginia. Jefferson had come to know and respect Latrobe during the time that the new federal city was being built and would consult with him throughout the development of his designs for the Virginia grounds.[13] Latrobe's conception of the national university—with principal academic buildings as an anchor to an open-ended space flanked by student and faculty quarters—is unmistakably reflected in the design of the academical village.

As Jefferson was developing his concept for the future university in Charlottesville, work was already underway in upstate New York on what Turner describes as "the most ambitious American college plan up to that time."[14] Union College in Schenectady, which had been founded in 1795 as a progressive, nonsectarian institution, was to be relocated to a new site on a height of land outside the town by 1812. The new location would allow Union's young president, Eliphalet Nott, to fulfill his vision of a familylike community "separated from the great world."[15] Nott's goal was to undergird the environment of free intellectual inquiry with a strong sense of communality by having students, faculty, and officers of the institution lodge and board together. In 1813, Nott hired Joseph Ramée, an architect and landscape designer who had recently emigrated from Europe, to prepare a plan for the new campus. Building foundation construction had begun in 1812 but was curtailed pending the results of Ramée's design.

Ramée's plan employed the now-common idiom of a three-sided central space open to the countryside but with bold refinements that could only have come from classic French and English notions of spatial organization. The campus was laid out in a broad U-shaped courtyard with a domed structure (originally conceived as a chapel) occupying the center of the semicircle at the apex of the space. The academic buildings framing the space were connected by arcades. At the ends of the U were two residential college halls for students and college personnel. Nott's idea of the familylike community, while "separated from the great world," did not turn its back on the world. Jefferson would have been aware of Ramée's eloquent scheme for built space to embrace nature and community as he advanced his own ideas for an academical village.[16] Ramée's basic organizational concept for the Union College campus is remarkably intact to this day. Much of that is owed to the fact that Eliphalet Nott was Union's president for more than six decades, remaining an ardent steward of the design idea that he and Ramée had forged together.

## The Antebellum Campus: Nature and Object

The four decades prior to the Civil War led to one of the most robust and tumultuous periods of collegiate growth in America. Upward of 800 institutions were founded, including many that failed in short order.[17] There were numerous cross currents at play during this period of burgeoning growth. The sense of national expectations for higher education appeared in the gradual development of practical scientific, technical, and agricultural curricula. Nevertheless, most institutions stood by the narrow classical teaching tradition considered by its critics to be irrelevant to the needs of an expanding, progressive society.[18] Students were frustrated by the limits imposed under the traditional systems, resorting to riots and vandalism that became deadly at some colleges.

Progressive changes in the college curriculum in Germany in the early nineteenth century departed markedly from the classical practices being observed in U.S. schools. Clark Kerr describes the changes that came with the founding of the University of Berlin as "the dramatic event" in higher education of the time.[19] Kerr notes that Berlin's emphasis on "philosophy and science, on research, on graduate instruction, on the freedom of professors and students," along with the creation of the academic department, brought an unprecedented vigor to Western collegiate life.[20] The United States was not wholly without its own progressive antecedents. Benjamin Franklin had advocated "a more useful culture of young minds" at the College of Philadelphia (now the University of Pennsylvania) in the mid-eighteenth century, where agriculture, commerce, and science would be studied; and Jefferson's curriculum at Virginia included science and mathematics as well as electives. Leaders at Harvard, Brown, and Michigan endeavored to introduce liberalization of curricula following the new German system, but at a national level, there were still few fundamental departures from the traditional approach practiced in America until Daniel Coit Gilman established a graduate research program at Johns Hopkins after the Civil War.[21]

On the other hand, students improvised a wide range of extracurricular activities on their own, including literary and debating societies, Greek-letter social organizations, and collegiate athletics. Turner observes that student groups occasionally created better library collections than those of their colleges, sometimes in separate buildings that became "almost an alternative student-run college within the college."[22] He makes the cardinal case that in this period, when the value of traditional higher education was being questioned from several quarters, the American college built "a kind of mythology" to sustain classical education as a noble and necessary model for the young country, ultimately benefiting all classes. A critical element of the mythology was to bring students together in a close community setting, surrounded by nature and removed from the distractions of urban life.

The emphasis on the natural setting in the nineteenth century was spurred by aesthetic considerations as much as by aversion to urban life, considerations that expressed "transcendental notions of nature as inherently more beautiful and uplifting than cities."[23] The campus that was immersed in what Turner calls "sublime nature" was seen as morally elevating to the character of its students.[24] New colleges were sited on hilltops and at the edges of water bodies where the greater expanse of the local natural environment could be brought into view. American campuses captured the sense of their native regional landscapes in ways rarely imagined in the ancient urban universities of Europe.

Still, less bucolic visions of the ideal campus were stirring in the decades preceding the Civil War. The urban campus had its champions, notably progressives such as Brown's President Francis Wayland, who advocated campus locations that would benefit by connections with and scrutiny by the host community. By the middle of the century, many colleges formed by various orders of the Catholic Church adopted urban locations in keeping with their tradition of service to the community. Campuses of the era adopted the Greek temple as a collegiate building form to symbolize the classical antiquity being taught in the schools. Buildings were designed as freestanding objects rather than as parts of building ensembles organized to frame central spaces, as at Virginia and many post-Revolutionary campuses. More significantly, the buildings were conceived to house a multitude of functions—classrooms, housing, offices—in a single dominant structure.[25]

Although "female seminaries," which were more like finishing schools, existed early in the nineteenth century, higher education was a male domain in America until late in the pre–Civil War period. Young women did not participate in American collegiate life in appreciable numbers until the 1850s, when about a dozen women's colleges were established.[26] Two Ohio colleges, Oberlin and Antioch, had inaugurated coeducational enrollment in the antebellum years, but it was not until the 1860s and 1870s that coeducation attained a firm footing. The new women's colleges, which proved to be popular from the outset, established a distinctive domestic character based on the then-dominant ideas of what a women's educational environment should be. The consolidation of the college's functions in a single building or closely grouped buildings reinforced the intended "family" atmosphere. The schools were located mostly in rural settings, removed from the dangers and temptations of city life. However, campuses were rarely located far from the secure, civilized presence of a town. The ideals of rural tranquility and domestic ambience were not very different from those of the campuses occupied by men. There was a compelling resonance in the idea of the college as a homelike setting that would influence campus place-making for years to come. One of the great exponents of that ideal would be Frederick Law Olmsted, whose influence is discussed in this chapter.

## Justin Morrill and the Convergence of Place and Populism

European immigrants had settled one end of the continent to the other by the middle of the nineteenth century, working the mills and mines of the American Industrial Revolution and tilling the land in every state and territory. Railroads, canals, and telegraph lines were being laid out across the land. Colleges, however, had not kept up with America's social, geographic, and economic changes.

President Francis Wayland of Brown University lamented in 1850 that among the hundreds of colleges that existed in the country, not one was "designed to furnish the agriculturalist, the manufacturer, the mechanic, or the merchant with the education that will prepare him for the profession for which his life is to be devoted."[27] A professor at Illinois College named Jonathan Baldwin Turner proposed a plan in the 1850s for a national grant of land for education, called by some a "common man's education Bill of Rights."[28] That proposal was never enacted. In 1862, however, in the same congressional session that passed the Homestead Act and the Pacific Railroad Act, the Morrill Land Grant Act was signed into law by Abraham Lincoln. First introduced by Vermont Congressman Justin Morrill in 1857, the legislation granted to each state an amount of public land, the income interest from which the states were to apply "to the endowment, support and maintenance of at least one college where the leading object shall be . . . to teach such branches of learning as are related to agriculture and the mechanic arts . . . in order to promote the liberal and practical education of the industrial classes in the several pursuits and professions in life."[29]

Morrill, the son of a blacksmith, sought to redress what he saw as a lack of practical learning at colleges in the mid-nineteenth century. Morrill's vision was not enacted without criticism. An earlier version of the Morrill bill was vetoed by James Buchanan, who argued that it violated states' rights.[30] People speaking for the agricultural community scorned the land grant idea as "book farming" even after it was enacted.[31] Once made into law, however, the Morrill Act proved to be revolutionary on several counts. It provided public higher education to a large segment of the population to whom access to college had been denied since before the country's founding. It steered American higher education in a more practical direction than it had ever taken. It enabled each state to create an institution serving the state's particular agricultural and economic environment.

Less than 20 years after the Morrill Act, 43 of the 69 public land grant colleges that exist in the United States today were already in place, including several previously existing institutions that were designated as land grant colleges.[32] The remarkable achievement of the Morrill Act was that it spawned a stunning diversity of colleges, shaped by local place and culture, whose aggregate effect was to forever change the civic role and the physical character of higher education institutions in the United States.

Speaking at the Massachusetts Agricultural College (later the University of Massachusetts) on the 25th anniversary of the land grant act, Justin Morrill recalled the intent of the act as being "founded on the idea that a higher and broader education should be placed in every state within the reach of those whose destiny assigns them to, or who may have the courage to choose, industrial vocations, where the wealth of nations is produced, where advanced civilization unfolds its comforts, and where a much larger number of the people need wider educational advantages and impatiently await their possession."[33]

## The Fortuitous Ascendancy of Frederick Law Olmsted and His Picturesque Populism

The period following the enactment of the Morrill Act is widely regarded as an extraordinary era in the making of a philosophy of the American campus. The campus became an anthem not just of the American land, but also of the ideals of a democratic higher education. One of the most fortuitous events of that time was the ascendancy of Frederick Law Olmsted as the country's most prominent landscape architect, ardently espousing his philosophy of the campus as a model for the betterment of democracy. Olmsted's notions of social reform were already imbued in his masterful design for New York's Central Park in 1858, with the theme of nature as a healthy, civilizing force for the common man. The theme was repeated in his designs for parks, public grounds, and communities throughout the United States. Even before he established his career as a self-educated landscape architect, Olmsted had written extensively about the need for civil institutions and outlooks appropriate for the still-formative republic. With the advent of the Morrill Act, it was inevitable that Olmsted would give his attention to campus design.

Olmsted was concerned not just with how the new land grant colleges would be made to function as democratizing institutions, but with how the sense of place for expanding campuses of all types could be shaped to make higher education a civilizing experience.[34] David Schuyler of Franklin and Marshall College, in a 1997 essay entitled "Frederick Law Olmsted and the Origins of Modern Campus Design," observes that:

> Olmsted's commitment to campus planning reflected his belief that the physical environment in which instruction took place was an essential component of the education students would receive. He hoped that a properly designed campus would influence the tastes and inclinations of students, who upon their return home would extend the civilizing mission that he attributed to higher education.[35]

Olmsted went on to draw plans for at least nine campuses after the Civil War, including new land grant institutions such as Cornell, the Massachusetts Agricultural College, and the Maine College of Agriculture and the Mechanic Arts (the University of Maine). His designs for the College of California (later University of California–Berkeley) followed the principles he had established in his work with the land grant colleges. His work at Stanford was a more formalistic departure. Schuyler makes the important point that while Olmsted never set down a book of rules for campus design, his work demonstrated several consistent themes that would bear on campus place-making in the United States to this very day. He intended that the campus should be an extension of its community and not a "cloistered retreat" from it. In his reports for California, Massachusetts, and Maine, Olmsted insisted that the campuses be located and laid out to make the higher education endeavor an integral part of the community, inculcating in students the "acceptance of social responsibility." He believed that for students to have a sense of communal responsibility, campus buildings should be "scaled to resemble a community." He summarily rejected the new generation of large, multiuse buildings that were being erected at campuses around the country, which he found to be "incongruous to the landscape."[36]

A corresponding theme often promulgated by Olmsted was that student housing should be of a kind similar to what students will inhabit once they go out into the world. Rather than building "large barracks and commons," Olmsted urged his clients to build housing that had the "appearance of large domestic houses," accommodating no more than 20 to 40 students. He saw such arrangements as having a civilizing influence on their inhabitants. Olmsted's plans avoided the quadrangle layout because it was too inflexible for future growth. As Schuyler observes, "Olmsted articulated a vision of the college as an organic entity, with buildings arranged to allow for future growth that would not compromise or destroy the beauty of the campus."[37] Olmsted applied to campus design picturesque notions of the landscape similar to those that had been successful in many of his plans for public parks, although he was not beyond formalism, as he elegantly demonstrated in his later design for Stanford in 1887. Olmsted's ultimate theme was that the campus, including its buildings and landscape, is an integral part of the civilizing mission of higher education. This was his universal theory, the foundation for his ideas of scale, nature, and community. He urged his clients at the new land grant colleges to recognize that the campus experience would be as important to the education and later behavior of students as any of the subject matter that they would learn during their college years.[38]

Olmsted demonstrated a practical theory of place that was attuned to the great wave of social and economic change sweeping over the nation in the last half of the nineteenth century. He perceived, in America's rapid urbanization, the need for natural surroundings offering a physical and visual counterpoint to the din of city life.[39] He sought the restorative power of nature and spaciousness in the design of parks, public spaces, and campuses. "Openness is the one thing you cannot get in buildings," he wrote.[40] He was ever mindful, however, that the public realm had to foster a sense of common cause if it was to contribute to the development of a civilized urban society in America. His term for this social ideal was "communicativeness," manifested by the creation of places that would invite people of all classes and interests to be together.

In a sense, "communicativeness" and the restorative properties of nature had been implicit elements of campus design in America all along, but in the later nineteenth century, Olmsted and his contemporary thinkers and activists were giving public voice to a philosophy of place in a democratic, urbanizing society that would have a sustaining influence on the character of campuses for the next hundred years. Although Olmsted was involved in the design of a mere handful of the many campuses that were created or expanded in the decades after the Civil

War, he brought to the field of campus design an original philosophy that coupled the American land with a vision for a civil society.

## The Campus for an Urbanizing America

At the beginning of the nineteenth century, the U.S. population was barely more than 5 million. The few cities of any size were situated on the Eastern Seaboard, none having a population larger than 60,000. The geographic center of the U.S. population, as calculated by the Census Bureau, was less than 20 miles west of Baltimore. Colleges established in the first two decades of the century, such as Dickinson, Union, and Virginia, were located in still rural areas east of the Appalachians. By 1880, there were more than 50 million Americans living throughout the country's continental expanse. Although the majority of the population was still concentrated in the East and Midwest, thriving urban centers were emerging in all parts of the country. Industrialization and commerce were in full throttle, absorbing a massive new wave of European immigrants who were mainly drawn to the expanding cities. The census of that year showed 20 cities with populations of at least 100,000, and one, New York, with more than 1 million people. There were 115,000 students enrolled in America's 800 colleges and universities.

Higher education institutions, especially the universities, were already evolving into more complex organizations. The German higher education model that had been dismissed earlier in the nineteenth century was now more broadly accepted, bringing in its wake a new, multilayered conception of the university, with emphasis on graduate and professional education and research. The new Johns Hopkins University in Baltimore was in the vanguard of this adaptation in the late 1860s.[41] Harvard followed not long thereafter, adding the elective course system. As other institutions across the country followed suit, the modern university was born.[42] Although Johns Hopkins and Harvard were both in urban locations, neither represented a radical new idea of urban campus form to match their educational transformation. Hopkins merely built its structures along Baltimore's streets, making the campus an indistinguishable part of the city fabric. Harvard's campus, by now more than two centuries old, actually ceded a part of its domain back to its Cambridge neighborhood by permitting students to live off campus.[43] Along with Johns Hopkins and Harvard, other older colleges such as Yale, Pennsylvania, and Columbia were becoming engulfed by their expanding cities in 1880.

For the most part, however, new campuses were still being located in rural and small-town settings. College life in the midst of nature's beauty was firmly established as a moral and aesthetic foundation of the American higher education experience. That, however, was about to change. A convergence of circumstances gave rise to new visions of what an urban campus in America should be like. The urban population was growing at a breathtaking pace. Industrialization had created a new generation of wealthy, cosmopolitan benefactors. The Beaux-Arts design movement in architecture and urban planning, with its formal arrangements of buildings and open spaces, became popular. Americans were ready to build a grander civic environment that, by then, had powerful cultural underpinnings.

The period from the late 1870s until 1938 was known as the American Renaissance, an era when "America's architects, landscape architects, painters, sculptors and craftsmen joined together to create an iconography that would represent their nation as the rightful heir to the great themes of civilization."[44] The search for an American cultural and artistic identity was in keeping with the country's economic ascendancy in the late nineteenth century. Seeking to transcend what they criticized as national provincialism, architects, artists, and writers found the inspiration of the Renaissance in European academies such as l'Ecole des Beaux-Arts and the French Academy in Rome. American architects drew freely from European classical styles, while developing original forms and details appropriate for the new U.S. industrial age. Exponents of the American Renaissance would have a prominent hand in U.S. campus design for nearly three-quarters of a century. The period after World War I marked the decline in American identification with the Renaissance, although most of the country's architecture schools tenaciously held to neoclassical design principles up to the eve of World War II. The American Renaissance in architecture effectively ended with the appointment of the German modernists Walter Gropius and Mies van der Rohe as deans, respectively, of the architecture schools at Harvard and the Illinois Institute of Technology in 1938.[45]

## The Campus and the City Beautiful Movement

Near the end of the nineteenth century, campuses were adding more programs and support activities, drawing larger student bodies to individual campuses than ever before.[46] The village analogy could still apply to the traditional liberal arts colleges, but the universities were now being described in the terms of a city. This coincided with America's urge to create a new civic realm in the decades bridging the nineteenth and twentieth centuries, adopting the formal principles of urban design embodied in the Beaux-Arts method and its distinctly American manifestation, the City Beautiful movement.

The City Beautiful movement, born of the 1893 World Columbian Exposition in Chicago, had as significant an influence on campus design in the late nineteenth and early twentieth centuries as it did on the planning of cities. The exposition was the largest and most dramatic example of Beaux-Arts planning and design ever built in the United States. The chief architect of the exposition, Daniel Burnham, later coined the term *City Beautiful* in the report of his renowned plan for the city of Chicago that was adopted in 1907. His plans for Chicago, San Francisco, Cleveland, and Washington, D.C., each resulted in the creation of formal civic spaces on a grand scale, usually framed by equally grand public buildings. His visions of public space were intended to convey civic strength.[47]

Frederick Law Olmsted, who designed the Columbian Exposition's landscape, was credited with the conceptual originality of the plan. Although more formally organized than most of his civic and campus designs up to that time, the exposition bore the Olmstedian stamp. Openness and nature were skillfully employed to make the exposition an enjoyable experience for the millions of people attending the fair. The exposition's Beaux-Arts design idiom was illuminated by Burnham's civic symbolism and Olmsted's emphasis on the human experience. It had an indelible influence on the design of cities, public places, and campuses for the next two generations. The powerful aesthetic resonated with the urban perspectives that were taking hold in the country's institutions. Paul V. Turner views it as "therefore natural that many of the new American universities, large both in size and ambition and thinking of themselves as cities of learning, should turn to the newly fashionable Beaux-Arts system to create their physical form and self-image."[48]

The City Beautiful era, lasting until the Great Depression, was a golden age in American urban design. Formal as its expressions and organizational patterns were, the City Beautiful movement drew from an eclectic range of historical styles and analogies. Embedded in the movement were ambitious social goals for the betterment of civic life.[49] The movement was perfectly suited as a design motive for the new generation of urban campuses that were constructed during the period. The new campuses for Columbia in New York, the Massachusetts Institute of Technology in Cambridge, the University of California at Berkeley, and the University of Washington in Seattle were laid out in classic Beaux-Arts patterns.

Each campus was defined by the strong axial symmetries embodied in the movement, but varied the expression to fit the terrain and the functional organization of the institution. Welles Bosworth's 1913 scheme for MIT eschewed the notion of separate buildings framing axial open spaces, being organized instead as a vast single building whose wings formed courtyards overlooking the Charles River.

The 1899 plan for the University of California at Berkeley by John Galen Howard was laid out as a series of building areas paralleling the contours of the Berkeley hillside along a terraced axial open space that ascended the hill (Howard's plan superseded a competition-winning scheme for the campus by Emile Bénard that exhibited a stunning mastery of the Beaux-Arts idiom). The 1908 Minnesota plan by Cass Gilbert, set in the Minneapolis urban grid, featured a system of open spaces along a formal axis descending to a park along the edge of the Mississippi. Many of these campuses drew inspiration from Jefferson's academical village design, representing something of a "rediscovery" of the Jefferson plan at the beginning of the twentieth century.[50]

The formal principles of Beaux-Arts design were adapted to numerous campuses that had been established before the movement took hold. It took a generation of bold architects to convince equally strong-willed campus leaders that it was time to superimpose classic axial order on campuses that were already substantially built up. In 1908, Paul Cret fundamentally redefined the informal organization of the University of Wisconsin campus in Madison by superimposing a system of formal open space axes and cross axes along which new buildings were subsequently located. Cass Gilbert redesigned the campus of the University of Texas at Austin in 1910 by absorbing a number of randomly positioned buildings into a formal campus arrangement laid out on two intersecting axes with building quadrangles in each of the four quadrants formed by the axes.

The University of Illinois, which began as the Illinois Industrial University in 1867, was originally laid out around a large, informally landscaped open space within the street grid of the towns of Urbana and Champaign. The grid provided the geometric framework within which Beaux-Arts design principles were applied in successive plans for the development of the campus during the first 30 years of the twentieth century. In this case, the Beaux-Arts order was matched with the Midwestern gridded landscape, enabling the campus to grow in increments along a powerful prime axis and cross axis. Plans prepared by Clarence Blackhall in 1909 through 1912, James White in 1913 and 1919, and Charles Platt in 1922, progressively established a civic structure for the campus that was the very essence of the City Beautiful era. Although the details of the plans were not followed to the letter, the basic order has been the framework for the growth of the institution for a century.

Far from being an arbitrary set of design principles imposed without regard for the distinctions of locality, the Beaux-Arts system was tailored to the topography, to natural features, to the views of surrounding local landmarks, and to the civic fabric of the adjacent community. The bold diagrams brought civic unity to campuses that were, themselves, becoming fair-sized cities. Open space was the defining element, as it had been from the time of the colonial colleges, but now was structured as a formal network of civic spaces and axial streets that acted as an armature for the buildings that would be added to the campus over time. The significant contribution of the period was that the discipline of urban design was introduced as a way of making and remaking campuses as whole places in increasingly complex settings. In that era, the campus attained a level of civic expression necessary to mark higher education's standing in an urbanizing society.

The era of Beaux-Arts-inspired campus site planning coincided with the period in which several major universities in the American West were founded or undergoing significant expansion. The powerful landscapes of the West were both an inspiration and a challenge to the spatial formality of the Beaux-Arts order. But in keeping with the American ethos that nature should be an integral part of the campus experience, Beaux-Arts formality was adapted, often ingeniously, to the grandeur of the Western landscape.

Leland Stanford's vision for the new university he intended to build on his estate in the Santa Clara Valley south of San Francisco was that it should have a formal, monumental character, laid out with grand vistas of the nearby foothills and the valley. The campus was to be a memorial to a recently deceased son. Stanford, a onetime transcontinental railroad builder, governor, and U.S. senator, was accustomed to planning grand-scale projects in the wide expanses of the West. In 1886, he commissioned the two preeminent designers of the time, Frederick Law Olmsted and Henry Hobson Richardson, to execute his design vision. Olmsted, as might be expected, proposed a relatively modest building layout nestled in the foothills, but Stanford insisted that the campus be built in a formal manner on the plain of the valley. Over the next few years, Stanford, Olmsted, and Charles Coolidge (a young partner of Richardson's who succeeded him on the project after his death in 1886) developed a design for the campus that held to the bold formality sought by Stanford.[51]

The plan was a remarkable blend of ideas that fully engaged the campus with its magnificent setting. The larger-scale formality insisted upon by Stanford established the important vistas that have given the campus its enduring prominence. Olmsted's Mediterranean landscape metaphors respected the semiarid California climate. He arranged for the site plan to make the transition into a more naturalistic composition as the campus spread toward the hills. In the design of the university's first buildings, Coolidge adapted the stolid Richardsonian Romanesque style of his predecessor to the locale by introducing yellow sandstone façades and red tile roofs. The architecture was arranged to form a series of arcaded quadrangles and courtyards reminiscent of California's Spanish missions. The Stanford plan advanced campus design in America by demonstrating that the new civic ideal of the campus could be adapted to the extraordinarily diverse environments of the continent-spanning nation.

In 1919, the eminent Philadelphia architect Charles Klauder was called upon to prepare a new plan for the University of Colorado's Boulder campus at the base of the Rocky Mountain Front Range. The campus consisted of a loose and undistinguished assortment of buildings that had been constructed from the university's beginnings in 1876. Klauder was one of the leading exponents of the resurgent collegiate Gothic style, represented in buildings that he had designed for Princeton, Wellesley, and other colleges. He also adhered to the Beaux-Arts planning principles of spatial symmetry and axial order, which he readily incorporated in his plan for Colorado as a way of restoring coherence to the disorganized campus. Klauder's conceptual breakthrough at Colorado was in matching architecture with the environment. Not unexpectedly, his initial building proposals followed the neo-Gothic style. But he realized that the style, which worked well in the serene East Coast landscape, was ill suited to the dry, rugged environs of the Front Range. In what Turner describes as Klauder's "most innovative stylistic experiment,"[52] Klauder crafted an architectural idiom for Colorado that he called, at various times, "rural Italian" and "Tuscan vernacular." With its sandstone walls and pitched red tile roof forms, the rural Italian style brilliantly set off the foothills backdrop. Klauder arranged the buildings around arcaded courtyards, a gesture toward his neo-Gothic disposition that complemented the bright, airy atmosphere of the place. The resonance between the natural environment and the architectural character of the Boulder campus as conceived by Klauder was so powerful that it stands today as the guiding principle for buildings designed at Colorado.

The collegiate Gothic design style espoused by Klauder, James Gamble Roberts, and the style's most ardent proponent, Ralph Adams Cram, flourished from the 1890s to the 1930s. Neo-Gothic and Tudor architecture had a magnetic appeal during that period with its genteel scale, refined detailing, and use of iconic towers and spires that gave campuses an appealing collegiate identity. More than architectural style, however, the collegiate Gothic idiom's signal contribution to campus form in America was in organizing architecture to create enclosed courtyards, quadrangles, and loggias reminiscent of the cloistered spaces of medieval Oxford and Cambridge. This reflected an educational philosophy of the time that sought to restore a sense of fellowship between students and professors, a more communal, introspective environment free of the distracting influences that many educators saw in the growing complexity of universities. The urge of those educators to return to classical norms of learning was a reaction to the specialization and vocationalism that prevailed around the turn of the last century. In some places, that urge was to recapture a sense of exclusivity. Regardless of the institutional motivations implied by the enclosure of campus spaces, the collegiate Gothic order became an important part of the American campus vocabulary that still inspires ideals of scale, texture, and tranquility in campus place-making. It could be executed with Beaux-Arts formality at campuses such as Duke, the University of Chicago, and Washington University in St. Louis, or be informally tailored to the shape of the land as at Princeton, Swarthmore, and Bryn Mawr. It restored a coherence and compactness to campuses, or parts of campuses, that had eroded in the expansive last decades of the nineteenth century. In so doing, it fostered a reconnection between academic and residential life. In the 1920s and 1930s, in a kind of outgrowth of the revival of the cloister, the residential house system sprang up at places such as Harvard and Yale as a means of integrating academic and residential life.

At the beginning of the twentieth century, fewer than one-quarter-million students attended America's colleges and universities. Nevertheless, the new century ushered a change that would prove to be as revolutionary as the Morrill Act in making practical postsecondary learning widely available to Americans. The new stage was the emergence of the community-oriented, two-year college system. Its champion was William Rainey Harper, the first president of the University of Chicago, who had already established his position as an innovative force in higher education in the 1890s. Harper was one of the first university leaders in the United States to integrate the German graduate research system with the English undergraduate collegiate tradition and was an early proponent of extension programs.[53] He also held that high schools should develop two additional years of postsecondary instruction to prepare students for practical lives in their communities.[54] At his urging, Joliet Junior College was formed in 1901 out of a high school in that Illinois city, becoming America's first community college. In the view of George Boggs, president of the American Association of Community Colleges, Joliet began a "community-responsive movement that has opened access to higher education to the most diverse student body in history."[55] The explosive rate of growth in the number of two-year postsecondary institutions in the first four decades of the twentieth century exceeded that of any other type of collegiate institution that had been formed in America up to that time. By 1920, the United States had 52 junior or community colleges, and 450 at the beginning of World War II.[56]

## The American Campus Legacy: The First Three Hundred Years

In the 300 years from the founding of Harvard until the eve of World War II, the continental American settlement pattern went from being largely the domain of indigenous people living in a natural environment to being an agricultural mosaic interspersed with towns and cities, and then to a constellation of urban regions rivaling those of Europe. The degree-granting colleges that were established in that remarkable period of national expansion chart the social, educational, and economic metamorphosis that occurred in the various regions of the country through time. The elite private institutions of the Eastern Seaboard reflect that region's early adherence to higher learning as a cultural resource, abetted by its accumulation of wealth and national power from the eighteenth century on. The public colleges and universities of the Midwest, South, and Far West mirror the successive periods of agricultural and manufacturing growth fed by the continental migrations in the early nineteenth to early twentieth centuries. The great city institutions, public and private, signal America's vision for an urban society in the late nineteenth and early twentieth centuries.

Campuses were open to the natural environment around them, and they blended that environment into the campus itself. Campuses echoed the nation's reach for a visible horizon. There was no need in this country for the campus to look inward on itself when nature had provided a bountiful, expansive, in many ways sublime, setting for a people declaring themselves unfettered by old-country limitations. The soul of the new American campus was the land. This ubiquitous theme is captured in Turner's observation that "Americans normally have preferred open and expansive schools that look confidently outward to the world."[57]

Buildings were set in the landscape; they enclosed the landscape only as campuses filled out and attained urban character from the late nineteenth century on. The campuses that were built in towns and cities, or where the towns and cities later grew up around them, were as open to their community surroundings as those that were sited in the countryside. They became important parts of the civic fabric of their communities. American institutions eschewed the monastic introversion of the old European universities until around the turn of the twentieth century, when the movement toward enclosed, cloistered spaces took prominence. Even then, the adjustment was meant to strengthen communal links on the campus. Nature was not so much excluded as it was captured, while the urban world built up around campuses.

It was a period in which much of the grandest, most dignified, best-composed architecture in America came into being on college campuses. Buildings and building arrangements were in large measure derived from the historic revival styles borrowed from Europe. We were, after all, as much a part of European culture as the Europeans themselves. Classically inspired architecture brought to the place-making of campuses an intellectual discipline and sense of order that gave the campuses powerful visual strength. To be sure, there were splendid, uniquely American adaptations of form and style shaped out of the materials and vernacular of various parts of the country. There was, in that great period of campus formation, a profound interplay between the rules and passions of architecture and the environments in which it was built. Those 300 years taught Americans much about how to create built places that can exalt and are exalted by the settings around them.

From the birth of the British colonial colleges to the appearance of the public colleges and great research universities, American higher education was in a constant state of evolution. It had grown to a national enterprise, housing nearly 1.5 million students in 1,700 institutions on the eve of World War II. Despite the breathtaking variety of institutions that were formed in American higher education's first 300 years, amidst a continent-wide range of settings, the central characteristic of each campus was that it was an inextricable part of its locale. It developed in the language of its locale. Those place characteristics became the benchmarks for understanding what there is about the campus environment that is distinctively American in its meaning and its image:

*Nature and Openness:* Nature is a defining feature in the American campus environment, whether expressed by the visual and spatial connection of the campus to the larger natural setting beyond or in contained spaces threaded through the campus itself. Nature, represented in landform, water bodies, and vegetation, provides repose, respite, aesthetic pleasure, and a unifying fabric for the campus. By being open to nature, campuses are open and integrated with the world around them. By making nature the center of campus order, institutions make regional authenticity an integral part of the campus experience.

*Inclusiveness:* In spite of the ivory tower stereotype, the signature trend in the historic development of American campuses through the early twentieth century was the accommodation of more diverse student bodies, more varied economic, cultural, and political expectations, more and larger roles in the service of their constituencies. The level and pace of that accommodation picked up when the Land Grant Act when into effect, culminating by the twentieth century in the community college movement. As late as the 1930s, American institutions still were not the everyman's schools that they would become after the war, but the trend from the mid-nineteenth century on was always toward places that were inclusive and democratic. Exclusive schools held their own, to be sure, but that only added to the diversity of the mix.

*Urbanity and Civic Character:* American campuses became civic places in function and image. They achieved a civic purpose by virtue of the educational, cultural, and social offerings that they provided to their constituents on and off campus. Campuses were organized with a civic order that supported and encouraged the interaction of campus citizens. They conveyed a civic presence to their community in the stateliness of their architecture and their spaces. The more complex some institutions became, the more cosmopolitan they became, the more they acquired an atmosphere of urbanity.

*The Strength of the Campus Idea:* The character and image of most campuses were determined by the strength of the original idea around which the campus was formed, or, in some cases, a transformative idea executed at some later, significant stage in their development. The original ideas around which campuses were designed were linked to the culture and environment in which they were located, and those original design ideas almost always ended up being preserved in some form as campuses rapidly grew in the postwar era. Princeton, Virginia, and Stanford are among hundreds of campuses whose basic character is defined by their original ideas, even as a host of later changes occurred. They provided the foundations for the transformations that were to come in the second half of the twentieth century.

# two

# The Postwar Twentieth Century:
## When Tradition and Transformation Intersected

## Remaking Place at Berkeley

The setting for the Berkeley campus of the University of California is at once complicated and breathtaking. The 175-acre core campus area is draped on a hillside location rising up to the Berkeley Hills that form the eastern backdrop of the campus. Two forks of Strawberry Creek descend the hill in meandering courses, providing the primary natural interventions in what is otherwise a heavily built-up domain. The university is bordered on three sides by the eclectic urban milieu of Berkeley, which owes much of its vitality to the existence of the university. The steep upper slopes of the Berkeley Hills emphatically define the eastern boundary of the core campus, although the larger university holdings extend far up the hillside.

The occasional vistas west to San Francisco Bay and the Golden Gate Bridge are, to say the least, stunning. The mellow East Bay climate supports the lush vegetation that graces the lawns, courtyards, and niches between buildings. The great white campanile of Sather Tower is a visual rallying point for the university and a landmark for the entire East Bay metropolis. At few universities in the United States does the physical setting influence the gestalt of the campus as much as it does at Berkeley.

The dramatic nature of the site was paramount in Olmsted's 1866 "picturesque" plan for the fledgling College of California, as it would be for successive plans of the campus made through the twentieth century. Near the turn of the twentieth century, the sense of optimism in the emerging promise of California inspired the idea that the state's university should embody that promise by imbuing the

Sather Tower at the University of California–Berkeley. (Sasaki Associates, Inc., Mark R. Eischeid.)

campus with the civic spirit of the time. Toward that end, the regents decided to conduct an international competition for the campus design in 1897. Phoebe Hearst, the mother of William Randolph Hearst, was so taken by the idea of a competition that she offered to sponsor it. Most of the more than 100 entries from around the world embraced the Beaux-Arts formality that had come to exemplify civic expression in America and abroad. The winning plan by French designer Emile Bénard was a classic urban plan organized around a network of boulevards and squares. The primary stream was rendered as a linear fountain that cascaded over descending basins to an informal park at the base of the campus. Although Bénard's scheme was a dramatic civic interpretation for a campus, it proved unsuitable for the topography and to contemporary notions of what an ideal college should be. Bénard's role rapidly diminished for various reasons, ultimately being transferred by the regents to John Galen Howard in 1902. Howard, who had placed fourth in the competition and was already designing the Hearst Memorial Mining Building, served as supervising architect, revising the plan and designing buildings largely in the Beaux-Arts tradition for more than 20 years. In his designs for the core campus at Berkeley, Howard achieved what many regard as the most complete combination of Beaux-Arts neoclassic architecture in a picturesque landscape to be found anywhere in the country. Campus development in the period leading up to World War II maintained a delicate balance between the natural features of the site and an architectural pattern that was sympathetic to the site, despite the fact that the university grew from 2,200 students to more than 17,000 from the start of the century to the end of World War II.[1]

The clarity of the relationship between nature and development at Berkeley was overtaken by Berkeley's growth after the war. Between 1945 and 2000, university enrollment went from 18,000 to more than 30,000 students, with most of that increase occurring by the 1960s. In the post–World War II years, the university established itself as one of the world's premier research institutions, increasing the ratio of graduate enrollment from 18 to 36 percent in the 20 years after the war. Hemmed in by the city and the foothills, there was nowhere to grow except by building high and filling the gaps in between. Land expansion near the core campus included a contentious plan in the 1950s for some 45 acres of urban-renewal-type purchases, clearances, and construction on adjacent city blocks. The eventual property acquisition, less than the planned amount, was used for student housing, parking structures, and recreation facilities. Academic buildings were not built on the expansion parcels. Large-scale buildings of the postwar period, many designed in the austere *brutalist* idiom of the 1960s, were located on core campus sites that cut off vistas, displaced natural landscape, and overwhelmed adjacent older buildings. By the turn of the twenty-first century, the building space constructed in such abundance in the 1950s, 1960s, and 1970s had already surpassed its first cycle of depreciation.

In 1997, the university undertook its most extensive assessment of the changes in facilities and grounds wrought by campus growth in the twentieth century, largely prompted by an act of nature. That assessment would lead to the crafting of a twenty-first-century vision for the Berkeley campus. The Loma Prieta earthquake on the nearby San Andreas Fault in 1989 shook the Berkeley campus, but the university did not sustain the kind of damage experienced elsewhere in the Bay Area. However, Berkeley straddles the Hayward Fault, with its estimated 32 percent probability of a rupture during the next 25 years[2]—a sobering prospect that prompted the university to make a seismic evaluation of all its buildings in 1997. The study found that more than one-quarter of the campus building space would require seismic remediation, concluding that it would be more economical to demolish some structures than to renovate them.

Chancellor Robert Berdahl called for a major capital initiative to make the campus facilities seismically stable. Berdahl, in announcing the initiative, said that if "UC Berkeley were put out of business by an earthquake, recovery for the state and the region would be hindered, and the impact locally and nationally would be felt for years afterward."[3] The approach anticipated a 25-year renovation and rebuilding program expected to cost more than $1 billion. The university prepared an academic plan that was coordinated with the building rehabilitation program so the capital investment strategy would be aligned with academic goals. Inaugurated by Chancellor Berdahl in 2000, the New Century Plan established a vision of renewal for the university's future, taking into consideration the academic plan and related expansion and the issues related to the campus and its context. Growth limits capped enrollment at the level of 33,000 students, to include Berkeley's share of statewide student growth. Measures contained in the plan to maintain the contiguity of academic and research functions and to design buildings and spaces that would promote a high degree of collegial vitality on the campus. The plan called for investment in new student and faculty housing in close proximity to campus to further enhance campus interaction.

The physical development plan was embellished by a landscape master plan and a landscape heritage plan, so that by 2004, Berkeley had created a visionary framework for the new century based on the restoration of the very qualities of the campus established in the early twentieth century. Some of the "offending" buildings from the postwar boom would be replaced by buildings in more graceful forms and positions and by the resurrection of landscape spaces to reunite the natural features of the land. Strawberry Creek, with its edges reforested, would once again wrap the campus in a green necklace. Roads and parking areas would be simplified by removing commuter spaces and forming a less-obtrusive network for service vehicles, building on the work initiated in the 1950s by landscape architect Thomas Church to rein in a clutter of traffic and surface parking lots. The landscape heritage plan judiciously recalls the best of earlier eras—the picturesque, the Beaux-Arts, the modern—recognizing that Berkeley's heritage is an eclectic layering of architectural styles, spatial arrangements, and landscape palettes that will go on to enrich campus life for future generations.

Berkeley, like scores upon scores of American campuses, entered the postwar twentieth century as a place whose scale, texture, and character still reflected a civic vision exquisitely orchestrated with the natural landscape. In an explosive growth period of barely three decades, the campus was transformed into a place that was more confusing and more congested, where the sense of collegiality was eroded by the sequestering of disciplines in big, indifferent boxes. The spectacular natural features of the place were too powerful to be totally eclipsed, but the natural amenities were diminished, nonetheless. It was not until near the end of the twentieth century that the penalties of unbridled growth and change were fully comprehended and that it was considered that the wages of growth should be redressed, so that the Berkeley of tomorrow could be the better place it once was. In all of this, Berkeley is the perfect metaphor for the transformation of the American campus in the last half of the twentieth century.

## The Engines of Postwar Change

The years after World War II marked a watershed that would forever alter the character and the dimensions of most of America's colleges and universities. In the quarter century after the end of combat in 1945, higher education in the United States underwent unprecedented expansion, institutional change, and physical transformation. The change was driven by four momentous forces: the GI Bill of Rights, the "Sputnik effect" on national science policy, the baby boom generation reaching college age, and the forging of a national "idea" on the postwar role of higher education.

### The GI Bill of Rights

The enactment of the GI Bill of Rights in 1944 provided federal tuition funds to veterans of World War II and, later, to the veterans of the Korean Conflict. Between 1945 and 1949, more than 2.2 million returning GIs were enrolled in

U.S. colleges.[4] Taking up residence in hastily built temporary dormitories on the edges of most campuses, the GIs and their families accounted for the first great wave of campus sprawl. This was the first time that family housing at a large scale appeared on U.S. campuses. The GIs shattered the traditional college student image. Mature, toughened by the experience of the war and intent on building a new peacetime life, they brought a pragmatic sense of purpose to their quest for a college education. Most of them were in the first generation of their families to go to college. Many would not likely have gone to college without the GI Bill. They injected American higher education with an egalitarian flavor not felt since the rise of the public universities after the Morrill Act. Many who became business and professional leaders would later become higher education benefactors.

Although the GI Bill was intended to reintegrate veterans into civilian life, the program did not, at the outset, receive unanimous acclaim from the higher education community. The leaders of several private institutions felt that the program should be limited so that the elite character of higher education would not be undermined by a massive infusion of federally supported students. Public institutions were concerned that full reimbursement of tuition costs by the government would induce veterans to attend private institutions. Ultimately, skeptics in higher education were assuaged by provisions of the bill ensuring the independence of the institutions from government control.

Few anticipated the magnitude by which returning soldiers would take advantage of the program. Veterans' enrollment was initially estimated to be no more than 700,000 over the life of the program—more of an experiment than a fundamental change in American higher education.[5] Higher education was transformed by its capacity to rapidly absorb unprecedented attendance levels and, more significantly, to broaden the academy's franchise of social responsibility to the country. The role of the federal government in financing higher education was firmly established with the return of America's war veterans.

### The Sputnik Effect

In the fall of 1957, the Soviet Union unwittingly altered the contours of American education when it launched the world's first successful orbiting satellite. The steady beep emanating from Sputnik alerted the United States that it had fallen dangerously behind in the cold war race for scientific and technological supremacy. Competition with the Soviet Union permeated every aspect of life in the 1950s. America's ability to prevail in the world in a wide range of critical areas—space, defense systems, weaponry, agriculture, communications, industrial development—was dependent on its scientific and engineering resources. The government immediately set about rebuilding science education from the elementary to postsecondary levels, and nowhere was the escalation of federal investment more pronounced than in the basic research laboratories of U.S. universities.

The stage for significant federal support of basic science had been set during the war with the mobilization of the technologies needed to secure victory. President Roosevelt, recognizing the contribution that university-based research had made in the war effort, called upon MIT scientist Vannevar Bush to recommend ideas for federal support of university science that would have long-term benefits for postwar America. A report prepared by Bush in 1945, *Science, the Endless Frontier,* stated that "since health, well-being and security are proper concerns of government, scientific progress is, and must be, of vital interest to the government."[6] The report recommended the formation by the government of a partnership with America's research universities through what would eventually become the National Science Foundation. Bush saw the partnership as the "simplest and most effective way in which the government can strengthen industrial research"[7] by supporting basic science and developing scientific talent.

With the scientific support infrastructure fully established through the National Science Foundation and other sponsoring agencies, the government quickly ramped up campus-based science as a cold war weapon in the late 1950s. That weapon evolved into one of the most important economic development resources of the American twentieth century, placing U.S. research universities in the vanguard of scientific and technological change across the globe. By 1960, the federal government had raised its investment in research, scholarships, and facilities loans to $1.5 billion a year, a hundredfold increase over the previous two decades.[8] At the turn of the twenty-first century, the government is still, by far, the largest source of research funds for U.S. institutions.

### The Baby Boom Generation

The size and number of America's campuses ballooned in the early 1960s when the first of the baby boomers reached college age. The offspring of the GI generation, born between 1946 and 1964, added a prodigious 78 million souls to the U.S. population. By sheer numbers and an unshakable sense of generational destiny, the boomers altered—sometimes distorted—the country's culture and economy at every plateau of their lives. They redefined collegiate life by their numbers and attitudes. Nationwide, college enrollment grew from 3.6 million in 1960 to more than 8 million in 1970, and would grow to more than 11 million by the end of the 1970s before the rate of enrollment growth leveled off until its resurgence in the 1990s. A major benchmark was crossed in the late 1960s when more than 50 percent of U.S. high school graduates went on to postsecondary education. On the eve of World War II, fewer than 15 percent of high school graduates went on to college. The number of higher education institutions expanded by more than 50 percent between 1960 and the late 1970s, from 2,000 to more than 3,150. Enrollment of women went from 36 percent of the college population in 1960 to 51 percent in the late 1970s. It was not unusual for established colleges and universities to expand by orders of magnitude in the period between 1960 and 1980. The University of Virginia grew from 5,000 to 17,000 students during that time. Missouri blossomed from a single campus in Columbia to four campuses across the state. Small public teachers' colleges became state universities. Institutions that did not exist in 1960 were sizeable places by 1980. New campuses of the University of California system in Santa Cruz, Irvine, San Diego, Santa Barbara, and Riverside were planned in the 1960s for student populations averaging 25,000 before the end of the century.

Demographics were not the only driving forces in the campus boom that started in the 1960s, but they added significant momentum to the increase in public support for higher education across the United States. Expanding federal support of postsecondary education with student grants and loans was a formidable stimulus to college attendance. But it was the states that engineered the expansion of existing campuses and the creation of new campuses at a magnitude unmatched in the history of American higher education. The need to accommodate an exploding college-age population was buttressed by a public policy that wholeheartedly embraced the economic development potential of postsecondary education. Glimpsing a postindustrial economy on the horizon, many states pegged their future prosperity to the value of a well-educated workforce. Higher education as a public good was at its peak until it collided with the student unrest and economic recessions that mounted in the late 1960s and early 1970s.

### Forming a Postwar Idea about American Higher Education

The U.S. higher education system thrived in the postwar period in large part because the country was experiencing an era of extraordinary social and economic buoyancy. The quarter century after World War II was the first time in American history when the economy and public social support policies coalesced to create a massive middle class that could enjoy unprecedented stability, prosperity, and job security. America's vast continental market had virtually no foreign competition for most of the period, enabling the domestic economy to thrive in fulfilling the pent-up demand for consumer products, housing, and capital goods that had been suppressed during the war and the preceding post-Depression years. The nation's employers, aided by government tax incentives, offered generous pension and health insurance plans, along with the prospect of lifetime employment. Government social policies, born of the New Deal era—and embodied by Social Security, unemployment insurance, and welfare—provided a more secure grounding against economic exigencies. America had the need, the means, and the incentive to support a vibrant network of independent and public higher education institutions. Stephen Cohen and Bradford DeLong describe the postwar period as one that "stands as a reference point in our popular economic history—a gold standard for rapid growth and shared prosperity." They also refer to the era as "probably an aberration, a confluence of events never before seen in our history and unlikely to be seen again."[9]

The educational policy debates of the early postwar period were reminiscent of the arguments that ensued in the nineteenth century between those favoring what was then the traditional classical education in America versus those advocating the more liberal German method. Two commissions in the late 1940s stood out in the discourse about the content of higher education and whom it should be serving. The President's Commission on Higher Education, chaired by George Zook, wanted to make higher education more broadly accessible and more oriented to society's practical needs. The Zook Commission, as it was called, favored more federal support of higher education. The Commission on Financing Higher Education, sponsored by the Rockefeller Foundation and the Association of American Universities, was less inclined to expand enrollment, emphasizing that the mission should focus on the cultivation of those showing intellectual promise and capacity for abstract thinking. The Rockefeller report opposed federal tuition support. The Zook Commission recommended that college facilities be expanded nationwide so that at least 49 percent of the nation's college-age population would receive at least two years of higher education by 1960. The Rockefeller report estimated that 25 percent of the college-age cohort could benefit from higher education.[10] As Richard Freeland observed in a summation of the two positions in *Academia's Golden Age: Universities in Massachusetts 1945–1970*:

> At the heart of the differences between the two reports were divergent views about the implications of "democratic" values of higher education. For the Rockefeller group, there was no conflict between democracy and elitism.

Admission procedures must be fair and accessible, but they could also be highly selective. The Zook Commission was less ready to accept a system that limited its advantages to the few. In its view, democracy implied not only fairness of treatment but also equality of status for a wide range of abilities and fields.[11]

No federal legislation was enacted in direct response to the recommendations of the commissions. Nevertheless, the discourse was fruitful in defining the benchmark ideas that would guide an extraordinary era of change in American higher education. More important, there was no disagreement on the imperative of institutional independence and academic freedom, ultimately fostering a great deal of improvisation in melding the values of merit-based education with societal purpose. At the same time, the government's role would be felt through a host of initiatives, ranging from growth in support for basic research, to student grant and loan programs, to support for facilities construction.

Affecting the debate on the direction of higher education was an uncertainty in the late 1940s and early 1950s as to what would happen to campus enrollment after World War II veterans completed their studies.[12] Enrollments did decline in 1950 and 1951 after veterans' attendance passed its peak. Private institutions were particularly affected by the decline. Then, college-age students streamed into the system, increasing enrollment by nearly 75 percent between 1952 and 1960,[13] only presaging the impact of the baby boomers who were still mostly in grade school. And then the deluge! In the decade of the 1960s, campus enrollment went from 3.6 million to 7.9 million, the number of campuses increased by a third, and the average college size tripled.[14] Clearly, the value of a college education had taken hold in America, vindicating the Zook Commission's advocacy of an expanded college-going rate. As Freeland noted, "the increasingly technical and bureaucratic character of industry, combined with the interest of employers in applicants with formal training and credentials, was convincing young Americans that college was an economic necessity."[15] Postwar affluence also made college more affordable to a much broader segment of the population.

Student enrollment became more diverse and the societal purposes of higher education institutions became more varied while, at the same time, the institutions themselves became more similar, according to Freeland.[16] They were providing more services of a similar order. Curricula became more standardized. It was inevitable that there would be a collision between the academy and the forces of student activism triggered by the Viet Nam War, and the rise of civil and environmental justice movements. Freeland noted that "For most of the period, the dominant view—inside and outside of higher education—was that expansion was improving the academy as well as the country, but the turmoil of the late 1960s raised fundamental doubts about the character of post-war change."[17]

## The Wages of Growth

Between 1945 and 2000, about 2,200 new campuses came into being and more than 12 million students were added to the college attendance rolls. The growth trajectory, however, was not consistent across that period. The transformation progressed in three distinct stages, each with commensurate impacts on the physical character of the nation's campuses. The first stage, the "golden age," from 1945 to roughly the mid-1970s, was the period of explosive growth—in student enrollment, in programs, in the size and number of campuses, and in the magnitude of facilities. The most profound impacts on campus form and scale occurred in this period. The stage from the mid-1970s until the mid-1980s was a period of relative stasis. There were pockets of growth, but national enrollment had reached a temporary plateau. Much of the momentum was stalled by the economy, the energy crisis, and the questioning of higher education that came in the wake of campus social upheaval in the 1960s and 1970s. The third stage of the postwar era, between the mid-1980s and the millennium, was a period of reformation. The competition for enrollments, revenues, and reputations forced institutions to renew their academic missions and to look again at the quality of the campus environment as an effective agent of the academic experience. Enrollment demand ramped up in the last years of the reformation stage, accompanied by higher student expectations for the quality of campus life, by growth in academic and ancillary functions, and by the need to remedy the decline in campus physical conditions.

Campus growth in the 1950s, 1960s, and 1970s took a multitude of forms. Campuses expanded in land area. They grew by filling in the interstitial spaces within campuses, making them more dense. The institutions that were on the most expansive paths, such as public universities and independent research universities, grew both outward and inward, literally superimposing new campuses onto old campuses. Campuses grew by dispersal to satellite locations nearby and spread around whole states. Entirely new college and university campuses were created to meet the educational, demographic, and economic demands of the period. The University of South Florida, founded on its own 1,000-acre site in Tampa in the late 1950s, added three branch campuses in one generation. In the 1960s, new community colleges opened at the rate of one a week. New campuses ranged from small liberal arts colleges to universities with enrollments upward of 30,000 students. Each approach to expansion affected the place qualities of the campus, and its home locality, in vastly different ways.

Most of the nation's public flagship and land grant universities doubled or tripled the land areas for facilities growth to meet the enrollment demands of the baby boom era. Public universities such as Ohio State, Illinois, Utah State, Penn State, Michigan State, Missouri, Massachusetts, and Auburn sprawled beyond their historic core campuses at distances that were no longer walkable. New dormitories were located at campus peripheries in mid-rise and high-rise enclaves separated from the heart of academic life. Athletic and recreation fields, field houses, and arenas were located farther out. Surface parking took up tens and even hundreds of acres at the perimeter of campuses and interstitial lots between the original campus core and the new dormitories and athletic facilities beyond. The functions became so distended that it became necessary to connect them with shuttle bus systems.

Campuses such as Michigan, Minnesota, Tennessee, and North Carolina State, running out of room in their core areas, located teaching and research facilities on satellite sites separated from their main campuses, requiring transportation to keep the outlying academic enclaves connected with the central academic cores. Agricultural fields, orchards, and pastures gave way to the facilities expansion. Properties were acquired by small colleges and large universities in the adjacent blocks of town, where houses were demolished or converted to offices and so-called institutes. New collegiate buildings popped up on scattered adjacent blocks, making town and city streets de facto campus streets.

A similar pattern occurred, usually at a smaller scale, at state colleges and teachers' colleges that took on the mantle of regional state universities—places such as East Stroudsburg University in Pennsylvania, East Tennessee State University, Northern Illinois University, and Eastern Washington University. These once-compact, bucolic places became more sprawling, with their edges blurring into the surrounding townscape and countryside, but their original core areas usually remained intact enough to maintain the historic identity of the schools.

### The Invasion of Vehicles

The impact of the automobile became a singular challenge on American campuses from the time that the returning GIs swelled enrollments, and never abated. Empirical experience suggests that parking has taken up 15 percent of developed campus land on the average, two or three times that amount at some campuses.[18] More land was given over to the storage of cars than to the accommodation of learning and living space. Property expansion was often driven more by the need for parking spaces than for other uses. Although most growing institutions attempted to keep parking areas on the campus periphery, the call for user convenience often won out, resulting in parking lots occupying interstitial locations in the heart of the campus and passenger drop-offs introduced near front doors of buildings. This, in turn, resulted in traffic congestion and conflicts in areas of the campus that had once been tranquil pedestrian domains.

Those institutions that chose to salvage the pedestrian environment closed interior streets or limited vehicle access to service and emergency vehicles and busses. It was popular, in making campus plans in the 1960s and 1970s, to surround the campus with a loop road system that would shunt campus traffic around the core pedestrian areas. Although that did allow traffic to flow more easily and kept vehicles out of central campus spaces, it usually created a further separation between the campus and the surrounding community. Commuter campuses and community colleges in suburban locations often took forms that were reminiscent of regional malls, with compact academic areas completely enveloped by parking. Such layouts often made for lively pedestrian cores, albeit isolated from the world beyond.

The accommodation of the car became an end in itself at many large institutions, where networks of broad streets were introduced as organizing frameworks for campus development, exacerbating sprawl and all but annihilating any semblance of human scale. Once enabled by having parking at the doorstep, faculty, staff, and students would become resistant to its displacement for new buildings or open space.

## Effects on Communities

The impact of campus expansion was often felt as acutely by the adjacent communities as by the institutions themselves. It was the rare institution that had enough land for a doubling or trebling of facilities expansion, so the only option, aside from filling in some of the voids, was to purchase property outside the campus. Occasionally, there was open and vacant land nearby, but, more often, properties with homes and businesses were involved. The prospect of campus growth by acquisition had a destabilizing effect on neighborhoods, where properties were allowed to run down in anticipation that they would eventually be bought up by the expanding institution.

In the 1960s and 1970s, when many central cities were in distress, it was frequently seen as a public good for institutional growth to offset the effects of neighborhood decline brought about by the flight of population and businesses to the suburbs. Colleges took advantage of special provisions of the federal urban renewal program, which was in its heyday at the time. Urban renewal funds were used to justify and subsidize public acquisition and clearance of land by eminent domain for the purposes of institutional expansion. Two cases had to be made: one, that the institution needed land for growth that would benefit the locality, and the other, that the adjacent property was "blighted." The latter case often involved stretching the definition of blight. (See "The Interdependence of Town and Gown" in Chapter 7 for further discussion of the use of urban renewal as a means of campus growth.)

There was always community resistance to campus expansion into nearby neighborhoods, but it continued to mount in the 1970s as more citizens insisted on having a say about the preservation of their communities. New federal and state laws contributed to their empowerment. The National Environmental Policy Act of 1969, augmented by environmental and planning legislation in several states, forced institutions to disclose the environmental and economic impacts of expansion proposals in public forums. New regulations on historic preservation were invoked to protect historic resources both in the community and on the campus. Cities and towns legislated more approval procedures governing campus development, requiring institutions to adopt more open policies for inclusion of community interests.

## The Academy Goes Modern

The postwar period was a heady time for modern architecture and planning on American campuses. It came as an unleashed force. Contemporary architectural design had, in fact, established a strong toehold in America in the decades before World War II, but its emergence on U.S. campuses was suppressed, not only by the Great Depression and the war itself, but by the fervent traditionalism that it encountered at U.S. educational institutions. The debate over traditional versus modern collegiate architectural styles raged in the 1930s on campuses and in the architectural press. Nonetheless, only a handful of strikingly modern campus designs had been initiated before the war, and those occurred in the late 1930s. They included Mies van der Rohe's plan for the Illinois Institute of Technology in Chicago, Frank Lloyd Wright's design for Florida Southern College in Lakeland, and the design for Black Mountain College in North Carolina by Walter Gropius and Marcel Breuer. The designs (or adaptations of the 1930s design, in the case of Black Mountain) were not fully executed until after the war, but they set a precedent waiting to be followed when the time was right.

The exuberant embrace of contemporary architecture on U.S. campuses was sudden. The International Style of architecture, which had surfaced amid controversy in 1930s America, became a design benchmark in the 1940s, 1950s, and 1960s. With its crisp, cubist forms; spare detailing; and robust use of concrete, steel, and glass, it was the embodiment of the new era of social and technological optimism that had swept the world. The technical capability to work in new materials and structures advanced rapidly. The United States was able to draw talent from all over the world, including European émigrés such as Mies van der Rohe, Walter Gropius, and Josep Luis Sert, who had been youthful central figures in the European prewar modern design movements such as the Bauhaus and the International Congress of Modern Architecture. I. M. Pei and Minuro Yamasaki were among the Asian-born designers who came to study in the United States and establish leading practices in campus design. Many of their landmark projects were built for American colleges and universities, as was the work of other pioneering European modernists who remained on the Continent. The Finnish architect Alvar Aalto demonstrated the gentle vernacular modernism of Scandinavia in his design for the Baker House dormitory at MIT. The only American building ever done by the legendary French modernist Le Corbusier was the Carpenter Center for the Visual Arts at Harvard. American-born contemporary leaders such as Louis Kahn, Paul Rudolph, Eero Saarinen, and Edward Durrell Stone made their distinct imprints on American campuses in the 1950s and 1960s with surprisingly varied interpretations of modern architectural form. Many of those men directed and taught in the leading architectural schools, begetting generations dedicated to the modern idiom.

The transition from prewar traditionalism to postwar modernism was a veritable sea change in the place-making vocabulary of the American campus. Optimistic young practitioners and educators of the postwar era saw architecture as a social undertaking bottled up during the dark years before. In a panel sponsored by a Boston architectural journal in 2003 to discuss the design environment of the 1960s, veteran architect Terry Rankine described the time as a personal educational transformation.

> This wasn't a revolution that happened overnight. . . . There were a lot of us who started our design education in the Beaux-Arts tradition. In my first years in college, I drew columns and entablatures. When I came back from the war, the revolution had begun. The Beaux-Arts training I knew was gone, and it was all Bauhaus. It was an amazing contrast, pre-war and post-war. But the change led to a growing excitement. . . . It was a heady time.[19]

It was a time of experimentation, in the design of structural systems, in the use of materials, in the conception of architectural forms expressive of the functions taking place inside the buildings, even in the ways that buildings were organized in the landscape. There were campuses to be built and buildings to be designed that had no traditional precedents. Moreover, the work had to be done at a scale and a pace that had no analogy in the collective memories of those charged with building the modern American campus.

Just about every campus in the country, existing or proposed, had to have a plan to guide its growth. The rapidly evolving complexities of the campus environment demanded liberation from the formal, stylistic prescriptions that had prevailed before World War II. Planning became a process of engagement with campus constituencies at many levels. Campus plans were approached more often as flexible frameworks that would allow for buildings to take their own shapes and positions rather than fit into a predetermined form. Paul V. Turner observes that postwar campus plans were often designed to reflect the autonomous nature of modern building:

> In a sense, the new attitude of freedom in campus planning, with each building standing on its own, was a return to the old American pattern—from the days before Beaux-Arts master planning—of separate buildings in large open spaces. But to the extent that the buildings on the traditional American campus were markedly different from one another in shape or style, it was normally because they dated from different eras. Given a chance, earlier colleges usually chose architectural unity over disparity. Only in the 1950s and 1960s did architectural variety on the American campus become a fully acceptable, even desirable, phenomenon. This change not only reflected the importance that modern architecture attached to originality (and its disdain of conformity), but it also expressed . . . the diversity of the post-war university.[20]

## The Juxtaposition of the Old and the New

As the need to provide new space became crucial, few institutions spared themselves from imposing awkwardly positioned new buildings on traditional spaces. The deleterious effects of careless sitting could be found on most campuses: the lost landscapes, the interrupted vistas, the imposition of behemoth architecture next to a century-old icon, or, alas, the demolition of the icon to make way for the behemoth. Few are the campuses that have avoided careless, sometimes unconscionable, lapses in the execution of change. Nevertheless, a fascinating thing happened in the transition from campuses being compact, humanly scaled collegiate places to becoming megacampuses. By and large, the old centers held. The historic hearts of scores of institutions were lovingly preserved because they embodied the image and traditions of the institutions. The sacred spaces had a powerful hold, one that could temper the layering of new objects on the campus fabric and even make campuses more intriguing by the contrast between old and new. If the original places were honored, it was because they were the bridges between generations. The parklike atmosphere of Michigan State's old college grounds on the north side of the Red Cedar River stands in clear contrast with the geometric order of the newer campus south of the river, defined by broad boulevards meant to move twentieth-century traffic. Ohio State's Central Oval and Mirror Lake Hollow provide visual and open space relief from the increasingly dense development occurring in the surrounding campus, and by providing an atmosphere of repose, they magnify the urban vitality of Ohio State's built-up academic precincts. Vanderbilt University is graced by two historic core campuses: its own and the one that it inherited when nearby Peabody College was merged with Vanderbilt in the 1970s. The historic areas impart a sense of collegiate tranquility in the midst of intensive development of medical, research, and nearby urban commercial uses.

## New Notions of the Campus/Nature Relationship

The American ideal of the campus as an integral, expressive part of its natural surroundings was under constant siege during the expansionist postwar era. Countrysides around colleges were disappearing, either due to campus expansion or suburban development, usually both. As new buildings and parking lots filled in the open spaces in the interior sections of campuses, the spatial connection with the natural areas beyond was broken. Visual ties with surrounding hills, woods, open fields, parks, and water bodies were cut off by buildings and roads. However, at the same time that nature was losing ground at many campuses around the country, it was being embraced in new ways at others.

New campuses created in the 1950s, 1960s, and 1970s made significant departures from the conventions of campus design practiced before the postwar boom, several demonstrating highly original ways of integrating the campus with the natural landscape. The mission of the institutions was uniquely expressed in the relationship. Consider three that took very different forms of regional expression.

The Air Force Academy near Colorado Springs, designed by Skidmore, Owings and Merrill in 1954, was the first new service academy to be built as a whole piece in the postwar twentieth century. The sturdy clarity of order required of a service academy was exquisitely fulfilled by its placement on a plateau framed by the backdrop of the Rocky Mountain Front Range. The buildings were laid out in a grid pattern around vast drill fields occupying broad terraces at the top of the plateau. The architecture was rendered in a crisp rectangular geometry, with simple metal and glass façades reflecting the Colorado sky. Most buildings project horizontal shadow patterns that set off the jagged verticality of the mountains beyond. Only the chapel, with its vaulting, folded-plane spires, was made to stand out as the academy's architectural icon. By sheer scale and startling visual contrasts, the academy has become one of the boldest spatial interpretations of a powerful natural setting to be found anywhere in the United States.

Tougaloo College was designed in 1965 by Gunnar Birkerts to replace a loosely scattered campus that had served the college's predominantly black student body for nearly a century. Birkerts chose a stunningly radical campus design to support Tougaloo's radical mission: to prepare young, rural black Americans for life in an urban world. The scheme was to mix academic and social facilities with residential space for students, faculty, and faculty families to promote a social environment emulating urban life. The design consists of a criss-cross layering of linear buildings, sitting on a hilltop and extended over the sloping hillsides on piers so that the floor levels remain constant for pedestrian circulation. Academic facilities are located in the lower floor layers, with residential facilities on the layers above. The natural open space of the hill weaves among and under the buildings. The urbanistic ideas embodied in the plan prompted Turner to remark that it was a "remarkable reversal of the traditional American ideal of the non-urban college."[21]

The plan for the Santa Cruz campus of the University of California approached the goal of fostering an intimate social community in a natural setting in a fundamentally different way. The Santa Cruz site consists of more than three square miles of undulating redwood forest terrain—more than four times the size of the Tougaloo property. To accommodate a target enrollment of 27,500 students, the plan prepared by John Carl Warnecke in 1963 envisioned a constellation of academic/residential colleges, with fewer than 1,000 students in each. The colleges were planned to be relatively independent of one another. The division of the campus into small academic clusters scattered amidst the woods was intended to emulate the social and educational virtues of the small liberal arts college, but to have the aggregated resources of a great university. Santa Cruz, in many ways, reprised the eighteenth- and nineteenth-century American ideals of an intimate collegiate environment surrounded by nature. As the Santa Cruz campus has grown, it has, to a large degree, fulfilled those ideals. In that respect, it is a university like no other. In spite of its idyllic setting, however, the campus has been criticized in recent years for lacking a sense of civic coherence, for having no central focus that gives the campus a sense of university-wide identity.

## The Postwar Urban Campus

The ideal of the campus as an urban social enterprise flourished in the 1960s and 1970s. It was a period of urban turmoil spurred by the accelerating flight of jobs and middle-class families to the suburbs, isolating poor and minority households in inner-city areas with diminishing economic prospects. In the flush of the Great Society, massive public investments in social service programs and urban revitalization projects were made in an attempt to stem further urban decline. Higher education was a principal player in the revitalization effort. State university systems established new urban campuses in cities such as Milwaukee, St. Louis, Memphis, Birmingham, Cleveland, and Indianapolis. In Michigan, new downtown public campuses were built in Detroit and Flint. Boston, the bastion of private higher education, hosted its first public university with the 1965 opening of a new branch of the University of Massachusetts. Urban private and municipal colleges were absorbed and expanded by state systems. Private institutions such as Chicago, Tufts, Marquette, and Johns Hopkins were associated with redevelopment efforts using the tools of urban renewal.

The Chicago Circle campus of the University of Illinois (now known as the University of Illinois–Chicago) was the most prominent of the new urban campuses built in the 1960s. At 106 acres, its site was one of the largest to be developed for new campus construction in an urban setting. Its location at the edge of one of America's most storied downtowns was unsurpassed in terms of accessibility and civic imagery. The design of the campus at its opening in 1965 was considered by many to be a prototype for the new American urban campus. The design by Skidmore, Owings and Merrill featured a two-level system of pedestrian walkways—one on the ground and one on elevated walks. The centerpiece of the campus was a common lecture center whose roof, connected with the elevated walks, consisted of four open amphitheaters (or *exedras*) in quadrants around a large central amphitheater. Surrounding the lecture commons were large buildings housing the student union, library, and laboratories; a 28-story high-rise administration building; and smaller classroom buildings.

Early critiques of the campus in the architectural journals praised the strength of the architectural forms and relationships as well as the concentration of activities generating student interaction.[22] The comments were less praiseworthy about the human environment of the campus and the disconnection of the campus with its urban neighborhood. The elevated walkways were criticized for stealing pedestrian life from the ground level of the campus because they diluted the volume of ground-level pedestrian activity and created obscure areas and obstructions in the campus landscape. The resulting environment was characterized as "hard, unyielding, vast in scale."[23] (The elevated walkways were removed in the 1990s, much to the enhancement of ground-level activity and amenity.) The layout of the campus, in a superblock lacking any engagement along the surrounding city streets, exacerbated the perception of its being a detached enclave. The university's relationship with the neighboring community was not helped by the fact that the urban renewal land on which it sits was initially earmarked for neighborhood housing.[24] ("The Entrepreneurial Campus" in Chapter 8 describes an initiative started in the late 1990s to construct a mixed-use urban village on several blocks of university land, melding city life with the campus proper.)

Other new downtown campuses built in the 1960s, such as Portland State University in Oregon, Cleveland State University in Ohio, and Wayne State University in Detroit, were designed to be part of the street and block structure of their cities. Urban campuses that were outgrowing their boundaries, unable or unwilling to engage in neighborhood expansion battles, decamped to outlying locations or found new land. Rochester Institute of Technology, unable to meet its burgeoning growth needs in a then-declining neighborhood near downtown Rochester, built an entirely new campus on a 1,000-acre farm site south of the city. Northwestern University, hemmed in by the surrounding city of Evanston, added 80 acres of land to the campus by filling the adjacent shore of Lake Michigan. In 1974, the Boston campus of the University of Massachusetts was relocated to a former trash landfill jutting into the harbor.

## The Late Twentieth Century: Stasis and Renewal

The period of booming campus development subsided in the 1970s as the baby boom student influx began to level off by the middle of the decade. Enrollment in American colleges had grown by 4.3 million students in the 1960s and by 3.6 million in the 1970s, most of it in the first half of the decade. In the 1980s, enrollment grew by 2 million students, much of that in community colleges and graduate schools. The oil embargoes of the 1970s and the ensuing energy shortages sparked what was called "stagflation." The country went through a series of recessions through the early 1980s, battering the stock market and the endowment portfolios of private colleges and universities. For the public institutions, state appropriations started to decline by the 1980s.

Financial and political difficulties for higher education began to surface in the late 1960s. Richard Freeland asserts that "the social position of higher education was weakened severely, and academic leaders were more concerned with defending their institutions against criticism than with shaping new demands for funding."[25] Moreover, the period through the 1980s was one in which the values of higher education were frequently questioned in books, journals, and the popular media. The labor market cooled off to college graduates, raising public skepticism about personal and public investment in the academy. Clearly, institutions were at the point where they needed to reexamine their missions and formulate strategies for dealing with a new "age of limits."

The period of stasis redirected the attentions of campus leaders to the state of campus facilities and grounds. Campus buildings erected in the quarter century after the war, upward of 2 billion square feet by some estimates, were reaching their first cycle of depreciation. Added to that, many of the prewar buildings on U.S. campuses, some dating back a century or more, had been neglected in the heady expansion years. Building renovation strategies were incorporated in the resurgent wave of campus planning that U.S. institutions undertook in the 1980s and 1990s. Regrettably, funding for facilities renovation did not keep up with the need, and has not to this day (see "The Cost of Place" in Chapter 6).

The main thrust of the campus revitalization campaigns that colleges and universities embarked upon in the 1980s was to meet the heightening competition for students and academic reputation. The downturn in the college-age population, although slight, was enough to trigger a rush to keep seats filled, especially for tuition-dependent private institutions. Public colleges, many of which were funded on the basis of enrollment, were also eager to maintain—even diversify—their demographic reach. The growing dependence on federal, state, and corporate research grants as a revenue source at public and private research institutions drove the expansion of graduate enrollment in science, engineering, and technology. The U.S. workforce, which needed to keep up with new and changing skill demands, provided a source of enrollment in continuing education, executive education, and technical upgrade courses.

Institutions entered this competitive environment with the realization that the quality of campus life would have to be reenergized to attract students and faculty. Demonstrated improvements in campus quality would be necessary to spur the interests of alumni and other public and private sources of financial support. "Quality of campus life" facilities deemed necessary to attract new students— housing, student unions, sports and recreation facilities, arts and cultural events spaces—dominated the renewal efforts at hundreds of U.S. colleges in the 1980s and 1990s. Many of the enhancements were financed by student or user fees and other sustained revenues, making campus improvements less dependent on uncertain capital appropriations. Such projects, however, strained the bonding capacity of many institutions. The level of amenity in the new facilities was often exceptional compared to what had been built in the earlier expansionist period. The gang dorms of the 1950s and 1960s were no longer adequate to meet the expectations of students in the 1980s and 1990s. Student housing was now in residence halls composed of suite-style and apartment units, with more single-occupant rooms.

Along the way to creating places more attractive to students, schools were reminded that the learning environment is improved when the quality of life is improved. Ideas about restoration of open space, reclamation of a walkable, human-scale campus, and creation of opportunities for interaction and chance encounter became the watchwords for the redesign of campus facilities and grounds. The value of the informal learning experience was expressed by the inclusion of generous amounts of public and common space in the design of teaching and research facilities. Campus plans were plentifully endowed with goals to foster the sense of place and the sense of community.

## Postmodernism and the Reprise of Historicist Roots

Planning and design concepts applied to campus renewal in the 1980s were mostly based on traditional formulations. The restoration of open space order, civic structure, and human scale was in keeping with campus design principles going back to the eighteenth century, when there were no cars, no high-tech laboratories, no massive sports and recreation facilities to consider. What made the old principles valid was their focus on the qualities of the natural setting and the character of space as a host to the human learning endeavor. Oftentimes, as campus renewal gained momentum in the 1980s, architects and planners applied literal or near-literal translations of historic forms and orders in their designs, adopting an idiom that was called *postmodernism.*

Seen simply as a revival of classical architectural principles, postmodern design was an easy fit in the campus domain, with all of its traditional reference points—a return to roots, so to speak. But there was more behind it than that. Postmodernism was born out of two interlocking motivations: It was a reaction to the austerity and lack of spatial and contextual resonance that modern design had come to symbolize by the 1970s; and it was a means of bringing representation and historical context back into the vocabulary of architecture. The social purpose of modern architecture had, somewhere, lost its way.

Interestingly, the genesis of postmodernism was attributed to ideas promulgated in the 1960s, a time when modernism in America was at its height and barely 20 years into wide acceptance. The American architect-scholar Robert Venturi is often cited as a seminal influence in the rise of postmodernism through his writing and the architecture that he produced from the 1960s on. Neil Levine, in an essay appearing in *American Architectural History: A Contemporary Reader*, credits Venturi as being one of the most influential architects of the last quarter of the twentieth century because of his "understanding of the role history must play in the restoration of a representational dimension to modern architecture."[26] Architects such as Philip Johnson (once in the vanguard of the modern international style) and Robert Stern became prolific exponents of classical references in their work.

For nearly 20 years, postmodernism was a dominant expression in campus design. Although it brought elements of stylistic continuity with the established architecture of older campuses, and a frequently welcomed reprise of ornamentation, it was too often executed in shallow, superficial ways. The intellectual intent of those like Venturi was frequently lost in the literal translation. Where campuses benefited from the revival of classical principles was not so much in the architectural style as in the urban design planning of campuses, much being reminiscent of the Beaux-Arts principles of a century earlier. Plans emphasizing a coherent spatial order, framed and animated by buildings of compatible scale, brought civic and human qualities back at least to parts of campuses recovering from the postwar free-for-all. Among the most eloquent examples of that urban design idiom were the plan and subsequent building designs for Carnegie Mellon University by Michael Dennis and for Rice University by Cesar Pelli. As the twentieth century came to a close, postmodernism was on the wane as a stylistic idiom, opening the door to crisp, but spirited, contemporary designs in glass, metal, and masonry that telegraphed the life inside the buildings. The turn of the new century gave rise, as well, to a new generation of self-conscious "rock star" architecture.

## Reflections on the Legacy of the Twentieth-century Campus

In a 1991 article entitled "Restoring the Values of Campus Architecture," veteran planner Werner Sensbach captured the challenges involved in remaking the qualities of place that had been eclipsed during the halcyon years of postwar campus expansion. Sensbach had directed facilities planning at the University of Virginia from 1965 to 1991, a period of unprecedented expansion there as at other institutions. He made a plea to campus leaders, academicians, and alumni to take up the banner of stewardship, acting as *enlightened patrons* to the design professional classes in whom colleges and universities had placed great faith in the postwar period. In his prologue, Sensbach lamented that:

> Even a superficial glance at the interior of most campuses reveals a break between the small scale of the pre-1950 buildings and the massive scale of the newer structures. The self-referential, fortress-like, nearly windowless, and often faceless structures of the past few decades that have muscled their way into the university architectural context are visually disconcerting. Some modern architects, by abandoning ornament, have felt a need to turn their whole building into an ornament, giving rise to some egregious and faddish forms.[27]

With a perspective that could only have been honed as the steward of America's most storied campus, Sensbach offered three lessons for making institutions better patrons of campus design: A renewed sense of the special purpose of campus architecture; an unswerving devotion to human scale; and restoration of the sense of delight that a campus demands. On his first point, he asserted that "no architect should be permitted to build for academe unless he or she fully appreciates that his or her building is an educational tool of sorts."[28] Sensbach reflected on the idea that the campus, and therefore its architecture, must fulfill a purpose unlike any other entity, which is to quicken the intellectual, sensory, and experiential capacity of students in the special process of making the transition from adolescence to adult citizenship. On the matter of human scale, he admonished his readers to recognize that higher learning is "an intensely personal exercise," of sharing and arguing ideas, beliefs, facts, and information. Human scale is an *imperative* that enhances the relationships that are so fundamental to collegial life. Scale, not style, he insisted, is the "essential element in good campus design." Sensbach acknowledged that *delight* is the hardest quality to define, being a matter of feelings that are evoked by the particular sights and smells and sounds of a campus. To achieve that quality, he asked campus leaders to choose and support professionals who are prepared to infuse their designs with surprise, elegance, whimsy, and wonder.

The Sensbach piece was one of many that appeared in journals and books assessing the state of the American campus at the end of the twentieth century. Current and former college presidents weighed in with important books on the institutional issues facing the academy, invariably touching on how the campus itself must reinforce the learning experience. Educators, planners, and designers were joined in a wide-ranging discourse, not just on the consequences of growth in the twentieth century that needed to be reexamined, but on qualities of the place-based campus that must endure as a learning environment in the face of societal changes already surfacing as the century drew to a close.

Most campus plans and designs in the late twentieth century focused on remedying issues of campus sprawl, the predations of the automobile, unsympathetic architecture, erosion of open space, backlog of physical plant needs, and neighborhood decline, but they also delineated ideas for the stewardship of place and enhancement of community necessary to sustain the campus environment in the future. Plans, mission statements, books, and articles reaffirmed the notion that place and community are interlinked, fundamental elements of the learning experience.

Any appraisal of the changes in the face of the American campus that occurred in the second half of the twentieth century must emphasize the extraordinarily powerful impact those changes had on the country as a whole. The central, overriding fact is that U.S. campuses became open and accessible to a larger, more diverse population of Americans and people from other lands at a level that can only be described as culture-changing. To move from a student body of 2.6 million infused by war veterans and their families in the 1940s to 15 million learners of every age, locale, and socioeconomic circumstance in less than three generations will go down in history as one of America's greatest social accomplishments. More than just embracing such huge numbers, the academy became more integrated into the life of communities and the country by the multiplicity of roles that it took on and by the range of constituent interests it came to serve. One can legitimately question the relevance of some roles that colleges and universities now play, but one cannot deny that they reflect a sense of how extraordinarily complex our society and our learning community has become.

The twentieth century gave the American campus a powerful civic presence in communities all across the country. We have 4,000 place-based institutions, with their branch campuses and outreach centers, their cultural and event offerings, their experiment stations, their academic medical centers, their arboreta and nature preserves, their far-flung research enterprises, their investments in real estate and community change beyond campus borders. We have community college storefront and online learning centers within reach of practically everyone. We have vast flagship campuses and research universities that define the culture and economy of whole urban regions and whole states. We have idyllic private colleges that have maintained a sense of genteel grace for generations. We have places such as Boston with more than two dozen colleges whose boundaries are so porous that one can barely discern where town ends and gown begins. The twentieth century gave America and the academy an interchangeable face.

As we look to the new century, we most certainly look to the revitalization and stewardship of the campus as a learning community, and we look beyond to how the campus and its community will be redefined by the forces of the new century while sustaining the power of place that is an essential part of the learning experience.

## Part Two

# The Seismic Forces Affecting the Shape of the Twenty-first-century Campus

The saying goes that nothing about the future is inevitable except change. That underlying fact of human existence is countered by an equally compelling desire for a degree of constancy in the lives of individuals and institutions. Change, of course, is a constant in American higher education that will not abate in the twenty-first century. Indeed, structural trends that took root in the last century are having seismic impacts on higher education institutions in this embryonic century. A structural trend, in this discussion, is considered to be one that is likely to last for at least a generation (if not indefinitely) and is of such import that it will permanently alter some aspects of campus-based higher education as we know them. Six such "seismic forces" are described in the chapters that follow:

- The revolution in digital information technology may be the most dynamic engine of economic, social, and cultural change in the world today. Nowhere is its impact more profound than in higher education, where the development and delivery of information is at the very heart of the learning enterprise. Technology will test basic notions of how place-based institutions teach in the campus setting and how they are to connect with students, other institutions, and communities for the broad dissemination of learning that this century will demand.

- Globalization encompasses the unprecedented movement of commerce, finances, information, jobs, people, cultural influences, and environmental change across international borders. Higher education, regarded as one of this country's most successful export endeavors, must adapt to the new roles, relationships, and competition embodied in the globalization of the academy.

- The diverse, ever-changing nature of the U.S. population, when coupled with the emerging demands of the highly competitive, knowledge-based economy, raises unparalleled challenges to the way that higher education is delivered in the United States. The challenge to place-based colleges and universities is in how they redefine themselves to serve demographic cohorts that are becoming more heterogeneous in their make-up and in their educational needs and expectations.

- The costs of a robust higher education system are colliding with limits in the ability of families to afford college and the willingness of governments in the United States to support higher education at levels that they have in the past. As future sources of education funding become less predictable, institutions will have to exercise more prudent stewardship to make the campus more effective as a learning environment.

- Many local communities will struggle to maintain fiscal stability and the quality of civic life in the volatile global economy of the twenty-first century. Nonprofit institutions will play roles in economic development and urban revitalization that traditionally have been the province of the municipal and business sectors. It will be in the mutual self-interest of the institutions and the localities to actively collaborate in community revitalization.

- In the quest for students, revenue, research dollars, and brand identity, colleges are engaging in entrepreneurial ventures outside the conventions of the academy. The development of university research parks, commercial and residential real estate projects, and campus amenities in partnership with private enterprises is changing the face of the campus and blurring the boundaries between the campus and the surrounding community.

Treating each of these structural trends as individual discussion topics is merely a way of conveying the substance of each trend and its implications for the higher education environment. They are interwoven in many layers. A campus cannot function as a globally relevant enterprise without a robust digital infrastructure. Technology and global connectivity will be key to engagement with demographically diverse learners and with communities undergoing economic transformations. The stewardship of institutional land and space resources, aided by technology, will contribute to the enhancement of the learning environment on campus and in the host communities. These relationships are explicit and implicit in the discourse that follows.

Technology, globalization, and demography (Chapters 3, 4, and 5) make up a composite "metatrend"[1] of the twenty-first century, driving cultural and economic transformation (and conflict) around the planet. Together, they will significantly affect the relationships among American higher education institutions, their communities, the nation, and the world, redefining the basic structure of place-based institutions.

Stewardship, community involvement, and entrepreneurial development (Chapters 6, 7, and 8), while closely connected with the metatrends described above, are practical responses to economic and societal demands that are directly affecting institutional operations. Their common thread is in the qualitative implications they hold for campus physical development and for the development of the communities around the campuses.

Numerous other forces for change, known and yet to be discovered, will affect the course of higher education in the twenty-first century. Radical concepts of pedagogy, possibly shaped by a convergence of technology and behavioral science, or by generational shifts in the teaching force, could alter the educational landscape forever. Unforeseen political, economic, environmental, and cultural shifts will very likely occur in the long term, some sooner than anyone can imagine. Nevertheless, the seismic forces described in the following six chapters are well underway. Their implications for the future of the American campus and its civic context are within the strategic horizons of today's educational leaders and planners.

The Drill Field at Virginia Tech. (Sasaki Associates.)

three

# *The Synergy of Real Space and Cyberspace*

## The Electronic Village

By most measures, the look and feel of the Virginia Tech campus is exactly what one would expect of a great American land grant institution. The Virginia Polytechnic Institute and State University, as it is officially known, is a superb example of a public university that evokes a distinctive, powerful sense of its place at three crucial levels: collegiate, civic, and regional.

In the typical pattern of the land-grant institution, Virginia Tech is made up of an historic academic core area bounded on one side by the town of Blacksburg and on the other by hundreds of acres of open land used for intercollegiate sports, intramural recreation, and agriculture. The central campus area, designed in traditional and modern variations of the collegiate Gothic style, surrounds a grand space known as the Drill Field. Most university buildings are clad in "hokie stone," a warm, light limestone quarried in the region. The Drill Field, recalling Virginia Tech's genesis as a military cadet academy, is an immense open oval at the campus epicenter. Residential spaces are concentrated on one side of the oval and academic facilities on the other. Few collegiate scenes are as compelling as that of the long streams of students crossing the Drill Field's broad green carpet in the hazy Virginia morning sun. Student commons facilities line the streets bordering downtown Blacksburg, animating street life from early morning until late evening. The university's agricultural fields blend into the farms and woods that line the New River Valley to the west. With the inevitable exceptions—sprawling parking lots and massive sports and laboratory structures—Virginia Tech matches the texture and scale of its southwestern Virginia countryside.

Virginia Tech has pioneered making digital technology a vital part of its collegiate, civic, and regional domains. The university was one of the first institutions in the United States to require that students have personal computers so that digital learning could become an integral, broadly available part of the pedagogy. In the process, Virginia Tech wired its residence halls, student social spaces, teaching and research facilities so that students would have practically universal access to the university's network and the World Wide Web.

The Faculty Development Institute was initiated in 1993 as a large-scale effort to invest in the faculty at Virginia Tech by providing intensive workshops on instructional technology. The goal was to give them the opportunity to rethink their teaching and explore the potential of instructional technology for improving the effectiveness of the teaching-learning process. More than 4,000 faculty have participated in these workshops over the past 12 years, resulting in several major curricular reform initiatives.

### The Math Emporium

The mathematics department is a core program at Virginia Tech, essential in the support of the school's highly regarded engineering and science curricula. Lacking the space and the financial resources to house the expanding program in the mid-1990s, the department decided to convert its large classroom lecture format to digitally based learning. The charge was to maintain—and even enhance—the level of face-to-face interaction between students and faculty. The notion of students doing all of their work on laptops in their dorm rooms or the library was rapidly discarded. Learning would have to take place, in part, in a space where students could have direct discourse with instructors. It happened that space had been vacated by a department store at the University Mall down the road from Virginia Tech, available for lease at a dollar per square foot.[1] Thus was born Virginia Tech's Math Emporium in 1997.

The emporium is a student-centered, advanced learning center, which provides an active learning environment for more than 7,000 undergraduates using interactive, self-paced courseware, diagnostic quizzes, small group work, and faculty-student tutoring. It operates around the clock, seven days a week, and is staffed by mathematics department professors, 80 hours a week. The 500-workstation environment enables students to take more than a dozen mathematics courses offered by the university online.[2] The workstations are arranged so that students can interact with one another in a variety of ways to set up mathematical problems and work out solutions.

In an essay on the application of digital technology in higher education, Carol Tomlinson-Keasey reports that in spite of initial apprehensions about being responsible for their own math learning, most of the Math Emporium students eventually found the arrangement more effective than the conventional lecture format. Moreover, faculty contact time remained about the same as it had been in the traditional lecture/office hour relationship, except that it shifted to more student-faculty exchange online and not on the emporium floor.[3]

As an instructor in the old system, emporium manager Chuck Hodges was available to students in the classroom somewhat less than three hours a week, plus office hours. Hodges was quoted as saying that some students had difficulty "meshing" with that arrangement, whereas with the emporium, "there is an enormous opportunity for different styles of help."[4]

Faculty teaching assignments were shifted from the annual numbers of the courses taught to the number of hours staffing the Math Emporium. Student performance has improved. Ninety percent of the students received at least a C grade in 2002, compared with 68 percent in 1997 when the course was redesigned for the emporium.[5] Early evaluations of the program indicate that the course failure rate in the Math Emporium declined about 10 percent compared to the traditional program.

The Math Emporium is not without its dissatisfactions. Some students look upon the software as inadequate, preferring to have more classroom time to interactively experiment with math concepts. Some complain that the computer equipment at the emporium is not compatible with the personal computers that Virginia Tech requires students to buy. The principal cause for complaint, however, is the location of the emporium in an old department store, a long, time-consuming walk from the university. The shuttle bus ride is ten minutes at best and frequently crowded. The consensus is that the emporium concept is good, but it would be much better if it were in the heart of the campus close to other instructional and social space. University staff do not disagree, but counter with the reminder that the campus was out of space when the idea was hatched in 1997 and without the funds to create it on campus. Space used for math courses in 76 classrooms was made available for other users after the emporium was established.[6]

The Math Emporium was a creative way for Virginia Tech to deal with a chronic financial challenge that the university shares with its sister public institutions in Virginia. State budget support has diminished at Virginia's major institutions at the same time that the commonwealth has asked the institutions to increase enrollments to serve its burgeoning population. The Math Emporium project was originally assisted with a grant from the Pew Charitable Trust that was designed to see how technology could be applied in the development of cost-effective models for teaching large introductory classes.[7] The idea has been adopted at the University of Alabama and the University of Idaho. The Math Emporium received the 1999 Xcaliber Award for courseware technology development from the Center for Innovation in Learning.[8]

### The Blacksburg Electronic Village

Virginia Tech was a prime mover in a community-wide online initiative that has received widespread attention for its educational and civic promise. In 1991, the university, the town of Blacksburg, and the Bell Atlantic telephone company formed Blacksburg Electronic Village, an initiative conceived not only to link the educational resources of the university with the surrounding community, but to provide inexpensive, easily accessible Internet access to Blacksburg's households, businesses, schools, and organizations. Users were able to connect worldwide through the program, purportedly making Blacksburg the most digitally connected town in the country at the time. The project spurred rapid technological growth in the community. With training from BEV staff, businesses and civic organizations experimented with, and realized the benefits of, online transactions with their customers and constituents. Within two years, area entrepreneurs were wiring apartment complexes and supplying Ethernet services to residents, further increasing demand for network access and services.

Most businesses in the area have long since moved their Web sites to commercial hosting services with the growth of the commodity Internet, but remain accessible via a link in the electronic village directory. Meanwhile, BEV continues to focus on community and to host a seemingly limitless number of community organizations and applications. All schools in the district have high-speed access to online courses and are collaborating on the Internet with schools elsewhere in the country. They are able to maintain day-to-day Web communications among parents, teachers, and administrators. Citizens can shop, bank, pay fees and fines, select library books, check local event calendars, and monitor public proceedings. Local human services organizations serving the needy coordinate client intake and referrals over the Internet using software developed through the BEV, thus saving time and money for all concerned

The Blacksburg Electronic Village provided the means for Virginia Tech's 30,000 students, faculty, and staff to connect with one another and with the educational resources of the institution on campus or at home. The university provides

Web-based courses and educational services to its students and the community. The school district and the university have collaborated in a number of research projects measuring the classroom learning outcomes of networked technology.

With the Math Emporium and Blacksburg Electronic Village, Virginia Tech has taken the lead in creating two flourishing prototypes for blending digital technology into the educational and community life of the institution. Virginia Tech places a high value on those qualities of place and community that have long distinguished the institution. And yet, the university, with the Math Emporium and the Blacksburg Electronic Village, has been bold in weaving digital technology into the fabric of the place, expanding and refining the meaning of community in a collegiate setting. Technological innovation is an essential component of Virginia Tech's educational mission, but in describing technology-based initiatives such as the Math Emporium and the Electronic Village, the university reiterates that its central promise (and central challenge) is educational, not technical. It could be said that the promise would be more difficult to attain were the place and the community not valued as highly as they are. In the offing, Virginia Tech has created a worthy example of the synergy between cyberspace and real place.

## Digital Technology and Its Discontents

The literature about digital technology in academe is filled with opinions and predictions on the effects, good and bad, that the digital revolution will have on place-based higher education. It is a debate that is as highly charged as any confronting the academy today. Passions are predictably high, fed by the wide disparity of feelings about technology's meaning for the learning experience in the campus setting. Militant digerati insist that the campus as we know it has been made obsolete. Traditionally minded educators counter that face-to-face, in-place learning, without digital mediation, is the only way that knowledge, as an aspect of human development, can truly be absorbed. Distance education and Web-based learning are seen by some as breathtaking opportunities to expand higher education's reach, affordability, and flexibility. For others, the Internet has a way of colonizing all forms of communication, including the classroom experience. The broader debate is not just about the disembodiment of place. Educational journals expound opposing views on technology's place in the academy: its impact on educational quality and accessibility, the benefits and perils of making higher education into a commercial digital product, and, not insignificantly, the issue of ownership of intellectual property that springs from online course programming.

We need to frame the ensuing discussion by citing these ineluctable facts: Personal interaction and hands-on/brains-on activity in real places is here to stay as a bulwark of the higher education enterprise; and the transfer of information through all forms of digital technology anytime, anyplace, is here to stay and will continue to grow as an amplification of, and, in certain circumstances, a substitute for real places. Real places will persevere, but they will change. The ivy-covered walls are not coming down anytime soon. Nor will desktops, laptops, and hand-held devices be thrown out of the classrooms, laboratories, offices, dormitories, and student unions, or out of the homes and workplaces of students whose lives are spent more off the campus than on it. The access afforded by online education is a boon to the nontraditional learner, the mid-life learner seeking to upgrade a technical skill or redefine a career to fit the changing economy, and the learner whose personal or locational circumstances prevent access to a place-based campus. On the other hand, there is no disputing the intrinsic value of the knowledge experience that is animated and illuminated by direct human interchange in a stimulating place environment. The challenge is how to make the breathtaking speed, capacity, visual quality, ubiquity, and flexibility of digital communication an organic, enriching part of the place-based collegiate realm.

James Duderstadt, president emeritus of the University of Michigan, sets out the fundamental question that the digital revolution presents to place-based institutions:

> Clearly, the digital age poses many challenges and opportunities for the contemporary university. For most of the history of higher education in America, we have expected students to travel to a physical place, a campus, to participate in a pedagogical process involving tightly integrated studies based mostly on lectures and seminars by recognized experts. As the constraints of time and space—and perhaps even reality itself—are relieved by information technology, will the university as a physical place continue to hold its relevance?[9]

Duderstadt goes on to acknowledge that the campus will prevail as the source of higher learning, with information technology contributing progressive enhancements to its traditional functions. Digital media will permit the creation of whole new learning communities on and off campus. Digital information access will be liberating in its capacity to accommodate intellectual exchange anytime and anywhere and by fostering more distributive and continuous ways of offering higher education. On the other hand, its ubiquity is opening place-based institutions to burgeoning competition from other nonprofit and for-profit institutions and commercial enterprises. That competition can stimulate greater availability of subject offerings, but it can also lead to more standardization, more concentration on high-demand subjects, and potential diminution of place-based programs that can be tailored to the specific needs of students. In *The Social Life of Information,* John Seely Brown and Paul Duguid cite a 1999 report claiming that "twenty-five packaged courses can take care of half of community college and one-third of four-year college enrollments."[10]

Steven Brint observes, in *The Future of the City of Intellect,* that the Internet has already "sunk roots deeper into the culture and practice of teaching and learning" than earlier communications media such as film and television that matured only as supplements to conventional instruction methods in spite of the revolutionary promise that many held out for them.[11] Brint, an ardent advocate of digital learning, asserts that:

> No force has a greater potential to transform higher education. In an immediate sense, the new technology allows far more creative teaching through a mix of visual, aural, and verbal information. But more dramatic outcomes are also easy to imagine. What, other than inertia and institutional legitimacy, prevents large parts of lower-division education from being absorbed by "all-star" faculties offering courses on the Internet and CDs? If accompanied by email question-and-answer sessions, would such an outcome lead to distinctively lower-quality undergraduate education than the lecture courses now commonplace at many universities that seat six to eight hundred students? How, indeed, will the ever-increasing number of students seeking higher education credentials be taught if not, at least in part, through these alternative media?[12]

The "death of distance" is an apt metaphor for the impact of technology because distance is no longer a constraining factor, either in the time that it takes to communicate information or in the shape and content of the information being communicated. The collegiate time schedule is dissolved, as well, because information is available and tradable around the clock and not on the set schedules of classes, labs, and faculty office hours. The evaporation of distance and time transforms, accelerates, and expands the capacity of the collegial learning environment to reach beyond its bounds.

The fundamental question remains: How does digital technology affect the quality of learning? Brown and Duguid posit that the qualitative dimension of the learning experience has to do with the distinctions between *information* and *knowledge.* They see those distinctions in terms of their value to the learner at a personal, individual level. Information is an impersonal tool—a resource—that is independent of meaning and "indifferent to people," whereas knowledge "returns attention to people, what they know, how they come to know it, and how they differ."[13] Knowledge, to Brown and Duguid, is "something we digest, rather than hold."[14] Knowledge springs from the personal, the experiential, the involved, the committed.

Brown and Duguid base their analysis on the proposition that people and information are integral parts of a "rich social network" that provides the energy for the cultivation of knowledge. Former Cornell President Frank Rhodes sees the relationship as being a transformative process in the institutional context: "At the heart of the university's mission, at the core of the concept of learning, will be the university's role in transforming facts" into useful information, information into meaningful knowledge, and knowledge into useful judgment.[15]

The distinctions between the personal and the impersonal are critical to understanding the transactions that are going on between the virtual place where technology resides and the real place that is the American campus. Cyberspace is a medium—a remarkably flexible medium for the exchange of information. It is profoundly transparent. Some would say its transparency makes it indiscriminate in the way that it can conflate fact, opinion, and ideology. It is a form of public space that can expand intellectual, social, and cultural communities of interest for the institution's inhabitants. On the other hand, the campus may be the last true public space that is deliberately organized for open discourse and hands-on discovery in the personal sense that Brown and Duguid say is necessary to develop knowledge. The campus is the working, experiential habitat of learners—students, researchers, faculty, and an ever-growing cohort of outside community participants—gathered where they see the eyes and sense the body language of their compatriots, where the resistance and reinforcement of human encounter is a tactile, sensory experience. It is where the senses and the intellect are honed by manipulating the tools of the laboratory, the studio, the field, *and* the technology. In the campus setting, learners are personally involved in the venues where they observe, argue, socialize, play, and reflect. The place and the interactions, real and virtual, conspire as stimuli to the learning process.

Brown and Duguid illuminate that point by noting that however well people are connected by technology, there is an advantage in the "implicit communication, negotiation and collective improvisation" that comes by working face to face. They refer to the observation by Cornell computer scientist Dan Huttenlochar that digital technology is better at maintaining the "dense" learning communities already established on campus than at creating such communities from scratch. This leads to the paradox that technologies "may do a better job on the conventional campus than on the virtual one."[16]

The digital revolution is only partly technological; it is also cultural. The issue is how the relatively conservative culture of the place-based institution deals with the power of the digital revolution and the influx of new generations of tech-savvy learners.[17] Barry Munitz, president of the J. Paul Getty Trust, holds that it is not just that technology is becoming more ubiquitous on the campus, but that it demands that institutions rethink how they educate and interact with students whose entire lives will be spent partly in a digital universe that transcends physical space. If the character of the campus is the reflection of longstanding institutional values and methods of teaching, immersion into digital learning can either reinforce or forever change that character. Munitz observes that, while traditional campus settings may *look* the same in the future, they may *be* very different places. He punctuates that observation with the cautionary reminder that, "Suddenly, and with apologies to Gertrude Stein, there is 'no there there' . . . institutions are being transformed into learning environments that are independent of both time and place."[18]

David Ward, president of the American Council on Education and chancellor emeritus at the University of Wisconsin–Madison, wrote in an essay entitled "Catching the Waves of Change in American Higher Education" that the transformation of the learning environment is necessary to advance today's higher education imperatives, prime among them being to address the widely varying needs of learners and to foster more collaboration and permeability among academic disciplines. From Ward's perspective, few academic programs have "systematically transformed themselves through the use of technology."[19] He also emphasizes that the digital domain is but one of a number of learning contexts that must be brought to bear in making the educational experience more flexible, transparent, and adaptable to diverse individual needs. Systemic change will require massive investment in both technology and training methods, calibrated to the requirements of the learners, whether for remediation, proficiency, or mastery.

## The Digital Face of Today's Learning Environments

The World Wide Web was literally born of academe in 1991. The first Web site was posted that year by a British computer scientist to stimulate computer-based networking as a medium for wider exchange of scientific information. Scientists accessed the nascent Web with browsers of their own creation until the Web went mainstream in 1995 with the advent of Netscape.[20]

The availability of Internet technology to today's learners has already expanded the market for higher education beyond the conventional campus setting. There are upward of 7,000 postsecondary learning entities of various sorts in addition to the 4,000 accredited higher education institutions. The greatest demand for course offerings in the future will be by learners who do not attend college full time and may never attend a place-based college at all. The growing cohort of learners whose attendance is facilitated by the Internet covers every age group from precollege to retirees.

Consider the standing of the digital revolution in postsecondary learning in the first years of this century:

- In 2002, more than 1.6 million students were taking online higher education courses. Of that number, about 600,000 students were taking all of their classes through the Web.[21] The Sloan Consortium predicted that more than 2.6 million students would take at least one online course by the fall of 2004.[22]

- A 2002 survey by the U.S. Department of Education estimated that as of 2000–2001, nearly 120,000 for-credit courses were being offered through distance education by two- and four-year degree-granting institutions. The survey found that 56 percent of two- and four-year institutions were offering distance education courses in 2000–2001—roughly 90 percent in public two- and four-year colleges and 40 percent in private four-year schools.[23]

- Spending on information technology by higher education institutions was more than $5 billion in 2004. Public institutions report annual investment in technology of $203 per student; private institutions, $553 per student. Despite early concerns about the effectiveness of technology spending, the promised productivity of technology is finally being achieved as spending swings to more efficient modes of technology. Nearly 80 percent of colleges surveyed in 2004 reported having wireless systems compared to 45 percent in 2002.[24]

- In 2004, the Massachusetts Institute of Technology was the first major university to post all of its 2,000 courses on the Internet for people who are not formally enrolled in the institution. Syllabi, lecture notes, exams, and other material are being made available, not as credit offerings, but rather to disseminate new knowledge and content, at no cost, that can be used as learning resources by others.[25] Other institutions offering at least some coursework for nonenrolled users include Harvard, Columbia, Stanford, Duke, and UNC–Chapel Hill.[26]

- Institutions have formed consortia and compacts that constitute, in effect, multicampus virtual universities. Western Governors University was formed in 1996, using the Internet to make course content widely and economically available. Other regional Web-based initiatives include the Electronic Campus of the Southern Regional Education Board[27] and the Great Plains Interactive Distance Education Alliance. Virtual statewide universities include the SUNY Learning Network in New York, the Ohio Learning Network, the Oregon Network for Education, the Louisiana Board of Regents Electronic Campus, and numerous others.[28]

- Scientific research, with its ever-growing computational demands, is a major driver of dedicated digital networking. Take, for example, National Lambda Rail, an ultra-high-capacity fiber-optic network that is being developed to link research universities across the United States to provide instant network transmission of experimental data that would literally take weeks to move in a standard dial-up connection.[29] The network's higher capacity and lower costs benefit from the fact that the system runs through surplus fiber-optic lines installed in the dot-com frenzy of the 1990s. The project, underwritten by participating colleges, higher education groups, and states, is independent of the Internet. Lambda Rail augurs a dramatic change in the capability of research institutions to expand and integrate their research with their sister institutions through digital technology.

Consider, as well, the Web-related and multimedia endeavors of other enterprises that will have revolutionary implications for traditional campus-based higher education institutions:

- In 2004, one of every 12 college students was enrolled in a for-profit institution.[30] The for-profits rely partly or wholly on digital course delivery. The University of Phoenix, the world's largest for-profit institution, announced in the summer of 2004 that it was lowering the minimum age of the students that it accepts from 21 to 18. With more than 200,000 students, half served by the Internet and half at locations in 30 states, the University of Phoenix has targeted older, working adult students for nearly three decades. Most other for-profit enterprises offering undergraduate instruction accept students under 21. One reason cited for the move into the traditional college-age bracket was the recognition that California will have a shortfall of 700,000 places in its higher education system within a decade.[31] According to some observers, the expansion of the student pool by Phoenix was conceived to offset a decline in the rate of online enrollment growth among for-profit institutions.

- Broadcasting, cable entertainment, and computer technology companies are engaged in a race for competitive market advantage, known as *convergence,* through mergers, strategic alliances, and cross-marketing, reaching an unprecedented level of concentration in the production and distribution of media content. The convergence phenomenon was estimated to support an interactive multimedia market approaching $1 trillion at the turn of century. This will give institutions extraordinary choices for the electronic distribution of educational materials; it also signals a formidable competitive challenge to traditional institutions. Corporations such as Microsoft, IBM, and Cisco deliver, or are poised to deliver, corporate degree programs.[32] Andrew Abbott of the University of Chicago sees the access and profit potential of the Internet as a huge stimulus for the entry of corporate enterprises into the higher education marketplace:

It is quite possible that all the major innovations in teaching will come from the commercial sector, which will view higher education as it has already viewed social service, health, and other eleemosynary activities—as a region for easy profit through downsizing and explicit product differentiation. The American higher education outlay is after all a quarter trillion dollars a year; the commercial sector has the necessary money, talent and desire to take it over.[33]

- In December 2004, the Internet search engine Google announced an agreement with five major research libraries (Harvard, the New York Public Library, Stanford University, the University of Michigan, and Oxford's Bodleian Library), to digitize upward of 30 million volumes from their collections for access on the Internet. The five- to six-year project is, by far, the most ambitious effort since the advent of the Internet to make vast academic library collections digitally available, including virtual access to rare historical volumes heretofore seen only by scholars working under rigorously controlled circumstances. The Google venture, a remarkable step toward making scholarly materials universally available, inevitably makes itself a symbol of the apprehensions of bibliophiles, who see in digital conversion the continuing erosion of the tactile, aesthetic experience of reading real books. Matthew Battle of Harvard's Houghton Library, musing on the impacts of the Google initiative, holds that "traditional books and their modes of reading" will not be supplanted by the digital library:

The book in its traditional form is a memory machine of surprisingly compact and enduring power. It carries in its bindings, its covers and the materials out of which it is made traces of its origins and its travels, both as an artifact and as a repository of images and ideas. As a physical object it has what the twentieth-century philosopher Walter Benjamin called an "aura," consisting of the host of ritual and metaphysical associations it calls to mind.[34]

The prospect of losing the aura of the book is a poetic analogy for the dislocations that have to be reconciled with the merging of cyberspace and real, tactile space.

## Seeking Synergy: The Digitally Enhanced Campus

The goal of blending real space and cyberspace to create a compelling, productive learning environment will depend, first of all, on the nature and culture of the institution. It will depend on the constituencies that the institution must serve, and on the willingness of the institution to imagine how digital technology can bring new vibrancy to the campus learning experience.

Because digital technology is time-free and place-free, it is more accessible to the varied circumstances of today's learners. Schools are routinely making more digital resources, such as laptops, hand-held computers, software, wireless access, e-mail kiosks, and expanded Web portals, directly available to students. Web-based technology's interactive learning capability is exquisitely matched to the expectations of the Net generation, which, of course, will be every generation attending college in this century. Today's learners are "sensorily bionic," having grown up with cell phones, computer games, hand-held messaging, iPods, and digital cameras as virtual extensions of their brains, eyes, and ears. In *Growing Up Digital: The Rise of the Net Generation,* Don Tapscott talks about those who have grown up with the Internet as being independent, active participants in interactive learning experiences—and in control of those experiences.[35] Higher education institutions will need to perpetually retool curricula and teaching methods to meet the expectations of the learner-centered generations to come. Campuses will be organized for time-free and place-free learning, and their environments will be more open, varied, and stimulating.

Digital technology is an integral part of the trend toward the "experience economy," taking immediacy, interaction, and visual/aural stimulus beyond the realm once exclusively contained in real places. This aspect of the technology is both a competitive challenge and an opportunity for place-based institutions. Other media enterprises, adept at maximizing the experiential properties of digital technology, are ready to convert those properties into widely accessible learning products. Technology has already demonstrated, through game applications, that it has a quality of play that can enliven the learning experience. The academy has to integrate the experiential qualities of technology into the learning system, on campus and in its virtual reach beyond campus. This connotes educational alliances with a variety of media enterprises, relationships that have to be approached with great care for the integrity of the academic mission.

Taking the challenge a step further, Richard Lanham asserts in *The Future of the City of Intellect* that today's higher education institutions need to recapture their historic role as exponents of the "economics of attention." He says they are still thinking in "an economics based on stuff."[36] Lanham reasons that the traditional educational institution is constrained by the "sequestration" model—"[the university] still conceives itself as a classroom landlord"—that inhibits it from fully embracing, through the Internet, the development of "attention-structures" that other enterprises are rapidly introducing into the new economy.[37]

William Mitchell, in his book *e-topia,* argues that place is a persistent power in a human milieu that is becoming vastly enlarged by digital technology, but that its power as a magnet for human encounter and community vitality will continue to depend on its capacity to invite, inspire, and stimulate such encounters:

> Since place retains this sort of power, it follows that place-based enterprises will compete for our presence, attention, and dollars in a digitally mediated world by attempting to add as much value as possible to the face-to-face experiences that they offer. They will emphasize the unusual, the elsewhere unobtainable, and the things that cannot (at least yet) be pumped through a wire.[38]

When asked which aspect of digital technology will have the most profound long-term impact on the place-based campus, Mitchell, head of MIT's Program in Media Arts and Sciences, told me that "clearly, ubiquitous, wireless connectivity will have the most powerful effect" because it will break the psychological barrier between real space and cyberspace. He characterizes such technology as an "extension of the people," in which access to information and ideas is as mobile as the users themselves.[39] The technology already comes in the ever more versatile hand-held objects that fit into people's pockets.

Mitchell believes that wireless technology in the academic environment will foster a more "nomadic pattern of occupancy," whereby students and faculty are less tethered to traditional workspaces in their interactions with one another. Interaction can occur more informally and in a greater variety of settings. The conversation can be one on one, with either or both parties referring to information on a portable instrument, or with a third party being brought into the conversation from afar. This synthesis of cyber connectivity and face-to-face connectivity will give rise to more "transparency" in the spaces in which collegiate exchange occurs: common spaces for informal gathering, auditoria that are more flexible and open, classrooms that are more informally arranged. Such space qualities are already in demand in colleges and universities seeking to invigorate the level of intellectual and social encounter. There is a cautionary tale in this. The institution must be very deliberate in determining how best to achieve social and intellectual value in marrying technology and place. In an earlier writing, Mitchell postulated an example:

> Where opportunities for connectivity are abundant, the locations of those opportunities may still be socially significant. If a university simply wires dormitory rooms, for example, it will almost certainly encourage students to stay in their rooms working at their computers, reduce general social interaction, and raise the incidence of conflicts among roommates. But if it goes for laptops rather than desktop devices, provides lots of connection points and power outlets in social spaces and library reading rooms, and implements a dynamic network addressing scheme that allows plug-and-play work anywhere, it will promote mobility among different hangouts, chance encounters and informal grouping.[40]

With wireless, it's an easier deal yet. Small-scale implements of wireless technology, functioning as "extensions of the person," do not have to be any more intrusive in the classroom setting than pencils, notebooks, and chalkboards. The most beneficial impact of ubiquitous wireless technology on the experience of learning in place could be the reduction of desktops, laptops, and other pieces of bulky equipment that get in the way of the social dynamic of the classroom. Mitchell envisions a payoff in the quality of academic life when technology and space are designed to prompt less hierarchical and more conversational interactions. Being in the place puts trust in the discourse. He observes, with obvious relish, the circumstance in many MIT classrooms when, as an instructor covers a particular topic, the students simultaneously surf the Web on their laptops to retrieve their own background stories on the topic. An animated conversation ensues when the students interject their instant—sometimes contrary—findings, making the classroom transaction all the more meaningful to the participants. This is the social use of technology in the classroom, energizing the sense of place that gives life to the learning experience.

Allusions to the sense of place and the heightened learning experience show up in numerous conversations with academic respondents when they are asked how cyberspace and real space can work together. The large lecture is a fascinating case in point. Although some feel that the content of large lectures could be better packaged in visually inviting, interactive programs on the Internet (as in the Math Emporium), others are as likely to suggest that media technology can give the large lecture an exciting quality of theater. Students armed with their own wireless electronic devices can be interactive participants in the lecture. It all depends on the creativity of the instructors and the vitality of the institution's media support. With advances in technology, media support is overcoming the stereotype of being the supplier of slide projectors for lectures. Media support programs will play more creative roles in designing the lecture hall and classroom experience, perhaps being more closely aligned with academic programs in the media and arts.

Digital technology is a revolution of means in American higher education. Technology is permeating classroom, laboratory, and dormitory halls with interactive cyber settings that permit more independent study, flexible scheduling, offsite field experiences, even virtual attendance at other institutions. It will enable college students to be as autonomous as current and future generations will expect to be. Digital forms of instruction will be applied as a means of mitigating the cost of higher education and probably as a means of addressing the onslaught of faculty retirements anticipated in the next decade. Technology will, of course, be enthusiastically embraced by the next generation of tech-savvy academicians replacing today's faculty.

Technology will affect basic roles and practices that have been the cornerstones of place-based education, notably in the relationship between faculty and students. A 2002 report by the National Academy of Sciences went so far as to say that digital technology will "alter the fundamental relationship between people and knowledge." The report anticipates that the undergraduate lecture format and use of common reading lists could be eclipsed as it becomes more routine for students to learn at distance and on their own time. Faculty could function less as teachers and more as consultants or coaches who are "less concerned with transmitting intellectual content directly than with inspiring, motivating and managing an active learning process"—interacting with undergraduates in ways that they interact with doctoral students today.[41] For institutions that seize on such a model, there will be a myriad of opportunities (and a fundamental need) to create lively places on campus that stimulate student-faculty discourse.

### The Digitally Distributed Campus

Web technology has hastened the making of individual colleges and universities into multicentered enterprises. The Web allows for greater integration of the elements that make up multicampus institutions. Furthermore, the capacity to create functional network links with other institutions and enterprises gives rise to the prospect of many new kinds of learning affiliations. The Internet will foster greater integration between colleges and their communities. Colleges will evolve into more "distributed" enterprises, virtually and physically. Remote places can become parts of campuses in a virtual sense. This, too, is not without precedents in the predigital age. Schools have, for many years, offered courses and programs to remote parts of their states and regions through extension services and by closed circuit telecommunications systems. The Web provides interactive capabilities and dynamic, sensorily stimulating modes of visual and aural representation that were not possible in earlier forms of telecommunication.

Dispersal is already a fact for many institutions, whether they are multicampus community college districts, flagship universities with branch campuses, or colleges with venues abroad. The home campus has to be the center of gravity for the virtual hinterland created when institutions disperse functions, relationships, and activities outside the borders of the core campus. In William Mitchell's words, "the more global the enterprise becomes, the more integrity and intensity the mother ship must possess."[42] The robustness of the learning environment on the home campus is crucial for the multicentered institutions of the future because it is part of the pedagogical glue that holds dispersed institutions together. As an advisor to a new university in California that had determined that half of its student body would be served by distance learning, I recommended that those students be required to spend time on the campus for some interval so that they could attach the image and identity of a real home place to the mediated experience of distance learning.

Competition and economics will prompt institutions to use digital technology as a means of promoting their particular strengths and niches. A course in medieval literature at an elite liberal arts college, an advanced program in nanofabrication at a research university, or a course in the management of food co-ops at a community college—each could be a program of premier standing sought by students and other institutions around the country and the world through the Internet. On the other hand, courses and departments in institutions across the United States could be put out of business by nonprofit and for-profit competition in a fiscal environment where programs are called upon to meet standards of financial self-sufficiency.

Digital networking among higher education institutions has its own set of place implications for participating institutions. High-speed, high-capacity network access has changed everything for the academy. All institutions are networked through the Internet, not only among themselves but with all of the other organizations and individuals who are on the Internet all over the globe. In this complex relationship, the learning capabilities that do not physically exist on any given campus now exist in a virtual state. A small college such as Bethel in Minnesota does not have a medical school, but if one of its history professors wants to demonstrate how epidemics have affected the cultural development of southern U.S. cities, the professor has instant network access to a score of epidemiologists in medical schools around the country who can describe the nature and pathology of epidemics. Better yet, the professor's students have instant access to the literature that is recommended by the epidemiologists (and to history departments in other colleges with expertise in the socioeconomic history of the South). Bethel has a virtual epidemiology department at its disposal, without the bricks and mortar. It has virtual faculties and experts in every conceivable subject wandering around its tranquil lakeside setting.

Online interaction has a way of inducing demand for face-to-face familiarity with virtual colleagues scattered in other places. The desire to meet in real surroundings becomes a complementary aspect of digital communication, spurring periodic conversations in a physical place that can be nuanced by observing body language and facial expression. Place reinforces trust. Again, quoting William Mitchell, "You can get a lot of bandwidth, when you really need it, by transporting heads attached to shoulders."[43]

The future of the place-based college will be forever changed by the transcendentally powerful medium of digital technology. It is a seismic force that is both centripetal and centrifugal in its impact on the campus environment and on the larger community, as Virginia Tech's digital initiatives have shown. It can bring a new kind of energy and transparency to the way that things work in the campus domain. It can be an instrument of creative pedagogy and an influence on campus design. Because technology provides such extraordinary connectivity with the world beyond the campus borders, institutions will be fully integrated with learning communities locally, nationally, and globally, in recombinations and formats yet to be determined.

Some campuses may shrink as they convert academic offerings to forms of digital delivery. That would not be an altogether bad thing if the conversions are hand-in-hand with measures to enhance the collegial character and vitality of those campuses. We cannot discount the melancholy prospect that some campuses will be shuttered as they grapple with the competition from media enterprises and other institutions more adroit in adapting technology as a learning resource. The worst possibility is if technology facilitates a milieu in which the conveyance of knowledge becomes so media-based, so commercial, so standardized that the integrity of the academy is forever compromised.

Those and other futures depend on the *will* of the institutions, because the real change wrought by technology, as noted earlier, is *cultural.* The cultural roles of teachers and learners will evolve with coming generations of students, faculty, and administrators for whom technology is second nature. Technology can be destructive of place when it is seen as an end in itself, but the optimistic bet is that the academy will make digital technology an integral, stimulating part of the place-based learning experience. After all, as Barry Munitz reminds us, "Some form of classical university has survived for two and a half millennia, whereas virtually every other social institution has been broken or severely modified."[44]

Mt. Hood from Lewis & Clark College. (Photo by Robert M. Reynolds, courtesy of Lewis & Clark College.)

# four

# *Globalization of the Academy*

## Lewis & Clark College: Thinking Globally, Acting Locally

The present-day campus of Lewis & Clark College in Portland, Oregon, was established in 1944 on a former estate that occupied a height of land overlooking the city and the Willamette Valley beyond. The estate's manor house and formal garden, which have remained intact as features of the campus, lie on a direct visual axis with the white cone of Mount Hood on the eastern horizon. Douglas firs stud the steep ravines falling away at the north and east edges of the campus. Abundant stands of pine, fir, and rhododendron fill the spaces with a lush verdancy that can only be found in the Pacific Northwest. Lewis & Clark is an urban campus by geography and spirit, but its bucolic setting at the top of Portland's Palatine Hill makes the campus seem as if it could be in a small town miles from any city. In that respect, the college is a mirror of Portland itself, an urbane community whose legendary civic vigor is fortified by the surrounding natural setting. The college's urban spirit and verdant environment are important assets in its academic pursuits. Nearly 1,800 of Lewis & Clark's students are enrolled in the undergraduate College of Arts and Sciences. More than 1,200 students are in the School of Law and the Graduate School of Education. Lewis & Clark is well known for its environmental curricular emphasis in all three schools.

For more than four decades, Lewis & Clark has been building its undergraduate curriculum on a foundation of international understanding. The school highlights itself as "a national college with a global reach."[1] Lewis & Clark inaugurated overseas study in 1962, setting up faculty-sponsored programs in Chile, England, Japan, Mexico, and Peru. Since the program's inception, more than 9,000 students and 200 faculty members have engaged in more than 550 studies in 67 countries. Today, roughly 260 students, mainly undergraduates, participate in overseas programs each year. International study is a keystone of the college's academic mission. All undergraduates are required to take at least two courses in the area of international studies that explore global relationships, the values of other nations, and America's role in the world community. The program statement for overseas and off-campus programs declares that Lewis & Clark's philosophy is "to educate students to live in a future world that will be increasingly interdependent and complex—a world that will be shaped by external forces beyond purely national control."

The college's emphasis on cross-cultural understanding in a globalized world has become more central to the institution's identity and a highly successful recruitment tool. The overseas program ranks in the top 10 for institutions sending students abroad for a year and among the top 20 of those whose students participate in semester-long studies.[2]

Lewis & Clark's international students, numbering around 100 in the fall of 2004, come from nearly 30 countries. Visiting international scholars represent eight foreign nations. Although the percentage of students from abroad is not large compared with other institutions that enroll sizeable international populations, foreign undergraduate students at Lewis & Clark are as immersed in cross-cultural studies as are their U.S. counterparts.[3] Given the growing influence of the Asia-Pacific economy and culture on the Pacific Northwest, collegiate life at Lewis & Clark will continue to be energized by cultural diversity.

The college has dedicated itself to the development of a campus environment that will facilitate the cross-cultural educational experience that it is striving to achieve. One of the hurdles facing the college when it began to develop its campus improvement program in support of that goal in the early 1990s was that many of the students returning from studying abroad, as well as a number of the foreign students, chose to live elsewhere in Portland rather than on the campus. They had been affected enough by their overseas experience that they preferred a more adult, independent lifestyle than they would have in a college dormitory. As a practical matter, the college simply did not have enough student housing to accommodate the manner of living desired by mature students. The notion of sharing the fruits of cultural immersion in the campus living environment was thwarted, some say, by the college's quiet and idyllic setting removed from Portland's urban bustle. The college concluded that the creation of a more diverse and vital residential community was the key to making Lewis & Clark a more inviting collegial place for all of its students.

Since 1998, Lewis & Clark has undertaken a strategy, based on expansion and improvement of its residential environment, to integrate "living, learning and discourse . . . in a seamless college experience." Living at Lewis & Clark had to be as exciting as studying there, according to the charge of the board of trustees. Upper-class undergraduates, underserved by the existing housing stock, had to be brought into the college's residential community so that their broadened outlook on life could enrich the collegiate discourse. The college had already taken ambitious steps to improve academic, recreational, and social facilities on the campus, together with an upgrading of the already pleasing campus grounds, to make the campus a more vibrant student crossroads.

Lewis & Clark set a goal of expanding the housing stock of 960 beds to more than 1,400 beds so that at least 75 percent of the undergraduates could live on campus. A first-phase program of nearly 170 beds in three apartment-style residential houses was completed in 2002. As of 2005, the balance of the proposed new housing has yet to be built. Currently, no more than 60 percent of the undergraduates live on campus. Critically, upper-division housing is still short, meaning that most students returning from off-campus programs live elsewhere. Michael Sestric, the college's director of planning, reports that increased enrollments in recent years, coupled with the desire of students in the millennial generation to live on campus, has outpaced the goal to accommodate more upper-division residents. At least 300 more beds are needed to achieve the desired 75 percent campus residency. Sestric also cites another housing need that must be met, that being affordable residences for faculty in close proximity to campus. The college's aim is for faculty to take a more active part in the international academical village, a role that is difficult to sustain with long commutes to outlying suburbs.

Workforce housing affordability is but one of the matters that Lewis & Clark, other area institutions, and the city of Portland will be addressing to advance a common strategy for positioning in the global marketplace. The city has designated its knowledge institutions as *targeted industries* in the quest to consolidate its standing as a key American hub in the Pacific Rim. For its part, Lewis & Clark recognizes that to advance its standing as a globally conscious institution, it has not only to continue building a vibrant living/learning community in its idyllic setting, but also to forge new links with the aspiring global city that surrounds it. Lewis & Clark's experience demonstrates that the quality of campus life and distinctiveness of place are strategic resources in academia's engagement with globalization.

## It's a New World, After All

Picture the millennial image of the world's economic leaders sequestered in their plush conference hall while demonstrators raged against economic globalization on the Seattle streets outside that hall. The fervor of the demonstrations that have taken place at the gatherings of the World Trade Organization and other transnational economic forums underscores the anxieties attending to the economic integration of the world. Apprehensions about the new world economic order and its real and perceived social disruptions are fed by the explosive penetration of commerce, technology, and ideas into every corner of the planet.

Globalization, fueled by digital technology, is the economic and cultural phenomenon of the twenty-first century. It is affecting nations and cultures around the earth in profound ways, but perhaps none greater than the United States. Globalization, according to MIT economist Lester Thurow,

> is, in fact, changing America faster than any other society. Nowhere is production moving offshore more rapidly. Yet Americans hardly notice what is happening because their belief that the global economy will simply be an enlarged American economy is so strongly held.[4]

Of course, all nations are changing. Traditional cultures are being irrevocably altered by the effects of global economic and popular culture. Modern and developing nations are seizing upon the global knowledge-based economy as the pathway to their economic well-being. Those nations are embracing higher education as the bulwark of their quest for a secure place at the global table.

In *The World Is Flat: A Brief History of the Twenty-first Century,* Thomas Friedman makes the graphic analogy of a world economic order that is "flattening" as populous countries such as China, India, and South Korea are usurping America's vaunted strengths with their rapidly advancing educational systems and skilled labor forces. They are doing so by practicing what Friedman calls *extreme capitalism.* He likens the moment to the 1957 launching of Sputnik by the Soviet Union, except that now the wake-up call does not come from an economic system that is antithetical to American capitalism but from several economies with expanding capacities to do American capitalism one better. Friedman argues that the flattening world demands a rededication to the advancement of science, mathematics, and engineering, as in the post-Sputnik period, with a commitment by the United States to "building the infrastructure, safety nets and institutions that will help every American become employable in an age when no one can be guaranteed lifetime employment."[5]

The response to the new world challenge is, like the titanic competition that ensued in the cold war 1960s, an "education race." This time, the federal and state governments, businesses, and higher education must be mutually vested in an American culture of lifetime learning and relearning, from kindergarten to postretirement. The culture of the early twenty-first century will be one characterized by the continuous and widespread adaptive behavior that individuals and organizations have to make to keep up with the circumstances of globalization.[6]

The importance of higher education—indeed, all levels of education—cannot be underestimated as the world becomes more economically integrated. Higher education will foster not just the skills necessary to run the world's economic machinery, but the faculties of critical thinking that will be crucial in addressing the global challenges of environmental change, human health, economic disparity, political and cultural conflict, and a host of other issues that must be confronted in this century, and soon. Higher education, whose intellectual infrastructure spans the planet, will have to be out front in preparing global citizens. From a strictly nationalistic point of view, countries will look to higher education as the essential tool for gaining competitive advantage in the global marketplace. As Thurow observes, "with everything else dropping out of the [international] competitive equation, knowledge has become the only source of long-run sustainable competitive advantage."[7]

Let it be said that higher education has been a uniquely global enterprise from its inception as an organized endeavor. The medieval European university drew and disseminated knowledge from sources all across what was then regarded as the civilized world. Professors and students migrated from one country to another to engage in scholarly intercourse. Well into the Renaissance, instruction was conducted in Latin, a universal language that bound the Western world. Subject matter and teaching methods have been adapted and exchanged among countries of the world for several hundred years. The longevity of higher education institutions as seats of global influence is underscored by Clark Kerr's famous observation that of all the Western institutions that had been established by the early sixteenth century, only about 85 exist today "in recognizable forms and with similar functions and unbroken histories—the Catholic Church, the Parliaments of the Isles of Man, of Iceland and of Great Britain, several Swiss cantons, and seventy universities."[8]

The signature fact of globalization in the twenty-first century is in the "newfound power of *individuals* [not just nations or companies or organizations] to collaborate and compete globally."[9] It is the minds of individuals, the capital on which higher education is based, that are connected at a global scale. The academy today is, by definition, a single global entity. It is a networked, distributed entity made up of campuses throughout the world that share and exchange knowledge with one another, that welcome students and scholars from other lands, that undertake joint ventures and research projects with institutions in other countries, and that advise nations and organizations throughout the world. Today, every campus is a global campus.

### The U.S. Role in the Global Academy

Currently, there are between 1.5 and 2 million students in the world who are studying in a country other than their own (estimates vary because not all countries consistently report on educational travel). That number could grow as high as 8 million by 2025.[10] The vast majority of students studying abroad—perhaps 80 percent—gravitate from developing and third-world countries to colleges in the Western nations where most of the world-class institutions are located. The developing countries, where populations are growing most rapidly, already contain more than half of the world's college-level students. Philip Altbach, of the Boston College Center for International Higher Education, makes the point that "as academic systems become more similar and academic degrees accepted internationally, as immigration rules are tailored to people with high skill levels, and as universities themselves are more open to hiring the best talent worldwide, the global [academic] marketplace will expand."[11]

Higher education in the United States became the world's premier system in the twentieth century, both in terms of the number of institutions and the quality of programs. By the year 2000, 28 percent of Americans had a college degree and more than 15 million were enrolled in degree-granting programs. Higher education has been a central factor in the development of the country's economic and technological preeminence up to this time. It is also one of America's most successful export industries. The United States is by far the principal destination for foreign students, hosting more students from abroad than any other country—nearly one-third of all the 1.42 million students enrolled offshore from their home nations, according to a 2002 study.[12] The enrollment of foreign students in U.S. colleges and universities hit a peak in excess of 586,000 in 2002–3.[13] The majority of foreign students enrolled in the United States are from Asian countries, with India and China comprising nearly 25 percent of all foreign students in the country.[14] American universities hosted nearly 80,000 visiting scholars from abroad in the year 2000.[15]

Although the number of international students in U.S. four-year institutions is less than 3 percent of undergraduates and under 14 percent of graduate students, they constitute, nonetheless, an important economic, social, and intellectual resource for this country. Foreign enrollment in American institutions currently represents a $13 billion annual infusion in the U.S. economy.[16] Many colleges and universities enroll international students to promote cross-cultural understanding. Nearly three-quarters of international students studying in the United States are enrolled in research at doctoral and master's institutions and almost half are studying at the graduate level.[17] For some graduate departments in American universities, foreign students constitute majorities or near majorities. International students are major players in American scientific research. Foreign scholars represent more than half of the growth of doctorates earned in the country in the last two decades, and two-thirds of those receiving PhDs stay on to take academic and industry positions in the United States.[18] A large number of foreign-born students in America's colleges stay on in the United States, contributing to the country's scientific, technological, and artistic wealth.

The United States sends its own students abroad for study and research, although not in numbers comparable to those who come to this country for higher education. The 175,000 American college students who studied in other countries for academic credit in 2002–3 were only 0.2 percent of U.S. undergraduates in four-year colleges. Nevertheless, the number of American students abroad grew by 145 percent in the 10 years ending in 2002–3. The rate of growth of study abroad increased by 8.5 percent in the first full school year after September 11, 2001.[19] Most Americans study in host countries for relatively short durations—a summer, a semester, or programs of eight weeks or less that are extensions of the home campus curriculum, oftentimes at foreign branches of U.S. colleges and universities. Only 7 percent study for a full academic year. They travel to other lands mainly for academic and cultural enrichment, returning to their home colleges for the completion of their studies. This is in sharp contrast to the expectations of international students studying in the United States, most of whom seek their degrees here and many of whom have stayed here.

English as the language of international business and science gives an enormous advantage to higher education institutions in the United States. Most of the world's scientific journals are in English, as are most of the Internet transactions and databases involving science and scholarship.[20] English, as the dominant language of academia in the world, furthers the influence and visibility of U.S. higher education in other countries.[21]

America's prominence in global higher education is being challenged in the twenty-first century. This country's relative position is affected by issues of international security, economic change in developing nations, and educational competition from other nations. After the terrorist attacks of September 11, 2001, the

U.S. process for granting visas to foreign students was significantly tightened, creating delays in entry and re-entry visa approvals, more outright rejections, and more complex reporting procedures for the institutions hosting students from abroad. The visa measures have had a chilling effect on foreign enrollment in U.S. colleges, especially at the graduate level. After two years of reduction in the rate of growth of foreign enrollment in the United States after 9/11, the 2003–4 school year showed an absolute decline of 2.4 percent from the preceding year.[22] That was the first decline in 30 years. The number of students from the Middle East has dropped four times that amount. Significantly, the number of first-time applications for entry into American graduate schools by foreign students is showing declines of nearly a third in some surveys (of 230 member institutions responding to surveys by the Council of Graduate Schools, nearly 90 percent reported foreign graduate application declines for 2004–5, averaging 32 percent).[23]

According to Robert M. O'Neil, writing for the National Center for Public Policy and Higher Education, the most ominous result of a 2004 survey by the Council of Graduate Schools was that the decline in foreign applications to U.S. graduate programs was greatest at the 50 institutions that traditionally enroll the largest numbers of foreign students, all but one of which reported declines in 2002–3.[24] International student security screening will be a fact of life for the indefinite future. The degree to which it will be a sustained factor in the enrollment of foreign students depends on the trajectories of international terrorism and the geopolitics that follow in their wake.

The global higher education landscape could also be altered over time by regulations designed to govern international trade. The importance of knowledge-based enterprises in the world economy has prompted an international debate as to whether higher education should fall under the open market framework of the evolving General Agreement on Trade in Services (GATS). Fundamentally, the issue revolves around the interpretation of educational services—that is, knowledge—as commodities to be competitively traded and, therefore, regulated. A variety of knowledge companies, for-profit education service providers, and trade-oriented agencies in the United States favor inclusion of nonprofit higher education institutions in the restrictions that are being debated. Organizations such as the American Council on Education are vigorously opposed. Regardless of whether the provision in question is adopted, it signals that the output of American higher education may be vulnerable to international regulation as the knowledge-based world order becomes more integrated and competitive.

More pertinent to America's position in the globalization of the academy is the competition from higher education institutions abroad and how higher education will be delivered worldwide. A critical issue confronting the United States is whether American higher education can maintain its current level of predominance in the world in science, engineering, and technology as the twenty-first century unfolds. One-fifth of the nation's scientists and engineers are foreign-born, a large percentage of whom came to this country for their education and stayed. Fewer are being drawn by the American dream because many are now able to achieve their dream in their home countries. American universities are already witnessing keen competition in several areas of scientific and technological activity by education institutions in China and India, the countries that have been the largest source of foreign enrollment in the United States. They are seeing American companies with whom they have long had research affiliations gravitating toward the research capabilities emerging in those countries. China's 2004 enrollment of 17 million students in university and advanced vocational learning programs was triple the number of enrollees five years earlier. China produced 325,000 engineers in 2004, five times the number of new engineers in the United States where enrollment has been declining.[25] In 2004, foreign applications to graduate engineering schools in the United States dropped 36 percent.[26] India graduates 40,000 computer scientists a year, and the number is growing.[27]

Although basic research in the United States still outpaces that of the expanding economies of China and India by wide margins, the separation is rapidly narrowing in the applied technologies that those countries depend upon for their economic growth. By 2010, China will confer more science and engineering doctorates than the United States.[28] U.S. higher education is facing fierce competition from other English-speaking countries that are attracting foreign students in greater numbers. Britain, which drew about 225,000 foreign students in 2000, attracted roughly 275,000 by 2002. Canada went from less than 70,000 foreign students in 2000 to more than 100,000 in 2003. Australia's foreign enrollment nearly doubled between 2000 and 2004 to more than 125,000. The Bologna Accord, enacted in 1999, will unify the academic standards for institutions in 40 European countries by 2010, giving students a choice of high-quality education throughout the Continent. This will be a source of huge competition with the United States, once the countries finally agree to the recognition of credits across Europe.

The global marketplace for higher education is taking a multiplicity of forms that transcend localities and cultures. The authors of a report by Brown University's Futures Project observe that "across the world, institutions seem less affiliated with specific geographic and cultural regions and gradually more intertwined in a borderless market-driven system of higher education."[29] The report notes that while higher education on the planet is "not yet wholly devoid of place," it is evolving more rapidly than most people and institutions realize.[30] The driving force is a worldwide shift to a knowledge-based economy, not just in the developed world, but in developing nations that are striving to make their service and manufacturing sectors globally competitive. Digital technology has propelled the global delivery of educational content, making it economically attractive for traditional higher education institutions and for-profit enterprises to be purveyors of knowledge around the planet.

Corporate organizations are entering the global higher education system at a stunning pace. The University of Phoenix has already declared itself a "global education company."[31] The media conglomerate News Corporation has embarked on a joint venture with several universities to capture a substantial share of the higher education market.[32] Established place-based institutions around the world are broadening their global reach through online delivery. The Futures Project report cited Monash University in Australia as offering 106 distance courses in 80 countries, and the British Open University having 43 sites outside the United Kingdom.

The broader question is not whether American higher education institutions will maintain global dominance, but how they will fit into a global system of higher education that will undergo epic expansion and integration in the twenty-first century. The attendant challenge for American institutions will be in the roles they must play in sustaining the U.S. position in the global economy. The next phase of academic globalization will respond to the explosion in the number of students worldwide and the urgent need for new ways of accommodating their diverse demands. The number of degree candidates in the world was measured in 1990 to be 42 million, whereas the number of degree students is estimated to reach 97 million in 2010, growing to 159 million by 2025. The estimates are based on observable trends in economically advanced nations and the "transition" nations of Southeast Asia, Latin America, and Southern Africa that have been building technology-based industrial economies for some time.[33]

The profile for student growth around the world is not unlike the profile of the United States itself. The world's population of traditional college-age students for whom initial access to higher education must be made available is joined by a population of older, part-time learners for whom lifelong education will be essential to keep up with technological and economic change. Most analysts predict worldwide exponential growth in the latter group. The stunning conclusion of these predictions is that the equivalent of a whole new university would have to be created every week for the next several years to serve the global growth of degree students.[34] Planners and architects might salivate at that prospect, but the scenario for accommodating higher education growth in the world will likely be a combination of new and expanded institutions, institutional collaborations, new providers, and exponential growth of digital learning.

### Place, Permeability, and People: The Natural Resources of the Global Twenty-first Century

Globalization has two parallel narratives ultimately affecting the institutional and place character of American colleges. One is the growth of the knowledge-based global economic system. The other is the transformations that American communities and institutions will undergo in their quest to be globally integrated. American institutions, communities, and enterprises have had international ties for decades, even centuries, but globalization, by its current terms, has franchised virtually all organizations and individuals to be members of the worldwide network. They can be a multinational corporation, a high-tech start-up in New Mexico, an Inuit art gallery in Vermont, and any scholar, consultant, author, or blogger seeking a market or audience anywhere on the planet. Still, globalization is most evident in concentrated places whose economies are information-driven, knowledge-based, rich in the creative enterprises and population diversity. Cosmopolitan cities and higher education institutions are usually prime contributors to and dependent on the international enterprise.

The essayist Michael Elliott, referring to New York City's transformation as the archetypal international community, observes that there are two lessons to be drawn from the forces of change enveloping the world:

> The first is that globalization, the greatest theme of our time, is driven not just by technology, economics or trade in goods and services, but also by the restless movement of people—millions of them, on a scale the world has never seen before. The other is that with good humor, sound institutions and tolerance, that swirl of humanity can create a vibrant culture and unparalleled opportunity to dream of a better life for themselves and their families.[35]

A large complement of Elliott's "restless movement," seeking its place in the world economic system, will navigate through the world's colleges and universities in growing numbers. They will attend the diverse and expanding choice of institutions here and abroad. They will avail themselves of the power of the Internet. They will do these things in various sequences and combinations throughout their lives. As they do, they will accelerate the worldwide integration of higher education and the formation of alliances that will make most, if not all, institutions parts of a world university.

The discourse on the relationship between globalization and place in America concentrates to a large degree on the effects that global economic change is having on local economies. The argument is not that the impact on localities is a new phenomenon because, indeed, it has been underway for decades. The main concern is that the deleterious effects are accelerating as jobs flow offshore and as enterprises grow larger, more transitional, and more remote from the welfare of localities.

Saskid Sasser of the University of Chicago examines the matter of economic globalization and its relationship to place with the premise that globalization must be understood by its "multiple localizations" as much as by its "macro-level processes." With the authority of the nation-state being unbundled by the forces of globalization, the prospect is that *subnational* and *nonstate* entities will ascend in the constellation of global actors. She affirms that place does matter in this constellation, and her prime candidate among geographically centered subnational players is the city—specifically, the emerging *global city*.[36]

The global city brings together the strategic relationships of international finance, media, culture, and technology, buttressed by an agglomeration of human and cultural resources in a dynamic setting. In broad terms, Sasser's global city has its direct analogy in the great American university. It is not entirely coincidental that the American institutions drawing very large numbers of international students are located in cities such as New York, Chicago, Los Angeles, and Boston. Indeed, the typical large university possesses the characteristics of the global city: a strategic orientation to the international exchange of information, knowledge, and research; a cosmopolitan outlook; a concentration of human brainpower; and a physical setting organized to undergird the vitality of those functions. It is significant that institutions playing a vigorous international role are more numerous than global cities and that many of them are not in what we would consider international hubs. Many American institutions have had international spheres of influence for decades, conducting collaborative research and studies with institutions abroad, hiring scholars from all over the world, sponsoring cultural, economic, and strategic initiatives that have affected countries everywhere. One could readily substitute the idea of the American university in the definition that Sasser gives to the emerging international city: "This is space that is both place-centered, in that it is embedded in particular and important sites, and transterritorial, insofar as it connects sites that although not geographically proximate are intensely connected."[37]

There is a splendid irony in the power of individual places and face-to-face contact as cohesive, energizing forces in the global, wired economy. In spite of the diffuse character of the new worldwide society, its strength lies in the places that provide physical propinquity—a critical mass of person-to-person exchange of sensitive knowledge and innovation. This is the classic *agglomeration effect* that has always drawn like enterprises together, except that now the resource base is the accumulated and constantly renewing knowledge found in industry, institutions, and creative professionals.

The globalized system points to a new economics of place in which postindustrial enterprise depends more on human access and intricate human networks and less on easy access to natural resources.[38] The agglomeration effect of the twenty-first century is most evident in global hubs such as London, New York, Paris, and Chicago, places that possess unmatched depths of expertise in the knowledge-driven economy and an extraordinarily high density of venues and organizations in which that expertise can interact. The formal and informal boundaries of human exchange are exceptionally permeable in these places. Centers of technological and intellectual capital, such as Boston and San Francisco, though not dominant players in the global economic order, harbor concentrations of knowledge resources that are, in fact, critically important to the world. Such places lie at the center of constellations of cultural, social, entertainment, natural, and recreational resources that further nourish the creative, knowledge-oriented population. Colleges and universities are among the most notable of those resources.

In an essay appropriately entitled "Where I'm @," William Mitchell of MIT suggests that local governments will have to form "strong and effective alliances with major cultural and educational institutions, based upon common interest in attracting and retaining intellectual and artistic talent."[39] Mitchell refers to his home base in Cambridge, Massachusetts, as having many of the place attributes that make it a location of choice in the globalized world, not the least being the presence of several world-class educational institutions in a stimulating, historically rich setting. He points out how MIT, as a global institution, has been engaged in an ambitious building program to strengthen its own sense of place and quality of life, in order to draw "footloose, sought after intellectual talent."[40]

In *The Rise of the Creative Class*, Richard Florida of Carnegie Mellon University sees regional development in the global knowledge economy as being driven by concentrations of talented people, and by the factors that make those concentrations possible. One of those factors is a strong higher education infrastructure. He cites studies showing that economic growth in various cities through the twentieth century was based, to a great extent, on the levels of educated human capital that existed in those cities at the beginning of the century. The presence of talent attracted and sustained talent.[41] Florida makes the significant assertion that "place is becoming the central organizing unit of our economy and society, taking on the role that used to be played by the large corporation."[42] He says that such a place doesn't necessarily have to be a big city, but it must possess those attributes that appeal to creative people: quality of life, the interplay of culture and ideas, tolerance for strangers, and "intolerance for mediocrity."[43] In Florida's work, one finds a strong correlation between the intrinsic qualities of a place—as manifested in the beauty, vitality, and authenticity of the built and natural environment—and the diverse experiences, interactions, and associations that can be created (not just passively consumed) by inventive people drawn to such a place. Those very qualities are intrinsic to the American campus and even more so when the campus is a vital part of the cultural and intellectual milieu of the community around it.

Nevertheless, the globalized campus has an identity challenge. By adapting to the circumstances of a footloose international student body, and by cementing associations with international institutions and businesses, institutions have to be diligent in protecting their academic and regional identities as they reshape themselves to fit the new economic order. In *Country of Exiles: The Destruction of Place in American Life,* William Leach takes a less than benign view of the globalization of the American campus. Leach starts with the premise that American research universities are among semisovereign entities "approaching city-states in scope, having close ties with transnational business and foreign policies of their own."[44] He argues that the exponential growth of university research partnerships with transnational corporations has "accelerated the entry of the schools into a placeless global system, detaching them from the country . . . to which they owed their existence."[45] He laments that research universities "have exchanged what was left of an older form of open inquiry for a new internationalization tailored to the need of the marketplace and indifferent to the life of the country."[46]

## Worldly Campuses: Where Do We Go from Here?

The globalization of the academy in the United States is fundamentally about the responsibility of America's colleges and universities to help create a globally engaged, economically sustainable society. The most critical issues of the twenty-first century—environmental degradation, economic integration and disparity, migration, militarism, social disorder, cultural preservation, and advancement of human health and well-being—place an unprecedented demand on the U.S. higher education system to take America to the forefront of global understanding.

The U.S. public recognizes that global knowledge is a practical imperative, as evidenced by a survey reported by the American Council on Education in 2001. Ninety percent of respondents saw international knowledge as having importance to the future careers of young Americans, and the same percentage viewed it as very important to understand other cultures in global economic competition.[47]

### A Global Mission and Curriculum

By setting missions with a bold international perspective, U.S. institutions will enrich the learning environment for all their students. Michael Adams and Michael Sperling, president and associate provost, respectively, at Fairleigh Dickinson University, assert that beyond simply including an element in an institution's mission statement to "prepare students as global citizens," it is strategically important for institutions to craft real measures for accomplishing that end.[48] Fairleigh Dickinson implemented a policy of "ubiquitous distributed learning" to provide students with a globally oriented education, using the Internet to "reach out to the world" and "bring the world to the campus." The cornerstone of the university's strategy is the formation of a Global Virtual Faculty consisting of 45 scholars and experts from more than 20 countries and the United Nations who, through interactive distance learning, cover subjects based on unique regional and cultural perspectives.[49] The faculty from abroad work in collaboration with the university's on-site faculty. Fairleigh Dickinson requires that students take one Global Virtual Faculty course for each of the four undergraduate years. The estimated $12 million cost to implement the program over five years is more than 10 percent of the university's annual operating budget. Contemplating the value of such an investment, as well as the considerable institutional adjustments that are required, Adams and Sperling cite the pragmatic benefits of increased selectivity and retention, reputation-building institutional differentiation, and, most certainly, the development of globally conscious citizens.

### Being an Engine of Local Economic Sustainability

Globalization will drive the demand for continuing, lifetime higher education in the United States. The growth in job competition from abroad, especially in high-skill and technical positions that can be outsourced with the aid of the Internet, will have a growing impact on U.S. jobs requiring a college-level education. By the year 2018, it is estimated that 3.3 million business jobs will have gone offshore.[50] The magnitude of such a shift over more than a decade may not be large in the context of the vast American economy, but it is indicative of potential volatility in white-collar positions that have been beyond the fray in the past. As world job competition affects more skill areas, a divide could arise between "those that are highly educated and possess complex skills and those that are merely well educated and skilled."[51] Higher education institutions will need to be at the center of any domestic strategy to maintain upward job mobility. In such a future, learning and relearning will, itself, be a lifetime career. Personal entrepreneurship and continuing education will be essential tools in the uncertain global economic order. They will, however, not be enough if the educational, social, and economic support systems are not there to ensure access to a lifelong education system that is agile enough to keep up with the changes wrought by globalization.

Postsecondary institutions of every sort, from community colleges to research universities, will be fully integrated into regional economic strategies conceived to maintain a workforce capable of participating in the changing world economy. Campuses will become more borderless as they form associations with municipalities, organizations, businesses, and other institutions to provide new, pertinent, and ever-changing forms of continuous learning.

### Maintaining Leadership in the Global Academy

The globalization of the academy heightens the competition for talented students and faculty who will have a multitude of stimulating choices of places across the planet in which to make their intellectual pursuits. For America's place-based institutions to maintain leadership in tackling the theoretical and pragmatic challenges arising so rapidly in this century will require not just the financial resources of the sort that propelled them during the postwar academic golden age, but the capacity to attract and retain the best intellectual talent available at home and from around the world. They will have to provide stimulating, exciting academic environments on campuses designed to make scholarly discovery the most compelling of endeavors. They will have to be digitally integrated with institutions across the globe. The worldly campuses will have to strategically pool their creative and cultural resources with American cities, states, and regions committed to the cultivation of economic and intellectual niches that will be unique and highly valuable in the international learning community. A premium will be placed on the campuses and localities that are most open to new faces and new ideas. The successful global institutions in the United States will be in physical settings that are authentic in their regional character and beauty, that are set in urbane, eclectic, culturally robust surroundings where domestic and international students will find common ground. The successful global campuses will be those where academic life, student life, community life, and residential life are aligned to create a secure, welcoming, stimulating place for citizens of the world.

# five

# Is There a Place for Place in Higher Education's New Demography?

## Northeastern: A Streetcar University Goes National

The first American educational endeavor of the Young Men's Christian Association began in Boston in 1851 as a series of self-improvement programs for young workingmen. In 1898, the YMCA formed the Department of Law of the Boston YMCA, the genesis of what is now Northeastern University. The YMCA continued to add academic programs in the early twentieth century, one of the most notable being the day school of the Polytechnic Institute in which cooperative courses in engineering allowed students to have paid workplace experience in conjunction with their education. Cooperative education remains today as a signature program at Northeastern.

Northeastern attained university standing in 1922, separating from the YMCA in 1948. In the postwar years, the university steadfastly held to its mission of serving local students from blue-collar backgrounds. The focus on the practical needs of working-class and adult students was intended not just to sustain the university's institutional tradition of local service, but to carve out a demographic niche that Boston's other private universities were not pursuing. Richard Freeland (who became Northeastern's president in 1996) wrote in 1991 that, "Northeastern specialized in jobs other universities considered marginal: educating non-elite students who needed to work their way through college and cooperating with area businesses to provide technically competent middle-level employees."[1]

As baby boomers reached college age in the 1960s, Northeastern expanded its offerings. Service to adult, part-time students grew with three new colleges offering two-year, four-year, and nondegree continuing education programs. At the

Northeastern University's West Campus. (Len Rubenstein.)

urging of local groups, the university set up four professional schools by absorbing existing local programs or creating new ones. Other undergraduate, graduate, and professional programs were added. By 1967, Northeastern's total enrollment had grown to 45,000, making it the largest private university in the country, a standing that was maintained through the late 1980s. The school took on some of the trappings of its more elite academic neighbors by promoting modest growth in research activity and expanding intercollegiate sports, fraternities, and sororities. Development of new dormitory space signaled a nascent emphasis on out-of-state recruitment. By the late 1960s, a third of the entering freshmen came from other states and a third of Northeastern's undergraduates were housed on campus.[2] The cooperative program continued to be a trademark for recruiting.

Since the 1930s, the university had held to an architectural theme consisting of unadorned, spare buildings clad in pale gray brick. The buildings were laid out in the street and block pattern of Boston's Fenway district, with campus open space relegated to a few grassy forecourts at street edges. Surface parking dominated the west end of the campus. For the most part, the unpretentious character of the campus suited Northeastern's self-image as the college serving the educational needs of the region's working students. Campus boundaries were constrained by major streets and transit corridors and by the resistance of Northeastern's neighbors to campus expansion. Staying true to its urban mission, Northeastern was reasonably diligent in working out boundary issues. In that respect, the university distinguished itself from the more aggressive expansion practices of other large universities in the Boston area.

In 1990–91, Northeastern took in 1,000 fewer freshmen than expected, an early consequence of a steep recession in New England, a decline in the region's college-age population, and stiff price competition from public colleges in Massachusetts. Successive smaller matriculating classes in the 1990s were replacing larger graduating classes, causing gradual but painful stress on the institution. The university found itself between the proverbial rock and hard place—too costly for its traditional urban market and far down in the academic rankings compared to the stellar private universities dotting the greater Boston landscape. Because Northeastern was heavily reliant on tuition revenue, a financial crisis was at hand. Survival depended on a radical revamping of its mission and identity.

University leaders determined that the only way to remain competitive was to improve the quality of the academic offerings and appeal to a more national, even international, student body. The survival strategy meant significant contraction in enrollment and expenditures. The chairman of Northeastern's board of trustees affirmed the university's new motto as "smaller, but better."[3] President John Curry presided over the initial enrollment cutbacks, at the same time overseeing necessary improvements in the academic facilities. In 1996, incoming President Richard Freeland called for more stringent student selection, advancement of sponsored research, improved student-faculty ratios, and measures to enhance retention and graduation rates. With the promise of academic excellence, the campus would have to become more inviting, more in keeping with the new academic direction. Despite improvements in teaching, student support, and recreation facilities made in the early 1990s, the image of boxy austerity still prevailed. In a bold stroke, Freeland embarked on a campaign to transform the campus' gritty character while improvements in academic quality were still works in progress.

President Freeland points out that the university had to consider radical action in response to critical demographic and economic changes by strategically repositioning itself from being a regional campus to one that can attract a national and international student body. The college-age cohort in New England was in stasis. With its growing tuition costs, Northeastern could no longer compete with public universities in Massachusetts for its urban, working-class students. Student population was growing elsewhere in the country, especially in the Sunbelt, projected to peak in 2008. If Northeastern were to attain a sustainable national stature, it would have to be "securely repositioned" in that role by 2008 to remain competitive as the college-age demographic levels off in future years.[4]

Between 1992 and 2002, Northeastern invested $477 million in new facilities and campus improvements.[5] On land south of the rapid transit tracks flanking the campus, the university constructed residential space for 585 students and 75 sale units for the housing-starved Roxbury neighborhood. The most stunning change is in the area now known as the west campus (the site of the vast parking fields previously mentioned), where seven new residence halls housing 2,600 students have been built around the first true series of campus greens in Northeastern's history. The west campus contains a new health sciences building and visitor center with underground parking, mixing uses to create an extra measure of urban vitality. The development, facing Boston's majestic Museum of Fine Arts across Huntington Avenue, gives Northeastern an entirely new architectural expression of bricks and masonry in several warm hues punctuated with crisp, glassy façades projecting campus life onto the urban street.

Larry Mucciolo, Northeastern's Senior Vice President for Administration and Finance, acknowledges the high stakes involved in executing the repositioning strategy. "Borrowing $400 million to make the physical institutional changes leaves no margin for error ... the effort has required a real commitment by people at every level, but it's still a leap of faith." President Freeland adds that the strategic risks the university would have faced by not taking action to redefine itself would have been even greater. He declares that "you have to be single-minded in effectuating a difficult strategy like this."[6]

President Freeland stresses that the physical improvements made by Northeastern had to occur in an "interactive sequence" with the university's academic and institutional changes. He and others reasoned early on that prospective students and the community had to see tangible things happening on the campus to reinforce the message that Northeastern was making qualitative institutional changes. The university had to make a "new statement, different from the past." Initial changes—providing new library, student life, and recreation improvements—were designed to demonstrate a more vibrant and attractive campus environment. A new, more spirited architecture, organized for the first time to shape inviting landscape spaces, played, in Freeland's estimation, a powerful role in the university's strategic repositioning effort, emancipating Northeastern from its aesthetic conservatism of old.[7]

Northeastern has adopted a variety of measures to improve recruitment, retention, and graduation rates: increased financial aid, tracking students in academic trouble, easing the process of switching majors, and fostering more collaborative learning environments throughout the campus. Between 1991 and 2005, applications increased from more than 9,000 to more than 25,000. Mean SAT scores for enrolled freshmen in the same period increased more than 20 percent. The graduation rate for the 1999 entering class was 60.5 percent, compared to 40 percent in the early 1990s. The cooperative program remains as a key element in Northeastern's academic mission, emphasizing its experiential and financial benefits. In 2003, more than 60 percent of the university's students were offered jobs from businesses where they had interned under the program.

In 2004, Northeastern announced plans to spend $75 million to hire 100 tenured and tenure-tracked faculty over a five-year period. The positions are conceived to fill undergraduate teaching needs in growth areas such as business, communications, and health sciences, as well as to spur research growth in targeted areas including biotechnology, nanotechnology, sensing/imaging, and urban policy.[8] A key academic investment goal is to consolidate Northeastern's leadership in its core professional graduate programs in business, engineering, computer science, pharmacy, and counseling psychology. By 2004–5, external funding for research/projects had more than doubled since the early 1990s to more than $46 million.

President Freeland cautions that the university must be diligent in addressing the concerns of its traditional constituencies as the transition is made to a selective national student body. This is complicated by the perception held by some that the university has abandoned its urban roots. Alumni need to be confident that they could and would have attended the "new" Northeastern. Freeland points out the university's commitment to the admission of a certain proportion of Boston high school students and the imperative to continue to seek out pragmatic, entrepreneurial students who, through cooperative education experience, can ultimately contribute to the region's well-being. He notes, as well, the university's commitment to the higher level of student service necessary to sustain the institutional culture on a long-term basis.[9]

In reinventing itself to accommodate a new student constituency, Northeastern University had to grapple with the daunting prospect of improving intellectual quality, place quality, and attention to the quality of student life. As a dedicated urban institution, the university had to maintain its civic role in Boston. The strategy could not succeed without the integration of every part.

## What, Exactly, Is Higher Education's New Demography?

### The Next Twenty-five Years: An American Population Primer

To put the demographic discussion in proper context, a synopsis of projected American population change over the next generation or two is in order. The U.S. Census Bureau estimated the country's population in 2005 to be more than 290 million. One Census Bureau projection shows the population at nearly 325 million in 2020 and 351 million in 2030, a growth of 22 percent in barely a quarter of a century.[10] The expected makeup of the population reveals significant changes as well. Whereas members of ethnic minority groups represent about 31 percent of today's population, 40 percent of Americans will come from minority groups in 2030. In absolute numbers, 92 million Americans classified as minorities today will grow to 146 million in 2030. People of Hispanic origin will make up more than 68 million members of the population in 2030, with African Americans nearly 50 million. The Asian-Pacific population will nearly double to almost 25 million, and the Native American population will grow by roughly 40 percent to 3.6 million. The bureau's projections show an increase of nearly 46 percent in the U.S. population that is foreign-born, from about 30 million in 2005 to almost 44 million by 2030.

America's population will continue its trend toward "grayness." The median age will increase from today's 36.7 years to more than 40 by 2030. The aging of the baby boomers, and, to some extent, the earliest members of the X-generation, will drive the graying of the U.S. population. Sixty-six million Americans are 55 and older today. In 2030, that group will be made up of 108 million souls. Those in the 18-to-24 bracket, considered to be the traditional college-age cohort, number about 28.5 million in 2005. That number will increase to more than 29 million in 2020 (after peaking at 30.6 million in 2013) and rebound to nearly 32 million in 2030. In absolute numbers, the traditional college-age population will be a relatively stable cohort for the next 25 years. The proportion of the minority population in that cohort, however, will increase by more than 35 percent.

### Sixteen Million Signers of Higher Education's Social Contract

Higher education's new student demography is reshaping the American campus by its numbers, by its patterns of migration and mobility, and by the multiplicity of its socioeconomic, ethnic, and age groups. Just as important, the circumstances and needs of college-going groups are in continuing flux, as are the ways that the academy must find to respond to those needs.

In 2005, there were about 16 million people enrolled in accredited place-based colleges—make that 16 million *individuals*, each one possessing a particular need or desire to participate in the collegiate experience. Being enrolled in a college program is an individually important act, made with a deliberate motivation: to change one's life through education. Sixteen million individuals are making choices that lend credence to the admonition made by Gordon Davies that "education is not a trivial pursuit but a deeply ethical work that will determine the future of our society."[11] As 16 million college students seek to fulfill their individual aspirations through higher education, they are also signing a social contract. They must prepare themselves to be part of an increasingly complex society in critical need of informed, engaged, and thoughtful citizens. U.S. college students face an uncertain, but undoubtedly demanding, future as they navigate in the global, technology-driven society. They make up a population of learners who will spend a lifetime chasing, changing, relearning, and retooling jobs at a pace that has seen no precedent in living memory. In a generation, 18 to 20 million students will come to place-based colleges with the same aspirations, the same challenges, the same civil obligations.

When one contemplates the 16 million individuals attending college today, it is important to observe one of the striking demographic shifts that have occurred in the last few decades, which is the growth in the enrollment of women at U.S. colleges. In 1950, male students outnumbered women by more than two to one (which is not a surprise as the impact of the returning GIs was still being felt), but around the late 1970s, women began to surpass men in total college enrollment. Currently, female enrollment is 56 percent of the national total. Women became the majority of associate degree recipients at about the same time they surged ahead in total enrollment, soon thereafter becoming the majority of baccalaureate and master's recipients. Men still receive the majority of doctoral and professional degrees. Nonetheless, the growth in female college attendance in the three decades from 1970 to 2000 is stunning—136 percent overall; 168 percent in graduate school; 853 percent in professional schools. Much of this is attributable to reforms in gender equity policies that were effectuated in the 1970s. Today, the debate has swung to concerns about the stagnation in the rate of males entering college and attaining postsecondary level workforce skills.[12] Looking 25 years into the future, women will continue to outnumber men in the U.S. general population by two or three percentage points, although men are projected to be in the majority of the 18-to-24 age cohort by a slight margin.

## The "Traditional" College-age Cohort

The mythic notion of the American college student is that of the postadolescent 18-to-22-year-old, attending a resident college full time in quest of a baccalaureate degree. The resident collegian is the most traditional member of the traditional college-age category. However, the members of this archetypal collegiate group are in the demographic minority. The fact is that only one in seven students in American higher education institutions attends college full time, in residence.[13] Fewer than half of American college students are in the traditional population cohort of 18 to 22 years, but even that is deceptive because, as we shall see later in this chapter, a large proportion of that number is anything but traditional.

Notwithstanding their smaller share of higher education's demographic profile, the traditionals are still a growing population. An article by Sara Hebel in the *Chronicle of Higher Education* in summer 2004 cited the fact that the total number of students graduating from the nation's high schools will peak at nearly 3.2 million by the year 2009, after which the graduation rate will plateau.[14] The figure represents roughly a 10 percent increase over the number of high school graduates in 2002, the benchmark year cited in the article. The article went on to say that "even then, the crunch [leading to demand for entry into U.S. colleges] is not likely to ease because state and college leaders are pressing to increase the college-going rate, given the imperative of an educated population that can fuel state economies."[15]

The growth in the college-age population since the mid-1990s is nearly as epochal as when returning veterans availed themselves of GI Bill benefits in the 1940s and when baby boomers flooded U.S. campuses in the 1960s and 1970s. At the beginning of the current surge, most campuses had a bit of a cushion in their capacity to accommodate enrollment growth because of the dip in enrollments in the 1980s after the boomers had passed through the system. That trough led to aggressive competition for student recruitment in the 1980s and 1990s, spurring ambitious campaigns to upgrade campus programs and facilities. In the next quarter century, the relative stability of the college-age population suggests that colleges catering to traditional students will find themselves in a steady, but limited and highly competitive, student recruitment market.

### Continental Drift

The twenty-first-century demographic phenomenon is as much geographic as it is quantitative. America's historical migration to the South and West continues inexorably on, with huge portents for higher education institutions. The continuing drift to the Sunbelt will reach epic proportions over the next generation, causing profound reallocations of regional wealth and shifts in the burdens of population change in all parts of the country. In what is considered to be the "third great American migration," upward of 50 million people will move to the southern and western U.S. from the northern states over the next generation.[16] By 2030, California, Florida, and Texas are each expected to add between 12 and 13 million people to the populations they registered in the 2000 census. Of the 15 fastest growing states through 2030, all except New Hampshire are in the West and South.[17] The influx of college-age students in the Sunbelt over the next generation will be disproportionately greater than that of the Rustbelt states of the Midwest and Northeast. By the middle of the next decade, the number of high school graduates in the West and South will increase 18 and 12 percent, respectively, while graduates in the Northeast and Midwest will grow 8 and 4 percent.[18]

College expansion and the development of new campuses in the Sunbelt states such as California, Arizona, Nevada, Texas, Florida, and North Carolina will occur at a pace that could easily rival that of the quarter century after World War II. Arizona State University is planning to double enrollment to 95,000 students on its main campus and three new campuses. The University of North Texas' planned campus in Dallas anticipates more than 20,000 students. In many northern-tier states, public and private colleges will experience flat or declining in-region enrollments. Schools in the northern tier that have historically catered to students from within their regions are aggressively recruiting candidates from the Sunbelt. Those that are unsuccessful in creating new learning markets will likely downsize or consolidate with other institutions. Northeastern University is one of several institutions in slower-growing areas that have adopted strategies of selective, nationwide recruitment leveraged by substantial investment in the quality of academic offerings and campus life.

### Here Come the Millennials!

The typical college-age student on the campus in the next 15 to 20 years will be a member of the "millennial generation," those who were born between 1982 and 2000.[19] The 70 million millennials are the largest generational cohort entering college age since the 78 million souls who made up the baby boom generation came of age in the 1960s and 1970s. If the millennials possess the generational power exerted by the boomers, they will lead cultural change in every stage of their lives, not the least being their years as college students. The millennials come to college with a vastly different set of childhood experiences, values, and expectations than their parents and grandparents. More racially and ethnically diverse, a third of the generation is from ethnic and racial minority households that have been historically underrepresented in America's colleges. Roughly 20 percent have at least one parent who is an immigrant.

Digital technology is a natural part of the millennials' lives. They have grown up with the Internet and the other appurtenances of the digital age. They take connectivity for granted, by their comfort with digital communication and because they tend to be more group-oriented and collaborative in their relationships with others. They lean toward experiential activities. They expect to use technology extensively in their educational settings, but they still place value on one-to-one discourse with teachers, professors, and one another. They don't take things at face value because they have access to so many alternative sources of information. Being more diverse and more connected, they tend to accept differences in others more easily. They expect change in the world and in their lives. They have high expectations of their educational, civic, and work environments, but they have no illusions that those environments can predictably meet their expectations.[20]

### The Nontraditionals Will Be the New Traditionals

The largest, most complicated, and fastest-growing segment of postsecondary learners now and in the coming generation is the cohort of so-called *nontraditional* learners. A large component of this group falls within the typical college-age brackets, but their patterns of college participation vary significantly from those of the full-time, resident students. Nontraditional students are those who have delayed enrollment, are attending college part-time, are working full time, and have dependents other than a spouse, in any combination of these circumstances. They make up the largest single category of college enrollees, constituting three-quarters of all U.S. postsecondary students. Nearly 40 percent attend school part-time, compared to 28 percent who went to college part-time in 1970. The same ratios apply to those students who are older than 25—nearly 40 percent today as opposed to 28 percent in 1970. About 60 percent of today's college students are employed full time or part-time while attending classes.[21] More than half of America's collegians in the next generation will be working adults who are more than 25 years of age.[22]

Chapter 4 highlighted one of the most critical factors affecting participation in postsecondary education by American adults of all ages in the next several decades, that being the position of the United States in the increasingly competitive global economy. The knowledge-based economy of the future depends on a workforce that is educated and reeducated many times over to keep pace with economic and technological change. The twenty-first-century American workforce will be more freelance. Lifetime employment in one organization, one sector of the economy, or even one profession will be extinct for the vast majority of Americans, putting the burden to learn new skills and relearn old skills on people from their young adult years to retirement age. The age cohorts from the mid-20s to the 50s and higher will thus be the fastest-growing set of college learners. America's standing in the global economy will rely, as well, on the quality of primary and secondary education, the early preparation of youngsters to be cognizant of a more complex world and more agile in their life skills and vocational abilities. Those demands will lead to a more integrated continuum from K–12 through postsecondary and continuing education if the United States is to maintain its competitive position.

The traditional and nontraditional classifications are descriptive only to the degree that they distinguish between the cohort of young learners direct from high school attending a full-time undergraduate program and the much larger and faster-growing learner population of all ages attending part-time credit and noncredit programs. Most institutions serving both groups have the ongoing challenge of creating equitable, mutually engaging campus environments that will accommodate the needs of full-time resident students from within and outside the region and local, nontraditional adults seeking part-time education.[23]

## Academia's Underrepresented Demographic

The segment of the population still on the margins of full participation in U.S. postsecondary education is made up of those on the low end of the socioeconomic ladder. Low-income, racial, and ethnic minorities and immigrants are not represented in higher education in nearly the same proportions as in the U.S. population as a whole. Roughly 40 percent of U.S. households had a mean annual income of $25,000 or less in 2003.[24] Students from households with annual incomes under $25,000, a large proportion of whom are members of minority and immigrant groups, made up 20 percent of the enrollment of public two-year colleges, 11 percent of public four-year colleges, and 8 percent of private four-year colleges in 1999–2000. Ethnic and racial minorities, regardless of income level, make up about 30 percent of the students enrolled in postsecondary institutions, slightly less than their share of the total U.S. population. Although minority enrollment is growing in absolute and proportionate terms, it is not growing as rapidly as the minority age cohorts that will be eligible for entry into the workforce in the next generations. Millions of individual Americans will be as ethnically polyglot as the country itself, blurring the group distinctions of college participation to the point where they will probably be less relevant than they are today.

For better than two decades, more than a million people annually have entered the country legally and illegally. Unlike the European-centered immigration surge of the early twentieth century, the current wave of immigrants is made up of 45 percent Latinos and 40 percent Asians, bringing a new mix of cultural and socioeconomic demands to the higher education enterprise. More than 38 million immigrants, the majority of whom will be Hispanic, will be added if the current rates of legal and illegal immigration are sustained through 2020. For immigrants to recharge America's social and economic energies, as they have throughout our history, they will have to be mainstreamed into the educational system at all levels. In many parts of the country, first- and second-generation Americans, many of whom will be in ethnic minorities, will be the major participants in the new jobs that are created in the next few decades.

One of the most daunting challenges to America's education system in this century is to elevate the economic prospects of those at the low end of the income ladder. This is a matter of basic, enlightened social equality *and* global competitiveness. The economist Anthony Carnevale has estimated a need for up to 14 million more workers with some level of postsecondary education than are likely to be produced by colleges and universities by 2020.[25] Carnevale and others regard low-income and minority populations as an untapped resource in higher education. President Emeritus Peter Smith of California State University at Monterey Bay estimates that the nation's wealth could grow by up to $225 billion if African American and Hispanic students participated in postsecondary education today at the same rates as white students.[26]

The prospect for higher rates of college attendance by low-income and minority students is uncertain in the current picture. Rising tuitions, combined with the erosion of public support for needs-based financial aid, further undermines the ability of people in low-income and working-class households to attend college. Affirmative action policies in higher education based solely on race are under siege, but are shifting to the correlation between race and income to sustain diversity. The qualified finding of the U.S. Supreme Court in favor of the University of Michigan's affirmative action policy was predicated, in part, on evidence showing that the poverty rates for African American and Hispanic students are roughly three times that of white students. Public universities in California, Washington, and Florida, with policies weighted toward allaying economic disadvantages were cited in the court decision, auguring for a possible shift toward economic equity as a basis for affirmative action policies in the future.[27] According to polls conducted in 2003, Americans support preferences for poor and economically disadvantaged students compared to racial preferences by roughly two to one.[28]

If there are to be meaningful improvements in the college-going rate of low-income and minority students, they will most likely be driven by national and regional responses to worldwide job competition that will require a social and political climate less tolerant of income disparities in America than it has been for the last several years. To restore rising real wages in the U.S. economy, the bottom 60 percent of the American workforce will need to be reskilled and reeducated.[29] The most substantial change will occur at public colleges and community colleges charged to fulfill public economic development mandates, collaborating with secondary school systems on issues of preparation and remediation. Top-ranked private and public institutions have further to go in achieving economic equity. The most selective 10 percent of four-year schools fill 74 percent of their openings with students from the top economic quartile, and only 3 percent from those in the bottom quartile.[30] Many of the prestigious schools, including Harvard and Princeton, are endeavoring to mend that imbalance, recognizing not just the benefits to the nation of improving the prospects for economically disadvantaged learners, but of making socioeconomic diversity a measure of institutional quality.

## A Graying but Active America

The aging of American society is already having an impact on higher education. The average age of Americans is nearly 38 and rising. People over age 50, who represent 29 percent of today's population, will make up a third of the population in 2020. The over-50 generation, with more than half of the country's discretionary income, will be a potent higher education constituency. Lifelong learning, a well-established component of higher education, will continue to grow due to a number of demographic factors. One such factor is the increased longevity of Americans. The average U.S. lifespan has grown from 68 in 1950 to more than 77 in 2002. It is projected to be in the low 80s by 2025. The relevance of longevity in this instance has much to do with the lifestyle decisions being made by Americans who are enjoying sustained health and vitality well into the so-called golden years. Among the most significant changes is that of delayed retirement, a trend that began to reveal itself in the 1980s. Economic necessity and uncertainties over the direction of the U.S. Social Security system will have bearing on the decisions of older people to stay in the workforce, but surveys suggest that better health among older Americans gives them the motivation and the capacity to do productive work in later age.

David P. Snyder, contributing editor for *The Futurist,* cites a survey by AARP revealing that three-quarters of the baby boom generation intend to continue working into their 70s and 80s.[31] If boomers fulfill that aspiration, that would portend that a majority of the largest generational population cohort in America could still be in the workforce 15 to 20 years from now. If that happens, and if subsequent generations follow that trend, there will be an enormous demand for sophisticated continuing education as mature workers endeavor to stay in touch with the changing technical and intellectual requirements of the workplace. Much of that educational demand will undoubtedly be met online, but it is plausible to expect that people in their 50s to 80s will populate campuses in unprecedented numbers in the future. Mature citizens will have no less of a desire for face-to-face interaction and in-place intellectual discovery than their younger counterparts. The campus could become a seedbed for the renewal of the intergenerational compact that has withered over the last few decades as a result of family mobility and the widening gap of cultural priorities among generations.

Regardless of how many Americans continue to work in their later years, greater longevity and decreasing morbidity allow older people to actively pursue intellectual and cultural interests for their own intrinsic values. Those pursuits involve a huge assortment of cultural venues, travel, and learning activities, of which the higher education experience is but one part. Nevertheless, older Americans make up a growing component of those participating in continuing education and cultural offerings made by higher education institutions. The Cornell Adult University brings alumni and others back to campus to take courses that range from the purely entertaining to the intellectually demanding. Utah State University in Logan has long sponsored summer resident study programs for older and retired people.

Retirees are migrating to college towns in increasing numbers, attracted by the cultural, educational, and recreational resources that are offered in those locales. Many are drawn by the youthful energy that pervades college and university towns. Retired alumni are gravitating to the places where their alma maters are located. In 2004, the AARP reported 27 college-affiliated retirement communities in 16 states, located on or near campuses, having educational and other program ties with the colleges. More such communities are being planned and developed, some solely as campus real estate ventures without formal program affiliations with the institutions.

## The Community Colleges

Any discourse on the collegiate environments serving the diverse, changing student demographic profile of the twenty-first century has to include America's 1,200 community colleges. Roughly two-thirds of community college students are part-time and adult learners.[32] A tide of traditional-age, full-time students makes up the other third. Forty-four percent of U.S. undergraduates attend community colleges. Nearly half of all minority students enrolled in higher education are in community colleges.[33] For access to continuing education and career advancement, the community college is unsurpassed. The average age of students in community colleges for several years was 29 (although because more college-age students are electing to go to community colleges for economic reasons, the average has recently dropped to 27).[34] The 450,000 associate degrees conferred by community colleges in 2000 represented one-quarter of all higher education degrees, second only to the 1.2 million bachelor's degrees and as many as all advanced degrees combined. Although 5.4 million students are officially enrolled for credit in community colleges, more than 10 million people take at least one credit or noncredit course in a community college program.[35] Community college campuses, located within commuting distance of 90 percent of the U.S. population, come in a stunning range, from rural, tribal colleges of a few hundred students to metropolitan districts serving 20,000 or more students in multiple branches.[36] They are housed in former department stores, factories, and schools, in large suburban mall-like complexes, and old-fashioned ivy-covered campuses.

Nearly 1,000 of the U.S. community colleges are public, founded with a mission to contribute to the economic and social well-being of their client localities by supporting regional workforce needs. Their mandate, and most of their funding, draws from the city, county, or constellation of communities in which they are located. Although many community college districts in the United States are statutorily administered by the states, they are, as a group, the most locally oriented of any of the postsecondary educational institutions in the country. Academic programs are heavily infused with applied and vocational curricula to enable students to be job-ready in regions where the employment market can shift with each economic cycle. Community colleges serve those starting their postsecondary educations, those making career changes, those upgrading or sustaining careers by seeking state-of-the-art knowledge, those returning to the workforce after a hiatus, and those receiving education one course at a time while they maintain their day jobs.

The relationship between the schools and their host localities varies with the socioeconomic fortunes of the localities. The educational demands of an inner-city district or a rural Rustbelt county are vastly different from those of an upper-income suburb or a burgeoning Sunbelt metropolis. The rate of change in a region's economy can be abrupt, as when once-thriving manufacturing enterprises shut down, sometimes being replaced with new technologies, oftentimes with no clear replacement economy in sight. In the twenty-first century, America's community college will have to be nimble in meeting such disparate circumstances.

Community colleges offer courses in the liberal arts, humanities, and social sciences for degree accreditation, including offerings that are expressly intended for students who move to higher degree levels beyond the community colleges. Roughly half of the first-time college students in the United States attend community colleges,[37] a significant number of whom come with expectations of a relatively traditional college experience during and beyond the two years. Roughly 25 percent of students completing associate degrees in community colleges matriculate to four-year institutions within a few years. That progression is bound to increase in the future as an economical way for students to attend college and for cash-strapped state higher education systems to make postsecondary education more productive and economical.

States such as Florida and Washington have strategically positioned their community college systems as an affordable means of providing the first two years of education leading to baccalaureate and advanced degrees. Many states have established upper-division public colleges to accommodate students who have fulfilled two-year programs. George Boggs, president of the American Association of Community Colleges, told me that some baccalaureate institutions are directing applicants to community colleges with a promise of matriculation if the applicant succeeds at the community college level. Dr. Boggs reminded me, too, that many students are going to more than one school in a degree career, sometimes two schools at once.[38]

## Place Implications of Student Growth and Multiplicity: The Imperative for Engagement

The place character of many U.S. campuses will be affected not just by the diversity and fluidity of the twenty-first-century student body, but by the imperative to fully engage diverse learners in a society that will thrive only by continuous, broad-based learning. The engagement must encompass the communities in which the institutions are located because the socioeconomic vitality of large and small communities in the United States will increasingly depend on the depth and diversity of education available to their citizens.

College life in the twenty-first century is life enriched and challenged by the diversity of those who participate in it. Many colleges will have to rethink how their institutional and physical settings can be made to serve student multiplicity, including all of the differentiations that students bring to campus life—ethnic, racial, age, gender, economic circumstance, full-time and part-time attendance, resident and commuter.

James O'Donnell of the University of Pennsylvania holds to the view that older, part-time and economically disadvantaged students are ill served by what he characterizes as the "youth camp culture" promulgated by higher education institutions that favor the traditional notion of the 18- to 22-year-old attending school for four years.[39] From O'Donnell's perspective, campus environments, facilities, activities, and faculty loads are too often oriented to the college-age youth model (even at institutions that enroll both full-time and part-time students), much to the disadvantage of nontraditional students. "If student services dollars privilege the full-time adolescent and offer little for the single parent or the mid-career learner, colleges and universities are not doing their jobs."[40] He argues that campuses have to find ways—some technological, some organizational—to engage the range of ages and circumstances represented by the twenty-first century demography of higher education.

Eighty percent of students attending place-based colleges and universities in the United States come to campus each day from someplace else. They are the most varied in their demographic makeup of any college-going group. They can be in the college-age bracket, attending school full time while living at home or off campus. They can be older, part-time students with jobs and families. They can be a small minority on a campus or the entire student body.[41] They spend less time in the campus setting than their resident counterparts. Part-time and commuting students usually juggle campus time with a host of family and employment demands, but even full-time commuting students typically have less engagement in the collegiate experience than resident students. Spending less time on campus, they have fewer opportunities for social interaction and co-curricular activities. They have fewer opportunities to reinforce their coursework through social and intellectual exchange with faculty and peers. As Barbara Jacoby of the University of Maryland observed, "For residential students, going to college is a new life; home and campus become synonymous for them. For commuter students, attending college is an add-on to their present lives; the campus is a place they visit for short periods of time."[42]

Colleges will have to do a better job of addressing the sense of isolation and separation confronting part-time and commuting students by creating opportunities for meaningful social and intellectual engagement. The colleges that offer no organized intervention or support on behalf of commuting and part-time students or that provide a modicum of programs and facilities for their particular use leave them with the sense that their interests are still marginal rather than integral with those of the campus community as a whole. Students in those circumstances are consistently less satisfied and more likely to drop out. Barbara Jacoby advocates "significant steps to treat all students fairly and provide the same quality for all" by designing the institution's activities, events, programs, and places to make all students as much a part of the community as they want to be.[43]

In responding to the needs of an increasingly diverse student body, institutions will have to balance the demands of a more freelance learner-centered population, the expectations of the larger community, and their own strategic self-interests in maintaining their positions in a volatile, competitive academic environment. The place implications of higher education's new demography will be as varied as the institutional responses to demographic change:

- As we saw in Chapter 3, Internet-based programs will continue to expand, broadening access and affordability to the changing learner population and extending the virtual boundaries of campuses without necessarily increasing their physical dimensions. Some institutions that come to depend more heavily on distance education to reach a wider variety of students may actually consolidate or reduce the physical space that they need to conduct instructional activities, particularly if they are among institutions that face reduced public support for capital development and operations (see "Back to Basics" in Chapter 6). Others may find that providing more extensive digital instruction will free capital resources to provide other services to their learning communities.

- We will see schools becoming physically more dispersed and integrated into the larger community domain in the form of affiliations and partnerships with other institutions, organizations, and agencies. Institutions will join with other entities to expand academic offerings, to diversify the settings and resources for student engagement, to provide closer physical proximity to various segments of the learning community, and to achieve such economies as can be found in shared learning environments. States and localities that look to their regional institutions to more economically prepare an educated workforce at many skill levels may call upon their baccalaureate colleges and community colleges to merge more of their resources through closer operating affiliations or physical co-locations. We can expect the emergence of functional, possibly physical, links with primary and secondary schools and with agencies serving older citizens to accommodate cross-generational learning needs. Multigenerational campuses could easily become more commonplace.

• The quality and identity of the campus setting and its efficacy as an environment for student engagement will be paramount, regardless of the type of institution and the range of learners that the institutions serve. As institutions broaden their programs to serve more varied socioeconomic, ethnic, and age segments of the learning population, their campuses should brim with vitality, exuding a quality of place that heightens the learning experience for all. The experience of place needs to be welcoming, engaging, comfortable, and secure for students of widely varying backgrounds and ages, many of whom arrive with language difficulties or limited earlier education. The campus should possess a variety of casual spaces; quiet places where students can study, prepare materials on their computers, or nap; animated places with activities for the more sociable; secure lockers; snack services; library/resource centers that are compelling in the ways that they offer material and virtual information; and engaging as places where group and individual study can take place.

• Community-based colleges will have a more distinct civic identity in the twenty-first century. Many are already providing a panoply of community services and activities: developmental, remedial, and counseling programs; conferences and symposia; library and information resources; arts and cultural events; recreation; health services; daycare; job placement; and other functions that support the evolving needs of their students and their communities. As the societal demand for continuing education, career enrichment, and community service expands in the future, the civic role of community-based colleges will expand. The San Diego Community College District, for example, has developed an educational-cultural complex that includes, besides classroom space, a community theater, public library, and food services.[44] Collin County Community College in Plano, Texas, Anne Arundel College in Maryland, and Northern New Mexico College, serving the Pueblo Native Americans, are among numerous schools that have adapted their campuses to provide a wide range of community functions in addition to their basic educational purposes. The public functions of community colleges will affect their place character. They will become more active public gathering places; they will be more integrated with the fabric of the community.

- At colleges preparing students for the local workforce, instructional space will have to be flexible and adaptable to change because course offerings and instructional methods will evolve at a rapid pace. The vocational, technical, and professional workforce needs of localities can significantly shift in a decade or less. Space adaptability will be necessary to accommodate programs conducted by other institutions and business enterprises on campus as colleges form learning partnerships over short and long durations. Wired and wireless learning technologies will require spatial flexibility. Given the broad diversity of learners entering academia in the next generation, there will be a wide range of methods by which instruction is provided—from low-cost, distributive technology-based instruction to curricula that are individually oriented and mentored on a face-to-face basis.

- Many community college campuses will take on a more traditional collegiate character. Indeed, that is already happening in some regions where schools are responding to the desire of full-time college-age students attending community colleges to have a more collegiate campus experience. Sports and recreation facilities and student commons have long been features of campus life at most schools, but more are providing amenities, including student housing, that typically are found at four-year institutions. As of 2004, more than 20 percent of community colleges have built or are planning to build student residences and facilities that are ancillary to residential life. The schools that become more traditional as home to full-time college-age students will, at the same time, host the multiplicity of functions and community services necessary to serve part-time and continuing education students of all ages.

# six

# The Learning Environment: Accountability, Cost, and Stewardship

## Clarion University: Stewardship within Modest Means

Clarion University of Pennsylvania, like most of its 14 sister institutions in the Pennsylvania State System of Higher Education, is the reincarnation of a state college whose original mission was to produce elementary and secondary schoolteachers for its region of the Keystone State. Founded as the Clarion Normal School in 1887, the institution attained university standing in 1982, with an enrollment of 6,200 students. Teacher education, still a flagship program at Clarion University, was joined in the expansion years by business, science, and communications programs, as the institution was called upon to play an ever-wider role in building the postwar workforce in central/northwestern Pennsylvania.

A tour of the Clarion campus provides a revealing narrative of the currents that have shaped small public colleges and universities throughout the United States: their enduring missions as regional educational, economic, and cultural resources; the changing nature of the regions they serve; and, perhaps most graphically, the cyclic nature of the public resources available to maintain their missions. The tour reveals a small coterie of late-Victorian-era buildings that survive from the school's earliest years, rich in character, domestic in scale. Nearby, a handful of structures whose vintages span the first half of the twentieth century, more modest in detail than the original buildings, are laid out in a pleasing ensemble that retains some of the earlier collegiate atmosphere. Beyond these reminders of Clarion's days as a teachers' college, the architectural personality of the campus shifts to the predictably bland postwar buildings whose scale, design, and placements are largely indifferent to one another. Many of the newer buildings occupy locations in a complicated topography that rises and falls as much as

Clarion University of Pennsylvania. (Melissa Hollier.)

seven stories in less than a half mile. Buildings were also placed on parcels made up of former residential lots, packaged serially over a 20-year period by the commonwealth and conveyed to the university for campus growth. Clarion, like other campuses, shows the effects of the high-growth era when the priority was to produce occupiable space as quickly as possible wherever and however land could be made available. More than 72 percent of the university's 1.6-million-gross-square-foot building inventory was constructed in the 1960s and 1970s when Pennsylvania and other states were infusing capital into regional public campuses at levels not seen before or since.

If the tour ranges beyond the campus into the borough of Clarion, it will discover a pleasant community of well-kept residential neighborhoods and a main street that maintains a modicum of vitality in spite of competition from the malls that have sprouted up at the I-80 interchange south of town. The town betrays the signs of a more flourishing past when local manufacturing and commercial enterprises seemed to be in a virtuous balance with the population. Clarion shares its past and its future with other towns that dot the Allegheny countryside—towns such as Oil City, Franklin, Titusville, and Dubois. Small cities there and throughout the Rustbelt have watched their seemingly stable industries migrate to other regions and other shores. Population is static at best. Younger people head elsewhere to make their livelihoods.

The university has become the economic mainstream in the Clarion area. If Clarion and the other towns in northwestern Pennsylvania are to pin their hopes on a postindustrial future, they will look to the university as a prime source of the knowledge and skills required to sustain such a future. That aspiration, however, is tempered by the relentless competition for capital and operating funds that Clarion University has been waging with its sister institutions in the commonwealth for several years. Pennsylvania is no different from other industrial states in the Northeast and Midwest, struggling to meet an increasing array of budgetary demands while revenues have declined.

Clarion University's institutional and financial challenges are inextricably tied with its capacity to sustain the quality of its physical environment. By the mid-1990s, those many buildings that were put up in the heady 1960s and 1970s had gone past any reasonable cycle of depreciation without major upgrading. In fact, the depreciation of many of the university's facilities was on a fast track when the buildings opened their doors. When Clarion was expanding, the pressure to produce space was so intense that the money left over for building envelopes, mechanical systems, and finishes could barely provide for the enduring qualities that are expected of institutional buildings. Resources for landscape and infra-structure were even more marginalized. In this, Clarion merely repeats the challenges confronting hundreds of colleges that were involved in the race for space in the decades after World War II and the ensuing budget struggles for upkeep.

The university had reached the point where it was essential to bring its academic facilities up to a level commensurate with twenty-first-century teaching and research methods. On top of that, the support environment for students—housing, dining, recreation, an inviting campus setting—had to be upgraded to draw students from a wider area and engage them in campus life. Clarion was competing for faculty and students as well as for funds.

With planning funds allocated from university revenues, in the mid-1990s Clarion undertook a comprehensive campus renewal plan that coupled a modest amount of new construction with a systematic program of renovation and reorganization of space in existing buildings. Among the first steps were to assess building conditions across the campus to determine the level of renovation that would be required to sustain each building's usability for the next generation, and to project the quantities and types of space necessary to fulfill Clarion's needs under modern standards. The assessments enabled the university to determine where it would be most effective to upgrade buildings for their current use and where renovations would be appropriate for new, reorganized functions.

The process was fraught with difficult decisions. Although finances would weigh heavily in the determinations, the host of issues ranged from the most individual of expectations to the reconciliation of broad visions of what Clarion should be in the future: Who would have to move? How could essential proximities and affinities be strengthened? How would the quality and quantity of space for each department be affected? How would historic buildings be preserved? After establishing a set of principles for dealing with these issues, the university spent several months testing and negotiating options for renovation and space reorganization, pausing periodically to reanalyze the implications of the moves on Clarion's resources. The program that was eventually adopted was geared to making substantive improvements that would foster a higher degree of student engagement in places all across the 132-acre campus. The university adopted a strategy of using funded projects to start a sequence of improvements that could be done with annual operating funds. Thus, the expansion of the university library allowed the consolidation of functions from scattered campus locations, liberating space in those locations that could be put in line for needed renovation and reuse by other programs. Academic departments dispersed in various buildings could be brought together in renovated space. Lacking the revenue to expand residential capacity while dormitory renovations were being made, Clarion formed a partnership with a private developer to build housing for more than 600 students on a site near the campus. New, fee-based projects such as the recreation center were accompanied by site improvements for the pedestrian environment.

Still, the public funding climate has forced the university to improvise at each step in its stewardship of the campus. In 2003, the state's funding formula for distributing legislatively authorized appropriations among its 14 system universities reduced Clarion's share by a total of $2.5 million over a three-year phase-in period. This curtailed the pace of critical campus improvements. Concurrently, however, the university's hopes were raised when the commonwealth appropriated more than $27 million to replace Clarion's science laboratory facilities, crucial to bring the university's science curriculum up to twenty-first-century demands. Rapidly rising cost estimates are outpacing the university's ability to implement the science building program at the level anticipated when the funds were designated. Rather than compromise the needed program, Clarion is waging a campaign for foundation and industry support to take up the slack. The university envisions a future in which public-private partnerships will play a greater role in making campus improvements, reinforced by Clarion's policy of vigorous stewardship.

Clarion University stands out not because it is unique in confronting the challenges of campus stewardship and accountability, but because its challenges are so typical of those faced by colleges throughout the country. The university demonstrates that stewardship requires diligent leadership that can build a consensus on institutional values. Joseph Grunewald, Clarion's current president, who chaired the planning process in the mid-1990s as dean of the Business School, fends off those who would compromise the efforts to make Clarion a better place by asserting that the institution must "define a course of action that is sound enough to endure with the support created by a solid development process."[1]

## Expectations and Accountability in the Knowledge-based Economy

America is making a series of transitions from an industrial economy to a knowledge-based economy. The transitions cut unevenly across regions. In those parts of the country whose fortunes were long defined by the manufacturing of steel, textiles, appliances, machine tools, and a host of other goods now produced on other shores, the impacts of job loss have become ingrained over the last quarter century. In those areas that have thrived by the growth of technology, media-based services, and international trade, the pressure is to maintain their competitive edge. The new specter in all parts of the country is the outsourcing of once seemingly secure high-skill jobs to countries abroad. Higher education must develop the intellectual capital necessary to drive the new economy and sustain the social fabric. Although not a new role for the academy, it is a more crucial role because the critical sources of economic production are drawn from intellectual discipline and innovation. The groves of academe are the virtual mills and factories of the twenty-first century.

With that role come new visibility, competition, and expectations. Clara Lovett, president of the American Association of Higher Education, reflects on the transition that society is expecting the higher education community to make, and how the academy fares in making that transition:

> The status of higher education in U.S. society has changed greatly; the days of marginality and genteel poverty are definitely behind us. At every opportunity, the country's leaders tout the central role of colleges and universities in a knowledge-based society. We are, and we are perceived to be, both the producers of new knowledge and the gatekeepers on pathways to well-paid jobs in a knowledge economy. We honor our tradition of genteel poverty, but we seek material rewards comparable to other professions. We resist, and perhaps do not even recognize, the new obligations accruing to an enterprise that indeed now plays a critical role in the development of society. Rhetorically, we cling to the old culture, while in practice, we go after large federal research grants and congressional earmarks, enter joint ventures with corporate partners, and build massive facilities and endowments.[2]

Lovett goes on to say that higher education leaders must meet two challenges in this era of heightened expectations. One challenge is to lead other sectors of society, particularly in areas where higher education has, in her words, the "tremendous capacity" to help transform the performance and production capabilities of other sectors. The other challenge to academia's leaders is that of *holding themselves and their institutions accountable as never before* for the outcomes of the higher education enterprise. The challenges of accountability, according to Lovett, are predicated on the ability to view higher education's role "through the eyes of its external stakeholders rather than through the lens of academic tradition and dogma."[3]

The public's expectations of the U.S. higher education system in the early twenty-first century are determined largely by the fundamental values that the American public attributes to higher education—as a *public good* whose values accrue to the society as a whole, and as a market-driven *private good* that is conceived, in the main, to benefit the individual learner. The debate on the value of higher education in terms of access, affordability, and outcomes is especially acute for public higher education, where more than 75 percent of American college students are enrolled.

By most accounts, a shift in academia's value to the American public has occurred in the last 30 years, from being one that fulfilled largely public purposes in the postwar years to one that serves the socioeconomic interests of individuals in the intensely competitive and market-driven environment of the twenty-first century. The public good paradigm was enthusiastically adopted at the end of World War II, building on the consensus that was formed around providing higher education to returning veterans and restoring American prosperity. The public good model was reinforced by the federal government through defense-driven research funding and direct financial support for students attending college. The states escalated their support of higher education as an investment in their own social and economic productivity.

The private good conception of value derives from a consensus that education is the path to higher individual earning power and social well-being. College education as a private good is sustained to a greater degree by the willingness and ability of individuals and private sources to pay for it. Governments in the United States are ceding the support of higher education to the private good paradigm. The proportion of investment in public (and private) higher education by states and the federal government has declined while the proportion of revenue derived from students and nongovernmental sources has risen. Federal support through grants and scholarship aid to students is gradually being replaced by loans. States have, for the most part, lowered the funding priorities once allocated to higher education as appropriations for primary/secondary education, prisons, highways, and health care costs have risen among the demands that are being made on limited state budgets.

Robert Zemsky, chairman of the Learning Alliance at the University of Pennsylvania, observed in a *Chronicle of Higher Education* essay that institutions recognized in the 1970s and 1980s that "survival depended on being responsive to market forces," increasingly driven by individuals desiring to achieve the personal and monetary advantages of a college degree.[4] He blames the decline of public purpose in academia on the American public who, through its elected state and federal officials, has reinforced the idea that college education is primarily an investment in personal advancement: "Legislators and governors everywhere have become accustomed to letting higher education pay its own way—reminding those who balk at ever-higher tuitions that, from the perspective of a return on investment, nothing beats a college education."[5]

The increase in tuition costs from the 1990s is striking. The average annual tuition for four-year private institutions went from $9,640 in 1990 to $20,082 in 2004, according to a survey of the National Education Association. The survey showed yearly tuition at four-year public colleges rising from $1,900 to $5,132 in the same period.[6] The numbers do not include room, board, and fees, which have also risen astronomically. Student debt rose comparably. Loans made to students through federal programs increased from 4.8 million to 10.8 million students between 1992–93 and 2003–4, in total annual amounts rising from $19.8 billion to $50.5 billion, as reported by the National Association of Student Aid Administrators.[7] Federally supported loan volume jumped early in the period when Congress broadened loan eligibility and raised borrowing limits. The report also registered an increase in private borrowing for education of $1.3 billion in 1995–96 to $10.6 billion in 2003–4. More than 60 percent of baccalaureate recipients and half of the master's recipients graduated with outstanding federal loans in 2003–4.

Rising tuition is not just an encumbrance in the pursuit of the American dream; it is a potential denial to those whose aspiration is a middle-class lifestyle. In most of the country, a middle-class income is no longer attainable with a high school diploma. In 2003, the median full-time annual wage for an individual over age 25 with a high school education was just short of $29,000, whereas that of a person with a bachelor's degree was nearly $47,000.[8] Even a baccalaureate is considered to be insufficient to attain the earning potential desired by many.

In *Correcting Course: How We Can Restore the Ideals of Public Higher Education in a Market-driven Era,* a paper by the Brown University Futures Project, the authors contend that public colleges and universities are caught in a vise between decreasing state support and continuing expectations that the institutions will fulfill their mission to serve the public.[9] The authors cite the pressure confronting higher education institutions to "cut costs, measure and report on performance, and compete ever more strenuously for students, grants, funding and prestige." State policies are moving in favor of an open market that is resulting in a "kind of unhealthy competition that does not necessarily lead to increased access, better instruction, lower costs, or greater efficiency."[10]

Press accounts, commission reports, and congressional statements since the 1990s have tied academia's supposed lack of fiscal discipline with a national rise in tuition costs that has consistently exceeded increases in the consumer price index.

Critics have claimed that millions of college-qualified students will be priced out of the opportunity to attend college by the end of this century's first decade. The complaints have given rise to demands for great accountability in justifying the costs of higher education.

In an article entitled "Understanding Higher Education Costs," Michael Middaugh cites the results of a study tracking education costs from 2000 to 2003, indicating that there is no causal relationship between the expenditures by institutions for delivering instruction and tuition prices.[11] Middaugh's study, prepared for the U.S. Department of Education, found that instructional expenditures actually increased less as a cost per student credit hour than the consumer price index during the 2000–2003 period.

With instructional expenditures being about 40 percent of educational and general costs at U.S. colleges (the largest cost category), the study findings are not indicative of runaway costs in providing college instruction. Middaugh points out that tuition, together with other sources of revenue, does, in fact, contribute to the elements of teaching, research, and service that institutions undertake in pursuit of their missions. However, the rise in tuitions stems in part from factors over which institutions have little or no control, such as health care, energy costs, and unfunded mandates by state and federal governments. Add to that decreases in state appropriations to public institutions. On the whole, Middaugh concludes that colleges have been "responsible fiscal stewards in containing instructional costs," and that when tuition contributes to the "creation of knowledge through pure and applied research or extension and other service activity, the common good of society is served."[12]

The ascendancy of the private good model, paired with the diminution of public funding for higher education, is prompting institutions to formulate strategic plans around goals to elevate their positions in the academic marketplace. The emphasis, in many cases, is on *repositioning* strategies based on improvements in academic reputation to attract and retain the most promising students. Repositioning can result in downsizing or expansion, depending on what colleges deem necessary to achieve a competitive advantage. With the erosion of state appropriations, public institutions are engaging in ambitious private donor campaigns. Hand in hand with the strategy of academic repositioning are campaigns for the advancement of research standing by institutions with graduate and professional programs. An astonishing number of public and private universities aspire to be ranked in the top 20 or 50 research institutions in the United States. Those that elect for reputation building as premier research institutions usually envision an expansionist future, relying on aggressive entrepreneurism to generate research dollars through foundation grants, corporate collaborations, and federal earmarking.

Many colleges and universities have more modest strategic goals for enhancing their academic reputations, choosing instead to realign their resources around the areas of teaching and research where they already possess demonstrated strengths. This can be a frugal way to carve a distinctive niche in the marketplace, although it frequently results in the marginalization of programs that are not seen as essential to the standing of the institutions or that do not generate grants. The humanities and social sciences often suffer in these undertakings, a potentially serious blow to academia's charge to cultivate the whole person.

The strategic paths that colleges are taking in today's market-driven regime invariably call for new levels of investment to enhance the physical resources of the institutions. Improvements in the quality of place and facilities are clearly linked with the strategies that institutions are adopting to position themselves in the new century, as illustrated in the case descriptions throughout Part Two of this book.

### The Fiscal Squeeze on Higher Education Institutions

The status of financial support for higher education at the dawn of the new century is reflected in several areas. Federal funding for academic research through the National Science Foundation increased at an annual rate of about 2 percent in constant dollars between 2001 and 2005.[13] Practically all of defense research, which increased nearly 5 percent, is done by contractors, not higher education institutions. According to the 2005 Outlook Report of the *Chronicle of Higher Education,* Congress, in 2004, projected discretionary spending at a rate about equal to the current rate of inflation through the rest of the decade. Most of the increases in the Pell Grant program will go into reimbursement of the federal treasury for student grants previously awarded, with a minor amount increasing the number of grants. The federal student loan program will continue to grow.[14]

The projection of state spending on higher education in the same *Chronicle* Outlook Report shows a nationwide increase in fiscal 2005 of 3.8 percent, to $63 billion. In the preceding year, an annual decline of 2.1 percent was posted; the rate of increase in state higher education support had declined for the three years prior to that.[15] Most college and university endowments were projected to increase at "mid- to high" single-digit levels of return in 2005, according to the *Chronicle* review. Most institutions had failed by 2004 to recover from losses posted since 2001. The shift toward private giving is evidenced by an increase of nearly 12 percent in alumni support in 2003, to $6.6 billion. Capital fund-raising campaigns are regularly going beyond the $2 billion mark among large institutions, with one analyst predicting that the $3 billion campaign level will soon be breached. The competition for private funds will be increasingly ferocious in the ensuing years as more institutions embark on large-scale campaigns for endowments, mission enhancement, student support, and facilities improvements.

College indebtedness escalated in the heady 1990s when $100 billion in bonds were sold. Deficit spending was encouraged by factors such as lower interest rates, the eagerness of investors to purchase tax-exempt bonds, and by a 1997 congressional raise in the cap on tax-exempt borrowing by private institutions.[16] Low interest rates that were precipitated during the recessionary period have been powerful inducements for borrowing, enabling colleges and universities to reduce the cost of debt by refinancing old bonds. Much of the bonded debt was encumbered to support expansion and improvements in campus facilities—addressing deferred maintenance and renovation needs that have accumulated over decades, and creating new academic, residential, and recreational facilities, infrastructure, technology, and campus amenities for institutions to maintain their competitive edge. Most of the student amenity improvements (housing, student unions, recreation and fitness centers, event facilities, etc.) have been built with revenue bonds that could be amortized by student tuition and fees, residential rentals, concession revenues, and other predictable income streams.

The prospects for consistent, sustained sources of revenue for higher education institutions over the next generation or two are uncertain at best. Tuition cannot continue to rise if there is any hope of making college as accessible as it must be for a pluralistic population in a competitive global economy. The competition for donor support waged by nonprofit organizations of all sorts does not guarantee that all of the country's colleges will receive equitable or adequate returns. Corporate financial collaborations in research and technical training will be subject to the exigencies of the global business climate. A return to more generous, sustained public support of higher education will require a political sea change, a renewed public commitment to higher education as a critical national asset in a globally competitive environment. Such a sea change, if it were to occur, would take the better part of a generation, coming in uneven spurts in various sectors of higher education and parts of the country.

Indeed, there are many who call for a rebuilding of the compact between higher education and the public. In a 2005 talk given to the American Council on Education, Larry Faulkner, president of the University of Texas at Austin, declared that the higher education community itself must take responsibility for renewing the public trust by sponsoring accountability, not just grudgingly accepting it.[17] President Faulkner's point was that if the recognition of higher education's contribution to the common good is to be restored, it will depend to a great extent on the ability of colleges and universities to demonstrate continuous improvements in academic productivity, financial access for middle-class families, and control of educational costs.

Educational costs are clearly the challenge of the new century. Faulkner's ACE address culminated in the admonition to his fellow education leaders that the rate of growth of cost per student, at a "substantially inflationary" 4.5 percent annually, "cannot be sustained indefinitely."[18] Notwithstanding the intrinsically high costs associated with the propagation of knowledge in the collegiate setting, more education leaders agree that cost control must be a priority if education's public compact is to be revived.

## The Cost of Place: A New Mandate for Stewardship

The operation and upkeep of campus buildings, grounds, roads, and utility and technology infrastructure represent between 20 and 30 percent of the total annual operating costs at most colleges. Buildings, where people spend 80 to 90 percent of their time, add up to roughly 5 billion gross square feet of space nationwide that have to be heated, cooled, lit, ventilated, cleaned, and kept in good repair. The cost of place includes the investment made in new construction and renovation necessary to accommodate growth, new pedagogical and research initiatives, and qualitative improvements in the campus environment. Although facilities and grounds represent only a part of the costs of sustaining institutional vitality, the enlightened stewardship of the campus as a place will be essential in the uncertain economic circumstances of the new century.

The drive to attract students and improve ranking in the academic marketplace has brought with it an enormous investment in facilities and amenities, as noted earlier in this chapter. The trend started in the 1980s when the college-age population cohort was in stasis, and institutions (especially those that were tuition-dependent) were competing for a static or declining student pool. The college-age cohort today is on the rise in proportions comparable to the baby boom surge of the 1960s, reviving the need for new, expanded facilities just to accommodate student growth. Many institutions are now engaged in more selective positioning strategies that require higher-quality campus facilities. They are launching into cutting-edge scientific and technological initiatives so that able research faculty and graduate students can come together in state-of-the-art scientific environments. They are enhancing their public reputations by the development of facilities in which they can showcase their cultural, entertainment, and sports activities.

Physical improvement strategies have contributed to a college building boom over the 10 years ending in 2004 estimated to be more than $84 billion.[19] This massive investment in building construction and renovation is nearly a 40 percent increase over the physical asset value of more than $212 billion for all U.S. colleges reported in 1994–95.[20] *College Planning & Management,* in its annual review of college construction activities, reports more than a doubling in the yearly amount of campus building construction during the 10 years ending in 2004. The figure for building construction in 1995 was $6.1 billion, jumping to $13.7 billion in 2004, with most of the growth spiking up between 2001 and 2003, in spite of those being recessionary years in which annual higher education funding declined in most states.

Much of what is currently being built, whether to maintain the competitive position, enhance reputation, support new academic initiatives, serve new public purposes, or accommodate enrollment growth, has resulted in positive changes in the quality of the collegial environment. Notwithstanding the occasional apt criticisms that colleges are creating country-club settings, new and renovated student housing, social and recreational facilities have restored the vitality of campus community at numerous institutions around the country. Much of the new construction and renewal has improved the functional quality of learning and research spaces and has improved the quality and variety of individual and social learning environments.

Although the space inventory of schools of all types has been expanded and improved in recent years, a formidable backlog of space remains in need of renewal. Public and private institutions in all regions of the country are confronted with the built-in costs of deferred maintenance, renovation, and renewal. The vast majority of the buildings on American campuses have reached at least one full cycle of depreciation. Scores of buildings have outlived the functions that they were originally designed to accommodate. The need for rehabilitation of existing facilities is not just a matter of aging, but of keeping up with ever-changing code requirements, compliance with the provisions of the Americans with Disabilities Act, environmental regulations, energy conservation measures, and, most recently, mandated security improvements. Comprehensive estimates of the amount of investment necessary to bring U.S. college buildings up to parity are widely varied and not always current. A 1996 study estimated that the nationwide cost of remediating only deferred maintenance needs on college campuses was more than $26 billion.[21] The most comprehensive assessment of U.S. campus renewal and replacement needs was last published in 1989 under the foreboding title *The Decaying American Campus: A Ticking Time Bomb*. The study estimated the cost of upgrading college and university facilities to be $60 billion in 1988 dollars. Of that amount, $20 billion was cited as necessary to alleviate "urgent needs."[22] Although many institutions have adopted regular or episodic programs of renovation and renewal since the *Decaying Campus* report was filed more than 15 years ago, the nationwide need for improvement of existing facilities has not diminished. It is, in fact, increasing each year. Facilities have continued to age, and inflation has taken its inexorable toll on the financial resources required to keep up with the backlog.

### Back to Basics

The first line of attack in the stewardship of the learning environment is to get the soundest use of existing facilities. Although this makes common sense, programs to use existing space better face a whole suite of obstacles, not the least of which is that fixing up old space or using it more efficiently lacks the financial sex appeal of shiny new projects. As any campus facilities manager is quick to say, donors are not standing in line to put their names on rewiring, roof replacement, and asbestos removal projects. Therein lies the rub. Facilities renewal and deferred maintenance are typically covered by annual operating budgets allocated for such purposes. With the other demands placed on operating budgets, the backlog of deferred maintenance needs simply grows each year. Nevertheless, investment in renewal can not only mitigate long-term operating costs of space but can make for more productive learning environments.

As at Clarion, many institutions are renewing their environments by coupling renovation and deferred maintenance projects with strategies to reorganize and consolidate academic and support functions that have been scattered around the campus after years of *ad hoc* decisions on where to locate them. Projects involving new additions to old buildings typically provide the funding leverage for rehabilitation and reprogramming of the old buildings. Although such measures allow institutions to make incremental improvements, strategic campaigns to upgrade existing facilities will have to be put forth with the same ardor that new construction projects are promulgated if colleges are to make significant advances in upgrading their building stock.

Reductions in the long-term operating costs per square foot of campus building space will be but one of the incremental measures for cost control that institutions will have to address. The operating costs of space—where roughly one-third go into heating, cooling, and other utility expenses, more than 40 percent cover maintenance and custodial needs, and the balance reflects administration, construction management, grounds upkeep, and public safety—average nearly $2,400 for each student attending college.

Most institutions have embarked on programs to conserve in the use of energy, water, and other resources as cost control measures. The economic benefits of reductions in resource consumption are only going to increase in the next few decades as the United States confronts resource shortages, increasing energy costs, and climate change issues. Institutions have to make the mitigation of long-range operating expenses an integral part of the cost equation when designing for new construction and adaptive reuse of existing facilities.

One of the most elusive nuts to crack, but a significant one because it can result in large amounts of *found* space, is to streamline the scheduling and utilization of teaching and administrative space. The oft-noted space scheduling profiles at most campuses are those in which high peaks of use occur in three to four hours from mid-morning to early afternoon during an eight-hour instruction day, or in concentrations of instruction time during the first three or four days of the school week, leaving space underused for the remainder of the day or week. The declared reasons for such schedules range from the way that pedagogy is practiced at the institution to limitations imposed by the configuration of the space or by the work and attendance schedules of faculty and students. However, the acceptance of abrupt peaks and valleys in campus space use will be challenged more and more as institutions are forced to go to the well of cost control. Even a modest leveling of space scheduling disparities will lead to improvements in the allocation of physical resources. Reductions in peak space demand can be echoed by reductions in peak parking demand (*ergo,* less asphalt) and peak utilities demand. Broader use of instructional space that is hoarded by faculty and departments must be part of the formulation for colleges that are serious about the stewardship of their facilities.

Technology is coming into its own as a tool for stewardship. The value of the technological investment by institutions has been strenuously debated, with questions raised as to whether institutions have invested smartly or to just keep up with the latest applications coming through the technological marketplace. Space needs for the accommodation of academia's technological appurtenances have actually increased over the last two decades. On the whole, though, American institutions have built an infrastructure and culture of technology that can expand and augment the learning environment, especially by extending the reach of nontraditional learning modes. Investment in digital hardware systems and the space necessary to accommodate them will level off as wireless technology becomes more commonplace. Basic lecture courses can be substituted with more interactive, flexible, digitally based programs such as those at Virginia Tech's Math Emporium, or they can be designed for greater learning impact by creative augmentation with digital media. Wireless technology will make the whole campus, and beyond, a classroom. A good deal of in-place instruction is going to be replaced or augmented by interactive digital learning that can be accessed 24/7 by students demanding flexible, customized learning in lieu of conventional lecture formats. The acid test of accountability for a learning environment that relies more on the effectiveness of technology is to prove that it makes for better, deeper, more creative learning. If it does, it is accountable stewardship.

### Space as a Cultural Force: Reconceptualizing Collaborative Learning

Building space typically is viewed as a commodity, measured in quantity as a way to fulfill per capita standards for classrooms, laboratories, offices, and the gamut of space categories that are required to make the institution work. It is meticulously inventoried, scheduled, and hoarded. The amount of space possessed by a public college or university can determine how much support for upkeep or new construction the institution will receive in some states. Space is a tradable commodity, coveted by a host of eager bidders if its previous occupants depart for new quarters elsewhere. Building committees talk of space in functional and budgetary terms. Architects talk about it in those terms as well, but are careful to burnish its aesthetic attributes.

Stewardship will be more than seeking functional efficiencies and economies in campus facilities, as critical as those things will be in the unfolding century. Stewardship will have as much to do with how the assets of the campus can qualitatively foster learning relationships. William Mitchell, head of media arts and sciences at MIT, says that fundamental notions of space must go beyond all of that in the twenty-first-century campus. He asserts that space must be seen as a *cultural force* for the institution.[23] By that, he means that space has to be valued by how it reflects and shapes the dynamic culture of the institution. The cultural dimension of space is being redefined in the form and organization of facilities at campuses across the country as many institutions make strategic shifts to more interactive, interdisciplinary, social learning cultures.

Mitchell points to the new Stata Center at MIT as a facility conceived as a cultural force for the institution. The Frank Gehry–designed building is the subject of much media attention because of its controversial design. The flamboyant pile of slanted walls, cylinders, and cubes stands in eyebrow-raising contrast to the spartan aesthetic of traditional MIT buildings. It was described by one Boston journalist as a "freeze-frame of a Disney animation" whose playful forms are "something you associate more with Sesame Street than MIT."[24] That playfulness, says Mitchell, is deliberately intended to break down barriers and foster a vibrant culture of collaboration at MIT. In his view, the real story of the building is that nearly half of its 400,000 square feet are dedicated to common and public spaces, corridors, and lounges deliberately designed to force chance encounter and conversations. Much of the public space has large window views into the labs and classrooms and out to the campus beyond. That amount of common, interactive space is unprecedented. It is an intentional move to reshape MIT's research culture in the twenty-first century.

The Stata Center and other teaching, research, and social buildings on U.S. campuses organized to foster encounter reflect a substantive trend in the way that learning and research are conducted in academia in the twenty-first century. The trend, which alters the traditional reliance on single-use facilities, is particularly evident in the way that scientific research is conducted today. Many academicians assert that the most vibrant areas of scientific discovery are at the margins, where disciplines intersect with one another. Science and technology faculty are in the forefront of the drive for spontaneous connectivity among disciplines. This is considered to be a cultural transformation at institutions where academic disciplines have long been viewed as highly tuned specialties. The primary areas of scientific investment over the next decade, and probably beyond, will center on the life sciences. They are in a realm of discovery that depends on the morphing of disciplines, such as chemistry, molecular biology, nanotechnology, bioinformatics, and a host of scientific endeavors that did not even have names a generation ago. Cross-disciplinary team research is having a spillover effect in other academic areas. A provost at a Midwestern research university wryly observed to me that, ironically, the life scientists are out in front of the social sciences and humanities faculty in their zeal for more cross-fertilization between areas of intellectual inquiry. He is confident that the social scientists will one day see the light.

A growing number of colleges are promoting stronger links between undergraduate and graduate studies, encouraging undergraduates to be involved in laboratory, studio, and seminar activities in graduate programs. This is not a new phenomenon, but one that is being more vigorously pursued as an academic policy to cultivate undergraduate participation in more advanced levels of intellectual activity, especially where that activity draws from a robust mix of outlooks.

The place-making implications of the trend toward cross-discipline learning and research are profound. Terms such as *connectivity, openness, permeability,* and *breaking down borders* are often cited in building program statements, not just for new science facilities but for all manner of learning and social space. The *quality* of human interaction is a program priority. That mandate is a reminder that physical proximity, enlivened by sociable connecting spaces, continues to be one of academia's prime cultural and intellectual resources.

## The New Stewardship: A System of Learning

The goal for the new stewardship of academia's physical environment is to make the campus itself a productive, integral part of the learning experience. All of the standard performance measures—cost effectiveness, operating efficiency, resource conservation—will have to come into play in making the campus a productive learning environment in an era when the sources of financial support for institutions are, at best, unpredictable. Higher performance will come in response to the market forces confronting institutions, but, above all, it must be part of an institutional ethos for adding value to the learning experience. It will be oriented less to hierarchical forms of instruction and more to learning that is self-directed and interactive if the place-based campus is to be a resource that can meet the challenges of the twenty-first century.

David Ward, president of the American Council on Education, provides the proper context in which to define the terms of campus stewardship in the twenty-first century. In an essay in 2000, written while chancellor of the University of Wisconsin, Ward urged education leaders to rethink higher education's mission in terms of a *system of learning:* "Rather than continuing our efforts to rebalance teaching, research and service as if they were distinct, separate activities, American higher education must organize our priorities around three interconnected systems of learning: the learning experience, the learning community, and the learning environment."[25]

*Experience, community, environment*—these are the irreducible elements of place.

Stewardship of place in this age of accountability is all about the cultivation of an environment that infuses vitality and connectivity into the learning experience. The early twenty-first century may come to be known as the era of decline of single-purpose places on campus, the time when the academy was liberated from its silos. Consider the transformation of collegiate libraries. They are becoming multipurpose hubs, outfitted as interactive learning centers as well as repositories of books, CDs, computer terminals, and all of the other forms of informational entry to the world beyond. The Johnson Center at George Mason University in Virginia created a new paradigm for integrating academic libraries within the social fabric of the campus when the center was built in the mid-1990s to include not just the university's collection of undergraduate learning materials, but food service, a cinema, a travel agency, and other uses more typically found in student centers. It is a beehive of activity, although one of the principal criticisms of the facility has been that it functions more like a mall, soaking up the outside campus life. Later versions of multipurpose libraries and student centers have made more substantial connections with the campus around them.

Residential life, in a reprise of the earliest campus design ideas in America, is being organized to have more synergy with academic life. To enhance the quality of the relationship, institutions are designing residential facilities to include more formal and informal learning spaces and locating the living and learning domains of the campus in closer proximity to one another. The concept of the residential college or *house* system, with academic, co-curricular, and dining functions to foster social learning, is being revived at institutions all over the country. Vanderbilt, Virginia, Rice, and Union College are among the institutions that have adopted new variants of the system.

Propinquity and human scale are hallmarks of campus stewardship. Digital technology is a force that liberates a host of academic functions from the necessity of adjacency, but it does not supplant the spontaneous energy of face-to-face, hands-on engagement that comes with physical proximity and connection among the disparate activities of campus life. A major caution in planning facilities that combine functions and draw large numbers of people is to avoid megascale buildings that generalize interaction much like a shopping mall rather than nurture the many levels and variations of community that strengthen the learning environment.

Architecture is a critical element in campus stewardship. It gives the campus its three-dimensional form. It frames the open spaces in such a way as to define the distinctive character and order of the campus. The bulk of the day-to-day work of the campus takes place inside the architectural envelope. The placement of buildings and the activities within determine the movement patterns that criss-cross the campus terrain and the gathering places that energize collegial life. Together, the ensemble of buildings and open space can contribute vitality, unity, or chaos to the way that the campus works and the way it is perceived. Architectural design has its obvious obligations to the users of the building, to the program, the budget, and the functions that are destined to take place in the building. The stewardship challenge is to ensure that the design obligations to the campus as a whole are just as obvious.

Campus stewardship must always demonstrate care for those qualities of the place that make it unique and meaningful to its constituents within and beyond the campus boundaries. Stewardship is not about lavish or ostentatious design, but neither should it preclude bold, fresh, innovative forms that bring new energy and better performance to the academic environment. Stewardship is the protection of historic landscapes and buildings, the spaces and structures that have attained heritage value because of their character, location, and symbolic significance. Adaptive reuse of heritage structures sustains the cultural language of the campus, renewing the life of places that have brought generational connectivity to the learning environment. The institutional value of iconic structures and places is that they give the campus its distinctive, enduring sense of identity. Chapter 9 speaks to the importance of preservation as a means of maintaining the authenticity of place.

The idea of the campus itself being a synergistic, multifaceted learning experience is buttressed by the recognition that students learn in complex, varied ways. About 85 percent of the waking hours of the typical college student are spent outside the classroom.[26] That is, much of the day-to-day learning in the collegiate setting is individual and social learning that takes place in labs, studios, dormitories, and other residential settings, at the union, in the library, on the playing fields and courts and fitness rooms, in organizations, at work, and all of the other venues on and off campus that students are known to inhabit. Educators are being asked to recognize that learning is not unidimensional. People learn in different ways and at different paces. They absorb information differently and are motivated by different goals and circumstances. They possess *multiple intelligences*—linguistic, logical-mathematical, spatial, bodily-kinesthetic, musical, interpersonal, intrapersonal, and naturalist— that are stimulated by different settings and circumstances.[27] Active forms of learning engagement, collaborative and individual, blur the boundaries of responsibility and activity that previously separated teachers and learners. All parties are teaching and learning all of the time. In the final analysis, it will be the responsibility of America's colleges and universities to demonstrate to the public that, through campus stewardship, they can create value and vitality in the learning environment, making the campus itself a public good with an accountable civil purpose.

In the final analysis, however, the American public has to be a partner in the necessary revival of the public good model of higher education, welcoming academia's stewardship of the learning environment and investing in the means of making the learning environment the essential cultural and economic resource that it must be. In this century, the country and its educational institutions at all levels will be mutually accountable for ensuring the development of skills across the population, from the most basic to the most advanced, adaptable to the evolving demands of a global society. For its part, the academy must make it a strategic imperative to educate the whole person, the literate, value-centered learner with the core ability to make sense of the complexities confronting the world in this century. This will require new learning models and new linkages among institutions at levels of access and affordability fully supported by society.

The Wisconsin Avenue Portal at Marquette University. (Marquette University.)

# seven

# The Campus and the Community: The Civic Metaphor

## Renaissance on the Avenue

Marquette University is situated on a height of land at the western end of downtown Milwaukee on a prominent site straddling Wisconsin Avenue, the city's main civic boulevard. When the Jesuit institution was established in 1881, Wisconsin Avenue was lined with the great mansions built by Milwaukee's business titans. The area surrounding the campus was a flourishing white-collar and blue-collar residential community until the exodus of urban residents to the suburbs in the 1950s and 1960s, which set in motion a pattern of neighborhood change typical of what happened in the inner areas of many of America's industrial cities at that time. Family residences were subdivided into multiple units. Local commercial uses declined as the neighborhood edged toward a more transient, lower-income population base. The city of Milwaukee judged the area around Marquette to be blighted enough to merit a request for urban renewal assistance from the federal government.

Marquette, experiencing an enrollment growth surge in the 1960s and 1970s, took advantage of a provision of the federal urban renewal program that provided for the clearance and transfer of blighted urban land for institutional growth. The redevelopment of several blocks by the university helped to revitalize the area in the immediate vicinity of the campus. Marquette acquired a nearby hotel and other transitional properties for conversion to student residence halls. New buildings and campus open spaces served the influx of students coming to the university in growing numbers. Marquette's enrollment grew from just under 7,900 in 1950 to nearly 13,900 in 1980.

However, in the 1980s, the transient population in the neighborhood continued to rise in parallel with a rapid increase in absentee property ownership. By 1991, less than 5 percent of the residential properties in the blocks near Marquette were owner-occupied. The area absorbed one of the city's highest concentrations of social support agencies and organizations. Within a 90-block area around the university, there were at least 25 venues housing homeless shelters, soup kitchens, correctional facilities, detox centers, and halfway houses. Marquette, like other institutions, began to experience the drop in admissions applications that came about with the leveling of the college-age population in the late 1980s. In Marquette's case, the growing blight in nearby blocks placed the university at a further disadvantage in its ability to recruit students. Coverage of area crimes in the local and national press invariably cited the incidents as being in the vicinity of Marquette University. Marquette students were among the crime victims. Campus enrollment was dropping by 1991, and admissions applications were descending to the lowest levels in years.

The university embarked on an ambitious strategy in the early 1990s to rejuvenate its competitive position in the nation's academic marketplace. The strategy was built on a program of enhancement of Marquette's academic strengths, coupled with the renewal of the learning and living environment of the campus. A key part of the initiative was the university's proactive participation in an extensive program to upgrade the neighborhood in partnership with the city and community interests. Marquette's $50 million *Campus Circle* program of investment in community redevelopment at and beyond the campus borders received widespread national attention. Nearly half the outlay went into the purchase of 115 run-down and abandoned properties on urban land outside the campus, including 1,100 housing units.[1] Thirty-three buildings were demolished.

The university rehabilitated many of the run-down residential properties that it had purchased and sold them to developers for resale or rental at rates affordable to low- and moderate-income families. The university also participated in neighborhood renewal by offering social service and clinical programs administered by various academic departments. The city of Milwaukee undertook an extensive program of infrastructure, streetscape, and open space improvements to enhance the neighborhood setting.

The other half of Marquette's community real estate investment went into market-rate development on university property along Wells Street across from the campus. Marquette built more than 150 apartment units with nearly 50,000 square feet of street-level commercial space on a two-block stretch of the street.

An 1,100-space parking structure was built to serve the university and the new residential and commercial uses on Wells Street. The university coined the term *Campus Town* to give the area a neighborhood identity. Campus Town has offered students and neighborhood residents more nearby urban housing and more local options for dining, entertainment, and shopping where few such options existed before. The sense of urban vitality and safety has been restored by the 24-hour population in and around Campus Town.

The program of neighborhood rehabilitation has not only stabilized the area surrounding the campus; it has given it a renewed community identity. Vigorous, consistent code enforcement by the city reversed the blight occurring before the Campus Circle initiative began. By the end of the 1990s, the neighborhood crime rate had declined by 50 percent. Owner-occupied housing is increasing, as are the levels of community engagement and neighborhood economic development activities. Freshmen enrollment, which had plummeted by 1996 to its lowest level in 20 years at 1,420, has been on a gradual, consistent rebound into the new century. By 1998–99, Marquette saw the largest two-year increase in freshman enrollment in its history, and by 1999–2000, the freshman class had the highest average test scores and high school rankings in university history. Freshman enrollment was, in fact, capped at 1,800 in 2004 to ensure the maintenance of academic quality.

Parallel with the community revitalization effort, Marquette undertook a program of civic design improvements to strengthen the physical relationship between the campus and the surrounding urban fabric. A campaign in the early 1990s to unify the campus by converting Wisconsin Avenue to an urban open space was met with fierce resistance by the community, undermining the reputation that Marquette had built in its community revitalization efforts. The university redirected its design attention to aesthetic and safety improvements on the avenue. Entries to new academic buildings were located on city streets to animate sidewalk life. Landscape improvements on the streets and in campus spaces revitalized pedestrian life. Older buildings were renovated to create more transparency at street level. The university and the city collaborated in restoring the segment of Wisconsin Avenue through the campus to its earlier grandeur as an urban boulevard with new median planting, lighting, and gateway structures at the university portals, denoting the campus area as a distinct civic district. Milwaukee, under the leadership of then-mayor John Norquist, a national voice in revitalization through urban design, promoted thematic improvements in street character as a way of giving civic identity to urban districts throughout the city.

The old industrial flats straddling the Menomonee River south of the campus had fallen into a prolonged state of neglect as traditional manufacturing operations left the area. The city determined that its riverfront would be the centerpiece of a long-range urban revival from downtown through the Menomonee flats through the incremental development of a riverwalk providing public access to the water's edge. Marquette acquired 13 acres of defunct industrial land next to the river as the site for its new sports field complex. Intercollegiate and recreational outdoor sports could now be played within a quarter mile of the landlocked urban campus for the first time in decades. The university built the segment of the riverwalk adjacent to the playing fields, waiting for adjacent segments to be filled as the river is reclaimed as an urban amenity.

The strategic investments made by Marquette to renew both its academic standing and its environment during a period of reduced revenue meant that there would be an interval of lean times for the campus community. It was recognized that the university would not be able to recoup the monetary costs to purchase, demolish, and rehabilitate the derelict neighborhood properties necessary as those costs were in restoring the urban setting. The campus community understood the necessity of the commitment, but few anticipated the magnitude of the eventual costs. The debt encumbered by Marquette, coupled with the enrollment declines that bottomed out in the middle of the decade, would hang over the university through the 1990s.

With its massive expenditure of financial, political, and intellectual capital, however, Marquette has achieved most of its goals. Enrollment has increased. There is unprecedented demand for campus housing. The academic qualifications of entering students have steadily risen. Retention has improved. The social learning environment is more lively than it has been in years, and there is renewed pride in the campus environment. With the Campus Circle initiative, Marquette was engaged in a practical endeavor beyond the traditional core mission of the university, but certainly within its institutional self-interests. That endeavor, buttressed by the Jesuit institutional commitment to the urban community, has elevated Marquette's confidence in the legitimacy of its role as an agent for urban improvement. Other corporate and institutional entities in Milwaukee's Near West Side have followed Marquette's lead in helping to improve the environments in the neighborhoods around them. Marquette, with other public and private organizations, is a partner in the 15-year implementation program for housing, commercial development, public space, and transportation improvements delineated in the city's plan for the Near West Side area. There has been public and private reinvestment along Wisconsin Avenue and other streets between the campus and downtown, with new urban housing, hotels, and a convention center filling gaps once dominated by parking lots. Most of those projects would have occurred in any case. What the Campus Circle initiative helped to demonstrate was that a new urban confidence must be nourished by the institutions and enterprises that have an abiding interest in the long-term vitality of their community.

## The Interdependence of Town and Gown: An Old Story with New Twists

Marquette University's strategic participation in neighborhood renewal illustrates the powerful and complex interdependencies that exist between institutions and their communities. It demonstrates how much the vitality of the institution and the community are dependent on one another. The American town/gown relationship comes with a background of age-old cultural stereotypes: blue collar versus elite, real world versus ivory tower, grown-up world versus youth-camp culture. Towns and colleges have long lived up to the stereotypes; collegians and townies have historically possessed a ritual disdain for one another. Communities have resented the real or perceived indifferences to local concerns exhibited by colleges. Colleges have resented the real or perceived interference in their affairs by townspeople. But the towns have also recognized that much of their economic well-being and civic identity are derived from the presence of the colleges, and colleges have recognized that their towns or cities gave them a home, a place that provided civic and commercial amenities and a community life for their staff, faculty, and students.

The relationship between town and gown took an historic turn in the postwar twentieth century when explosive campus growth across the country was juxtaposed against a broad decline in the fortunes of cities and towns. Urban decline and population movement were significant factors in the town/gown relationship, hastened in the late 1940s and subsequent decades by public policy measures conceived to foster upward mobility in America. The FHA home mortgage program, initially intended to help returning GIs settle after the war, spurred the rush to suburbanization. Manufacturing continued to thrive in urban areas into the 1950s, sustaining the wartime migration of rural and minority workers to industrial cities and towns. But in the late 1950s, the interstate highway program accelerated the exodus of people and businesses from the central cities. The highways themselves broke up old neighborhoods, furthering the blight. As people moved out of older communities, jobs and businesses followed. Population movement to the western and southern parts of the country literally exploded in the 1960s. The 1950 census registered the peak in the population growth of scores of older municipalities throughout the country, the beginning of a relentless loss of population among older cities large and small. A shift in the socioeconomic makeup of cities and towns occurred in the same period. Those leaving for the countryside or from the Rustbelt to the Sunbelt were predominantly white and middle class. The proportion of poor, minority, and immigrant populations in the cities continued to rise.

The most significant federal intervention in the inner cities and towns since the Great Depression was initiated when Congress passed the Housing Act of 1949, the federal urban renewal program. Conceived to stem urban blight through government acquisition and clearance of deteriorated properties, making the land available for redevelopment by public and private enterprises, urban renewal attained a deservedly notorious reputation for indiscriminate clearance that demolished socially viable urban neighborhoods along with those that had become slums. In 1959, Congress enacted Section 112 of the urban renewal program to fund the acquisition and clearance of land in designated renewal areas for development by educational institutions. The program took advantage of the unprecedented campus growth of the 1960s and 1970s, legitimizing the development of higher education facilities as a stimulus for urban revitalization in what were reckoned to be blighted neighborhoods. Medical institutions subsequently became eligible for urban renewal credits.

The University of Chicago was among the first institutions whose expansion instigated the broadening of the urban renewal code to include campus development. Confronted with massive urban blight in the surrounding Hyde Park/Kenwood areas in the south side of Chicago, the university invested nearly $30 million of its own funds for acquisition and rehabilitation of neighborhood properties in the 1950s and 1960s. Institutions such as Vanderbilt University and Marquette doubled their land areas under the urban renewal program. In semirural towns such as Clarion, Pennsylvania, urban renewal was used for the growth of the local college. New universities such as the University of Illinois–Chicago, described in Chapter 2, were created entirely on land secured by urban renewal.

Whether campus expansion in the postwar period was facilitated by urban renewal, eminent domain, or land assembly by individual institutions, its impact on communities was significant, frequently galvanizing the ire of campus neighbors. Institutions could be stabilizing or destabilizing influences in their communities, depending on how they managed their growth in the neighborhoods; how they controlled high-impact activities such as parking, traffic, and off-campus housing; and how openly they engaged the neighbors in institutional decisions affecting the community. Neighborhood activism, which came into its own in the 1960s and 1970s, demanded affirmative engagement by institutions to demonstrate a respect for community interests.

Fast-forward to the turn of the new century and you find whole new facets of the town/gown relationship leading to what will be unprecedented levels of civic engagement between campuses and municipalities. Campuses are in a resurgent episode of growth and change that is pressing their traditional boundaries. This time around, institutions are expanding to maintain their competitive position: raising their enrollments or reorganizing to serve new types of learners, building facilities to stay at the leading edge in research and learning. Institutions are seeking economical forms of expansion by adaptive reuse of vacant commercial buildings off campus, often with the active support of municipalities eager to see the space occupied. They are upgrading deteriorated neighborhoods at their borders, in large part to preserve the appeal and safety of their campuses. They have to engage the community in these endeavors in an earnest way, recognizing that there is a powerful mutual interest in maintaining the long-term viability of the institutions and the localities.

From the vantage point of the localities, colleges and universities occupy a prominent place in what is otherwise a narrowing spectrum of enterprises that can contribute institutional leadership, economic stability, and social support. Communities that are beset not only by the steady erosion of core businesses but by the decline of the local tax base and of state and federal support are looking for higher education institutions to contribute more civic leadership and resources than ever before. A troubling aspect of today's world is that the bond between enterprises and localities is being severed by market forces. Recognizing that place-based institutions have a deep and lasting self-interest in the viability of the environment around them, municipalities are depending more than ever on the staying power that such institutions can contribute to the vitality of the community.

## The Borderless Campus

The campus, from a practical standpoint, is a borderless place. Although core activities—teaching, research, organized student life functions, and the administrative and operational infrastructure that supports the core activities—are concentrated within the campus boundaries, institutions have vibrant, extended lives beyond those boundaries. In most cases, the majority of students live off campus. The lion's share of student social and entertainment wants are met in the restaurants, pubs, pizza parlors, and shops that are located outside the campus borders. Faculty and staff are members of the outside community. As collegiate brochures are wont to report, money spent by institutions and by their students and employees has a multiplier effect on the economy of the community beyond the campus.

The impact of the borderless campus is not always benign. Institutions that gobble up neighboring residential and commercial properties and open land at even the most measured pace create anxieties in the neighborhood, making campus expansion rarely other than an adversarial process. The power of eminent domain is frequently invoked to secure new land for institutional growth, or, to avoid an escalation of real estate prices, properties are acquired by proxy purchases that mask the institution as the buyer. The imminent prospect of campus growth can undermine neighborhoods because it can trigger the neglect of properties in its path.

There has been a resurgence of campus expansion-related tensions arising across the country. Institutions, particularly those in urban locales, have run out of room to accommodate major initiatives in research, student life facilities, and other endeavors that they regard as necessary to maintain their operations. But memories of old encounters resurface on both sides. At this writing, Columbia University is staking much of its future on a plan to build a new $5 billion campus on 18 acres of land in Harlem, a mile north of the university's main campus at Morningside Heights. Declaring that it would be at a competitive disadvantage if it could not expand beyond its crowded borders, Columbia began a public communication process in early 2003 to make its case for development of the new campus over a 30-year duration. Many of Columbia's neighbors, chastened by what they regard as predictable university indifference to the community, are fighting the move. Others are prepared to make an accommodation, but only if Columbia commits to rigorous community benefits and promises on how the campus is developed.[2] At the beginning of 2006, the analyses of environmental and community impacts of the expansion plan were still undergoing public review and comment. Concerns about gentrification, neighborhood disruption, and economic impacts will be the subjects of continuing debate as the university pursues its quest for public approvals. Harvard, chronically constrained in its Cambridge environs, purchased 200 acres of urban property across the Charles River in Boston in the 1990s for institutional growth in the twenty-first century and beyond. The fact that most of the acquisitions were made by proxy purchases raised a firestorm in an area already hard-pressed by housing shortages and the turnover of local businesses. Harvard was able to overcome the initial animosity by underwriting a number of public benefits and committing to a joint planning effort with Boston that would tie Harvard's expansion to a phased strategy to maintain neighborhood residential and business activities. When the University of California at Berkeley issued its 15-year facilities expansion plan for more than 2 million square feet of new buildings on the campus to serve more than 4,000 new students, the city filed a suit requiring further study of the impacts of the plan. The suit was settled in May 2005 with an agreement made in a closed city council session more than doubling the annual fee that the university pays for city services. Among other facets of the agreement, the university would reduce planned parking growth by nearly 50 percent and pay half the cost of a downtown revitalization plan.

The tax-exempt status of nonprofit institutions has been a sticking point for years, particularly when urban land has been removed from the tax rolls by campus expansion. The erosion of state and federal aid to local governments is prompting towns and cities to be more aggressive in challenging the tax-exempt standing of colleges. Institutions find themselves negotiating or litigating over a growing menu of local government measures to retrieve payments in lieu of taxes, exact utility and parking fees, and impose taxes on revenue-producing activities on campus ranging from food service to sports concessions. The arguments typically end in some form of settlement, although satisfaction with the outcome is rarely unanimous. The tax-exempt standing usually holds up for activities that are proven to have an academic purpose, but community demands for institutions to pay more for local services will be a constant, and probably escalating, factor in town/gown relations. In Cambridge, Massachusetts, MIT and the city formed an agreement in 2004 by which the institution would annually increase payments in lieu of taxes and pay a penalty for removal of property from the city's tax base.

Campus traffic on local streets is a perennial source of community conflict, exacerbated when campus parking demand overflows into nearby neighborhoods. Communities are forcing the issue with a variety of measures, from instituting resident-only permits on streets near campuses to withholding zoning approvals and building permits until institutions agree to policies that provide more parking on campus, or that limit the amount of vehicles coming to campus.[3]

The impacts of students living off campus can cut several ways. Students, desiring to live independently or unable to live on campus, have long been a fertile market for landlords in campus neighborhoods without adequate oversight by the campus and the community. The pattern is predictable. Older apartments and rooms are rented to students at two or three times normal occupancy. New garden apartments are erected with minimum standards of construction. Absentee land-lords neglect upkeep, making the arrangement more lucrative but marginalizing the neighborhood into what is commonly called a student ghetto. Rowdy student behavior and parking congestion add to the deterioration of the neighborhood.

Even under the best of measures to enforce upkeep of property and police student behavior, student housing demand in tight rental markets can drive up area hous-ing costs and reduce the availability of affordable housing in the community. In high-cost areas such as Boston, this has led to demands by the city that colleges provide substantially more student housing on campus. Colleges and universities in Boston have constructed several thousand dormitory beds on their campuses in the last half-dozen years in response to the area's crowded housing market. Many institutions in the country are expanding their on-campus housing under regulations or agreements with municipalities. In some localities, the real estate community has come to rely on the off-campus student housing market as a lucrative source of income, often reinforced by the town or city that is depending on the real estate tax revenue generated by the housing. In those circumstances, it is not unusual that the developers and municipalities are vocally resistant to insti-tutional initiatives to build more housing on campus. This conflict can impinge on the needs of institutions that are striving to improve collegiate life with more housing on campus.

Mutual self-interest between the institution and the community comes into play when neighborhoods around the campus fall into decline. Marquette determined that it would invest in improving the conditions in its community as part of a strategy to upgrade its competitive academic position. In Marquette's case, the university worked closely with an economically stable city that had a shared interest in the revitalization of a neighborhood that had fallen into decline over several decades. Trinity College, in Hartford, Connecticut, was also motivated by self-interest to take a hand in the improvement of its urban surroundings. Trinity had to work with a city that had suffered not only a drastic erosion of its economic base for more than a decade, but one whose social infrastructure had deteriorated because of the loss of fiscal resources. Trinity's investment in com-munity revitalization had to address systemic issues of urban poverty and local educational needs transcending the immediate neighborhood.

Marquette and Trinity are not atypical. They echo the efforts of campuses nation-wide that are protecting their institutional interests by investing in the better-ment of their communities: by purchasing and refurbishing dilapidated housing, providing low-interest loans and incentives to campus staff to move into the neighborhoods, providing loans and grants to nonprofit housing organizations, supporting local schools, providing scholarships, assisting in neighborhood security and surveillance, participating in the development of local businesses, underwriting streetscape and lighting improvements, and a host of other measures designed to strengthen neighborhood life and thus the quality of the environment of the borderless campus.

Today, the federal government's financial involvement in town/gown collaboration is mainly through the Community Outreach Partnership Center (COPC) in the U.S. Department of Housing and Urban Development. The program, which came into existence in 1992, funds the formation of institutional partnerships with communities and local organizations that promise to become long-term working entities.[4] Central to the relationship is that of making community engagement an integral part of the core mission of the participating institutions so that the localities can count on the sustained help of institutions in community building. Although many of the partnerships established under the auspices of COPC are motivated by the desires of the institutions to improve their immediate surroundings, the program calls for inclusive relationships that will have lasting benefit to the communities.[5] The program has been used to leverage local, state, and private funding for community programs and projects. Whether programs such as COPC will endure in this era of tightening federal budgets remains to be seen, but the partnership model for community engagement should be adopted as a goal by enlightened institutions across the country.

Thriving higher education institutions are essential to the economy and social fabric of their host communities. That is axiomatic for traditional American campus towns whose existence is defined by the colleges in their midst—the Hanovers, the Amhersts, the Blacksburgs, Chapel Hills, Urbana–Champaigns, Boulders, and the Claremonts—but it is increasingly critical in urban communities whose economic bases have shifted from industrial to service and technology economies. In several American cities that were once diverse manufacturing centers, universities are now the largest single employers: Penn in Philadelphia, Johns Hopkins in Baltimore, Yale in New Haven, and the University of Alabama in Birmingham, among others.[6] Higher education institutions will become more central to the socioeconomic interests of older cities and towns, whether they become the dominant employers or take on more active roles with public, corporate, and other nonprofit organizations in measures to preserve the vitality of their communities.

The roles that higher education institutions play in fast-growing Sunbelt communities are no less critical to the future of those localities than they are to the cities in the country's mature regions. Campuses in high-growth localities are at the ground floor in contributing to the character and economy of those localities. They provide the educational, cultural, and social venues that are important in building up the still-formative civic framework of growing communities. In the burgeoning urban areas of the South and West, the emphasis is more apt to be on town/gown partnerships that reinforce the mutual growth aspirations of the institutions and the localities than on the revitalization of declining communities. Colleges are, however, involved in renewal and revitalization efforts in troubled inner cities and rural areas of the Sunbelt and will undoubtedly play more central roles with the maturing of Sunbelt communities. The predicted growth of the Sunbelt will provide opportunities for institutions and communities to shape one another that have not been seen since the halcyon years of the postwar campus expansion.

Consider Arizona State University President Michael Crow's plans for the growth of that institution in the Phoenix/Tempe area. The university, according to Crow, "is not going to be a place. It's going to be a force" in the evolution of the Phoenix region.[7] The university's plan for three new satellite campuses, including a 15,000-student campus in downtown Phoenix, will allow Arizona State to nearly double its enrollment to 95,000 by 2020 to keep pace with the region's burgeoning population. The downtown campus, in the early planning stages by the city and the university, will eventually take up 20 city blocks in the heart of the city.

Institutions collaborate with local planning agencies to blend their plans with community plans. In numerous locales, institutions are required under zoning to file campus plans delineating how and to what extent the campus is intended to grow before the institution can apply for approval of specific projects. However, as cities become strapped for the funds to support strong planning operations, some institutions are becoming de facto urban planners by dint of the campus expansion plans and projects that they are undertaking. *Boston Globe* architectural critic Robert Campbell declared in a March 2005 article that "universities are the new city planners."[8] Campbell cites major expansion and urban revitalization initiatives by Harvard, Columbia, Pennsylvania, and Ohio State, among others, that will redefine urban land use patterns and the character of the civic realm in the areas where those institutions are located. As more campuses become more integrated into the urban fabric, we will see hybrid forms of town and gown where borders are dissolved. The institutional mandate as an agent of social and economic change will surely intensify in the knowledge-based economy of the twenty-first century, as will the interdependencies between town and gown. The civic relationship will have to be a primary, integral part of the core mission of most American institutions.

Voices within academia have been pleading the case for more vigorous local involvement by colleges and universities, a return to civic purpose. In an essay entitled "Universities and the Inner Cities," Ira Harkavy and John Puckett of the University of Pennsylvania wrote in the early 1990s that

> What higher education requires is a qualitative leap forward, a leap that harnesses the university's broad array of academic resources to the task of contributing to the [revitalization] of our rapidly changing urban environment. No other institution in America has the prestige, intellectual power, and concern for humanity to lead the way.[9]

In the piece, Harkavy and Puckett assert that institutions in troubled urban settings cannot afford to "remain shores of affluence, self-importance and horticultural beauty at the edge of inland seas of squalor, violence and despair." [10] Former University of Michigan President James Duderstadt made service to society a key theme in *A University for the 21st Century:* "Historically our institutions have been responsible to and shaped by the communities that founded them . . . their curricula, their research and professional programs, their outreach activities, have all evolved to serve a public purpose."[11] Duderstadt offers a cautionary note, however, that higher education institutions must resist being all things to all people. The issue is not that colleges and universities are unresponsive to the needs of society, but that by trying to be responsive on so many fronts, higher education has "whetted an insatiable public appetite for a host of service activities of only marginal relevance to its academic mission."[12] His admonition is for the academy to find contemporary forms for addressing societal needs.

Academic institutions are, indeed, participating in community service and civic learning at record levels, according to a survey conducted by Campus Compact, a consortium of more than 900 campus presidents promoting higher education's civic role.[13] The survey for 2003 showed that, on the average, 36 percent of the students in member institutions were involved in community service activities and that the institutions were offering an average of 37 service-learning courses. A notable result of the survey is that a record 93 percent of the member colleges had educational partnerships with local K–12 schools.

Higher education leaders have to weigh institutional values with community needs every time they contemplate participation in community revitalization programs. Recounting the decision to invest in community revitalization in an essay entitled "Common Cause: Investing in the Community," Judith Rodin, president emeritus of the University of Pennsylvania, recalls that "well-meaning friends and colleagues" urged that the university not take on the seemingly insurmountable problems engulfing Penn's West Philadelphia neighborhood. Others, however, reminded her that the university had contributed to the decline and was responsible for turning it back.[14] Declaring that if Penn could "make discoveries that saved lives and drove the global economy, then surely we had the capacity to help revitalize our distressed neighborhood,"[15] Rodin steered the university on a multitiered effort with the West Philadelphia community to enhance neighborhood safety, stabilize housing, spur economic development, and improve the schools. One of the significant institutional outcomes of the endeavor, according to Rodin, was that "Penn's civic engagement with our neighbors has positively influenced the social and learning environment on our campus."[16] Students became "more socially conscious citizens," more adept at confronting divisive urban issues.

### Reweaving the Town/Gown Fabric in the Twenty-first Century

Institutions deploy their physical presence into the community for practical reasons. Consider just a few examples of the scores of initiatives that institutions are undertaking beyond the bounds of their campuses to effectuate practical institutional changes and elevate the level of community engagement.

The Rhode Island School of Design (RISD), sitting at the edge of downtown Providence, is locating more of its academic operations functions in downtown buildings. The school is tightly landlocked in its built-up location at the foot of College Hill. The growing downtown presence is part of a continuing relationship that the school has had with the city's campaign to make the arts a central theme of downtown development. Providence set the stage in the early 1990s with an ambitious redevelopment of the public realm that included opening up the three rivers converging on downtown after decades in which the rivers were covered by culverts under Providence streets. A new riverwalk, threading its way through downtown Providence, has spurred new construction and renovation along its edges, including the RISD campus, where the six-story RISD Center will house expansion of the school's highly regarded art museum, teaching, studio, gallery, and auditorium space.[17] The school's downtown expansion has taken place through the adaptive reuse of former office buildings in an area designated by the city as the Arts and Entertainment District. The adaptations included graduate studio space and a Center for Integrative Technology that houses academic programs in interiors, graphics, textiles, and digital media.[18] A Center for Design and Business, established jointly with Bryant College, has an incubator program that accommodates several design-oriented enterprises. The school's main library and expanded student housing have been relocated to the former Rhode Island Hospital Trust Building, a neoclassic gem in the heart of downtown, giving RISD a fivefold expansion of library space and the city a welcome increase in downtown foot traffic. The school's downtown presence as an academic enterprise reinforces its role as a catalyst for yet a new cycle in an old city's life.

Trinity College of Hartford, Connecticut, became a model for institutional collaboration with the community, in large part because of its position at the edge of the inner city. The neighborhood adjacent to the college's historic campus is among many areas of the once-thriving insurance city beset by a systemic rise in unemployment, poverty, and population loss to the suburbs. The city's financial plight in the 1990s was exacerbated by the erosion of state and federal financial support. Since 1995, Trinity has invested more than $7 million of its endowment in community revitalization in a 13-block area adjacent to the campus. The college donated its own land toward the creation of the 16-acre *Learning Corridor,* an exemplary civic redevelopment project that includes a Montessori Day Care Center (Grades pre-K through 5), a city magnet middle school, a math and science academy, and an arts academy. The site also includes a Boy's and Girl's Club, a community theater, and retail spaces. The project was jointly developed by Trinity and the Southside Institutions Neighborhood Alliance, a coalition of medical and public service organizations in the area with funds from the U.S. Department of Housing and Urban Development, the city of Hartford, the state of Connecticut, several charitable foundations, and local companies.

Opened in fall 2000, the Learning Corridor has brought a thriving pre-K through 16 educational experience program into the life of the city, and Trinity has institutionalized its academic links with community needs through a number of programs that go beyond traditional service learning. The Mega-Cities Institute, the Trinity Center for Neighborhoods, the Neighborhood Technical Center's Smart Neighborhood Initiative, the Institute for Living, the HART Job Center, and the Aetna Center for Families are all programs that involve Trinity faculty and students with community leaders to improve the economic, physical, and social circumstances of Hartford and the neighborhood.[19]

The University of Pennsylvania, through its Center for Community Partnerships, initiated a university-wide effort to improve the quality of life in the West Philadelphia neighborhood adjacent to the university. The center has undertaken an impressive range of academically based community services, support programs, and development initiatives. Examples include a community school built by Penn and turned over to the public school district with an operating contribution by the university, an urban nutrition initiative, a community arts partnership, neighborhood-level planning, neighborhood patrols and cleanups, education and job training for youth and adults, and minority entrepreneurship training. Penn participates in partnerships to foster continuing collaborations among community organizations, federal institutions, foundations, and other nonprofit groups.[20] (See Penn's neighborhood commercial real estate development activities in "The Entrepreneurial Campus" in Chapter 8.)

The Ohio State University in Columbus funded a public-private development entity called the Campus Partners for Community Development in the early 1990s. Campus Partners, whose membership encompasses the university, the city, neighborhood and business groups, is involved in community revitalization at several levels, including housing rehabilitation, public space improvements, assistance in code enforcement, and community service programs. One of the keystone projects is the revitalization of a depressed urban neighborhood adjacent to the campus, straddling High Street, the main thoroughfare connecting Ohio State with downtown Columbus. The High Street project, much of which is on campus property, will provide almost half a million square feet of office space, retail, dining, cinema, entertainment, student residential units, and apartments. The campus bookstore will be a key component of the new urban complex.

Clark University in Worcester, Massachusetts, was a forerunner of colleges promoting economic development and neighborhood revitalization. In the mid-1990s, Clark established the University Park Partnership among local residents, Clark organizations, Worcester public schools, government officials, local businesses, and churches to upgrade the rapidly declining Main-South area of Worcester surrounding the campus. The initiative was one of the first funded by the U.S. Department of Housing and Urban Development's Community Outreach Partnership Center program. Since the collaboration began, Clark and its partners have renovated more than 200 area houses and built 100 new residences for local residents and to attract faculty and staff to the college neighborhood with loans and other financial incentives. The partnership has guided the development of an education corridor similar to the one that Trinity College helped to develop in Hartford.[21]

Three Chicago colleges—DePaul and Roosevelt Universities and Columbia College—teamed up to build an 18-story residence hall on State Street in Chicago's Loop. The 1,700-student University Center, opened in 2004, is within a short walking distance of each of the school's downtown campuses, not far from the Art Institute of Chicago. DePaul initiated the joint project after finding that it could not, by itself, afford to build needed dormitory space on valuable downtown land. By aggregating their housing needs, the institutions were able to achieve economies of scale for financing and construction in the downtown setting. The $150-million project is being financed by 30-year revenue bonds. The city donated the 1.5-acre site, recognizing that the University Center would infuse new vitality in an area where Chicago is looking for more 24-hour activity. The colleges initially wrestled with concerns about whether the individual identities of the schools might be lost in the combined operation, but they concluded that having their students living within a block or two of their campuses, and in a vibrant urban environment, was a more valuable outcome.

## Town and Gown in an Era of Global Change

The vagaries of the global market economy are most immediately felt in the day-to-day life of cities, towns, and regions. That is where enterprises and jobs are created, where they flourish and decline, where they migrate elsewhere. Local and regional governments can, to some extent, moderate the cycles of socioeconomic change by providing the infrastructure, local tax structure, land use controls, public incentives, and institutional supports necessary either to guide growth or ameliorate decline. Invariably, state and federal government is enlisted in the process.

Within the next two or three decades, the effects of socioeconomic change on localities will be more daunting than ever. Business in the global economy will be more footloose and less tied to the interests and identities of localities because of mergers, acquisitions, outsourcing, and off-shore operations. Analysts predict that the working population will have to be more freelance, changing careers and venues many times over to keep up with rapid transformations in the enterprise system. Local communities will probably get less help from state and federal governments in mitigating the effects of local economic change, although some states will have more resources than others to deal with the needs of localities. In some regions, the economic disparities will not be cyclic; they will be structural—and lasting.

Localities will look more and more to the institutional sector to fill the breach. The institutional resources of colleges and universities are particularly compelling for local communities seeking new leadership and participation to replace what is lost to the volatility of the business sector. They have a rootedness in the community that is consonant with the community itself. They have the virtue of institutional longevity that transcends economic and political cycles. They provide an essential societal resource as purveyors of knowledge in an increasingly knowledge-driven economy. They support the local economy with jobs, the purchase of local goods and services, and the revenues that they generate. They support existing local businesses and spin off new businesses as outgrowths of their research and education. As place-based entities, they play an important role in defining the civic character and land-use pattern of the community. They bring to the community what John Sexton, president of New York University, characterizes as "locational capital," the synergy of place, people, and intellectual resources necessary to effectuate social and economic change.[22]

The plea for colleges to lend leadership to all levels of public education comes from university presidents, community advocates, representatives of business, and those who recognize that the country's future hinges on vastly improved, equitable, and innovative education systems from early learning through adult learning. Higher education will be asked to play a more proactive community role in the advancement of primary and secondary education in the United States, particularly in economically disadvantaged communities. Partnerships between colleges and K–12 systems are the linchpins of collegiate participation in communities all across the country. The Trinity College Learning Corridor mentioned earlier in this chapter is but one recent example of a private college's investment and participation in the betterment of children's education resources in its city. Studies cite a wide range of K–16 councils that are being set up in urban areas, such as the Phoenix Urban Systematic Initiative, under which colleges in the Phoenix area have formed partnerships with the schools to effectuate "systematic change."[23] Much the same can be said about public health, family services, workforce development, and other community support activities in which institutional resources are and will be joined in collaboration with public and private organizations.

In such arrangements, the concept of the learning community becomes an expanded, highly productive civic expression. The school systems gain from the resources and ideas of the colleges. The students in the colleges learn from exposure to the high-stakes, real-world issues of life and learning in the community. The civic environment of the community as a whole is elevated by the renewal of education at all levels as a civic resource.

Still, higher education institutions are limited in their capacities to replace the local roles best played by government and the private sector. In spite of their perceived staying power in the community compared to that of other enterprises, colleges are subject to many of the same political and economic challenges faced by government and business. It was pointed out in Chapter 6 that America's higher education institutions will confront an increasing need to be prudent in the allocation of their resources in the future, so that any investments that they make in the community realm have to be measured against their financial capacity to make such investments as integral parts of their core missions. They cannot make governing decisions for the community, although public colleges and universities can and do participate in the implementation of government policy. As charitable institutions, they cannot take the same kinds of financial leadership positions in the community that for-profit enterprises can take. Whereas corporations can be philanthropic benefactors to the community, colleges are typically the beneficiaries of philanthropy, often competing with other local institutions and causes for charitable giving.

Academia can contribute to the betterment of its community by measures that are consonant with institutional goals and limitations. Its civic role will be played out in the future, as it is today, in partnerships with local government, businesses, other institutions, and civic organizations. All public, private, and institutional entities confronting new and greater demands on limited civic resources will have to improvise the collaborations necessary to make healthy, sustainable communities in a fast-changing world.

## The Place Implications of the Civic Metaphor

For higher education institutions, engagement in community-building will have both centrifugal and centripetal influences on the physical character of their campus environments. The centrifugal forces—the scattering of institutional functions and investments across the face of the community—have been building for decades. Colleges will continue to collaborate in the development of schools, community centers, arts and cultural facilities, recreation facilities, clinics, day-care centers, and other basic community services. They will form more joint ventures with public agencies, developers, banks, and nonprofit organizations to rehabilitate neighborhoods. They will locate more campus functions beyond the borders of the campus to serve their expansion needs, helping, at the same time, to revitalize neighborhoods and communities. They will partner, and perhaps merge, with other educational, cultural, and medical institutions to expand and diversify their offerings to the community in more economical, synergistic ways. They will participate in real estate developments designed to improve their surrounding environments and to create the innovative settings that will spawn tomorrow's knowledge-based businesses (see Chapter 8 for more examples of institutional real estate developments beyond campus borders).

As colleges extend their physical and virtual presence beyond their campus borders, they will also place greater value on the civic character and identity within their core campus domains. The campus as a repository of civic culture will be manifested in stimulating settings that enrich the quality of community life—the museums, galleries, theaters, music centers, libraries, recreation facilities, arboreta, and botanical gardens—that have historically functioned as cultural bridges between town and gown. Some institutions, particularly community colleges, will provide whole new layers of on-campus community services such as daycare, elder care, counseling, and, perhaps, housing and dining.

Many colleges and universities will find it too expensive, politically and economically, to expand the boundaries of their core campus. Such containment may be the best way to sustain, and possibly improve, the character of surrounding neighborhoods that are established and stable, or that are on the upswing. Institutions will have to ensure that campus edges are open and compatible with the scale, character, and uses in adjacent neighborhoods. They will provide community-oriented uses along their campus boundaries, adding vitality and permeability to the neighborhood environment. Concentration of the academic, residential, and social functions of the institution within the bounds of the campus can only strengthen the collegial life of the institution, reinforcing the integrity of the mother ship, while being fully engaged in the collaboration, outreach activities, and institutional ventures necessary to secure the future of the larger community.

# eight

# The Campus in the Age of Enterprise: Civic Metaphor or Marketplace Metaphor?

## From the Halls of Ivy to Place-making at a Regional Scale

Princeton, New Jersey, is the archetypal college town. The colonial scale and texture of the town proper is vintage Currier and Ives. The tree-studded forelawn of Princeton University's historic Nassau Hall, called "the Campus," is barely indistinguishable from what it appears to be in eighteenth-century engravings. The pastoral image of the area is maintained in the broad meadows that frame the roads entering the town. The tranquil sliver of Lake Carnegie is a frontispiece to the spired campus skyline, setting the town and the university off from the busy highways and railways to the east that connect New York and Philadelphia with one another.

Princeton's midway location along the 90-mile metropolitan corridor was a bulwark of the university's decision in the 1970s to undertake a real estate venture on nearly three square miles of land the university owned surrounding its James Forrestal Research Campus on U.S. Route 1, two miles east of the campus. The Forrestal Research Campus, which had been the hub of the university's high-end research in areas ranging from aeronautics to fusion since the early 1950s, occupied barely more than 200 acres on the vast site in nearby Plainsboro Township. Aside from a short airstrip next to the Forrestal complex, the land was composed of rolling meadows, a former tree nursery, and a magnificent stand of beech and oak woods traversing the property along a tributary stream system.

The university's trustees envisaged the development of the proposed Princeton Forrestal Center as accomplishing several goals. It would be a long-term source of revenue in a period when institutional portfolios were being battered by a

Princeton Forrestal Center. (Landslides.)

series of energy crisis–driven recessions. Planned development would surround and protect the research campus, accommodating uses and activities that would strengthen the university environment. It would create a high-quality regional model for multiple-use real estate development, with offices, homes, and commercial functions intermingled in a natural, parklike setting that would redefine the character of development along the Route 1 corridor. The last goal was critical in Princeton's approach to the development of its vast landholdings. New corporate headquarters, office parks, and apartment complexes were erupting from the New Jersey farmland up and down Route 1 in a fragmented pattern rapidly obliterating the region's pastoral landscape.

As an institution that regarded itself as a long-standing steward of its environment, Princeton set about a land development process that would stand apart from the oncoming sprawl. Development would be incrementally phased so as not to overtax the road and utility infrastructure. Princeton was determined to develop the complex at a pace geared to the community's ability to absorb the effects of its growth. The university would help underwrite many of the public roadway improvements necessary to accommodate traffic growth. Building and pavement coverage would be limited to protect groundwater resources. The plan preserved the beech and oak forest as a natural habitat and stream protection zone. The woods would form a continuous natural backdrop to the building development, mediating the visual and environmental effects. The diversity of uses would enable people to live, work, and shop for conveniences in close proximity.

As a real estate endeavor, Princeton Forrestal Center has far exceeded the expectations articulated by the university in the 1970s. With subsequent land acquisitions by the university, the complex encompasses 2,200 acres, of which 675 are in dedicated or public open space. Names such as Bristol-Myers Squibb, Merrill Lynch, and American Reinsurance appear on the signs in front of national and regional headquarters facilities. More than 15,000 people are employed in 130 enterprises at Princeton Forrestal Center. Today, the complex contains 7 million square feet of corporate space, 820 houses and apartments, 200,000 square feet of retail and restaurant space in a *town center* known as Princeton Forrestal Village, five hotels with 1,200 rooms, and three day-care centers. A new continuing care retirement community near the retail village houses 300 independent resident units, with 180-bed nursing and 60 assisted-living units. Princeton Forrestal Center generates $25 million a year in local property taxes.

Princeton, as a land developer, has had a significant impact on the once semirural oasis that existed between Manhattan and Philadelphia. Development was destined to fill the gap in the megapolitan corridor, with or without Princeton Forrestal Center. What Princeton did was to redefine the Route 1 address. High-end companies were drawn to the site by the amenities of a planned development bearing the vaunted imprimatur of the university. More than 15 million square feet of office space and 25,000 housing units have been built in numerous developments along the seven-mile corridor of U.S. Route 1 known as the "Zip Strip" because it carries the prestigious zip code of Princeton. Housing growth in the area coincided in part with the landmark Mount Laurel decision of the 1970s, requiring suburban communities in New Jersey to facilitate the availability of more diverse housing opportunities. Nonetheless, regional growth sent housing prices through the ceiling.

Princeton has been criticized for inducing phenomenal growth and traffic congestion in the corridor by the development of Princeton Forrestal. Princeton argues that it has been a partner with the regional community in guiding the inexorable change making its way toward the area from the two huge urban centers less than an hour away. By planning an organized, high-quality development, the university advanced the sophistication of the regional development cycle by a decade or more by attention to open space and support infrastructure. Other developments had to meet the standard. With the largest proportion of open space of any development in the corridor, Princeton set a regional standard for natural resource protection. Princeton Forrestal Center spent more than $50 million in regional infrastructure improvements. Although much of the infrastructure development in the complex was in highway improvements, traffic congestion from all of the projects in the region, including Princeton Forrestal, has become a serious problem. Princeton, through the Forrestal Center operation, has participated in a variety of regional transportation planning initiatives and is encouraging regional development of a bus rapid transit system connecting the corridor's commercial hubs.

Revenue from land leases and sales significantly contributed to the university's endowment in the 1980s, but has become overshadowed by other investments in the last decade or two. Robert Wolfe, general manager of Princeton Forrestal Center, believes that the greater, more lasting benefits realized by the university and the area are the economic opportunities for two-career employment and the growth of the region's cultural vitality, which make it easier to recruit faculty. Wolfe describes Princeton as "not so much an ivory tower as it once was" because of the area's diverse population and economic vitality.[1] He also observes that Forrestal Center has become the university's voice in many regional economic development and land use forums because the center, as an enterprise, has such a significant self-interest in the quality of regional change. He laments that it is difficult to engage many corporate tenants in local interests because so few are locally based, but he says that Princeton's long-term presence is recognized as a regional asset.

## University Park at MIT: From the Old Industrial Economy to the New Knowledge Economy

When the sprawling Simplex Wire and Cable Company closed shop in 1970 after decades of operation in Cambridge, Massachusetts, it marked the loss of the last large industrial employer in a city that was once one of New England's most diverse manufacturing centers. Despite being home to Harvard and MIT, two of America's premier higher education institutions, Cambridge employed more people in manufacturing than education-related activities until well into the twentieth century. The 27-acre Simplex site is located between the two institutions, next to the MIT campus which had, itself, grown up in the midst of the factories, power plants, and railroads that filled the once heavily blue-collar east end of town.

Since the 1940s, MIT has been the major force in the transformation of eastern Massachusetts from an old-line manufacturing economy to one of the world's main centers of technological enterprise. The institute helped to create several off-site federal and independent research and development laboratories such as MITRE, the Lincoln Laboratory, Draper Laboratories, and the Instrumentation Laboratory, which, with their emphasis on defense and military technologies, became the springboards for dozens of new companies in the cold war period. Raytheon, Polaroid, Digital Equipment, Lotus, and scores of other firms, spawned by their association with MIT scientists and engineers, helped to reshape the region's economy in the postwar era.

MIT became a real estate entrepreneur in the 1960s in a joint venture with a Boston developer, creating Technology Square on part of 14 acres of campus expansion land to house the corporate and research headquarters for Polaroid. The Charles Draper Laboratories constructed research facilities on the remaining university land in the 1970s. Technology Square became the nexus of a constellation of corporate and institutional research facilities surrounding MIT, where successive rounds of technological innovation have been hatched for four decades.

Thus, it came as no surprise when MIT announced in the early 1980s that it had assembled parcels in and around the largely vacant Simplex property. The university's neighbors were far from pleased that the institution had taken over 27 acres of urban industrial and residential land in the heart of Cambridge. Even though the Simplex site had been long abandoned, the Cambridge community saw the MIT acquisition as a blatant disregard for the community's desire to have the area restored as a diverse urban neighborhood. The city worried that development by MIT would overwhelm the adjacent residential neighborhood with traffic congestion and increased pressure on the already tight supply of affordable housing. The university's proposal for mixed-use development of the area underwent a series of environmental impact reviews and at least a dozen rezoning battles, culminating in 1983 with a city master plan for the area that stipulated land uses, development densities, and building height limits. Permit agreements set forth limits on traffic, requirements for roads and utilities to be constructed by MIT, and a minimum housing quota of 25 percent for low- and moderate-income residents.

In 1983, MIT also selected Forest City Enterprises of Cleveland as the developer to whom the university would lease the property for redevelopment on a long-term basis. Construction began in 1985, but the controversy was far from over. Agreements with the city of Cambridge were revised as the development climate evolved and the work was scrutinized by the community. Protests were waged in the late 1980s over the size of the project and its effects on the nearby Cambridgeport neighborhood. Activity slowed to a crawl during the recession of the early 1990s, but by the end of the decade, the site was booming.

University Park reached the completion of its development program in 2005. Nearly 2.5 million square feet of office, research, residential, retail, and hotel uses fill the site, with more than 1 million square feet of space occupied by biotechnology laboratories, the two largest being Millennium Pharmaceuticals and Alkermes. The area includes the neighborhood's first supermarket in living memory. Nearly 700 residential units have been constructed, including 200 units of affordable and moderate-income housing. More than 250 of the apartments, the last projects to be completed on the site, were built in lieu of originally planned office space. Forest City claims that almost 4,000 people are employed at University Park. At completion, the $650 million development is projected to contribute more than $11 million in annual taxes to Cambridge.[2]

The old Cambridge industrial atmosphere is still reflected in the development of the area. A former shoe factory houses high-tech enterprises, and the bakery where Fig Newtons were once produced is now an apartment building. Adjacent to University Park, in a separate development, the bioscience giant Novartis AG occupies the former New England Confectionary Company plant where billions of Necco wafers and valentine conversation hearts were produced until the company's recent move to a nearby location.

University Park has won awards as an urban development. It has a substantial working population. Residential life is still growing. The decision to expand the residential component in the late stages was met warmly by housing-starved Cambridge. There are new parks and new boulevards where once there were blocks of gritty factory buildings. Still, there is criticism that the area lacks street life, that large research buildings do not lend themselves to a vibrant urban character. It will take time to see if the patterns of human activity at the street level imbue the area with urban vitality, making it a model of the knowledge-based urban community.

## The Academy as Real Estate Entrepreneur

The thrust of this chapter is to examine how institutions are reshaping the physical character of their environments and the surrounding communities as they promote income-producing developments within and beyond the campus. The role of higher education institutions in real estate development has deep and notable roots. In the early 1800s, the state of New York gave Columbia University 20 acres of land between West 48th and 50th Streets on what was then the northern fringe of settlement in Manhattan. Columbia chose not to build its campus on the property, but rather to subdivide and lease the land for urban homes, using the income from the leases to develop its campus farther north in Manhattan. In the late 1920s, the leases were picked up by John D. Rockefeller for a new complex of skyscrapers and an opera house to be built on the three-block site in what by then had become a rather seedy area in the heart of midtown Manhattan. The opera house never materialized because construction began in the depths of the Great Depression, but Rockefeller Center would become one of America's crowning urban developments. It could not have been built as a complete ensemble at that time had the prime urban land not been owned in whole by an institution with the staying power of Columbia University. The university leased the land to the Rockefeller Center Corporation on a long-term basis with options for renewal, ensuring a continuous source of income for the institution until the land was sold outright in the late twentieth century.

Stanford University started the country's first major land development for commercial research and technology enterprises in 1951 by establishing the Stanford Industrial Park on 655 acres of surplus land adjacent to the campus. One of the prime motivations for the venture was to encourage university research faculty to translate their discoveries into technology enterprises in the industrial park. The park's most legendary start-up by Stanford faculty was Hewlett-Packard. Later renamed the Stanford Research Park, the complex offered long-term land leases to a host of start-up and established companies such as Varian, Lockheed, and IBM. Today, there are about 30,000 people employed in companies on the property. The Stanford Research Park is the progenitor of the Silicon Valley phenomenon that communities all over the United States have been striving to emulate as they have migrated into the postindustrial economy.

The most ambitiously organized research complex was North Carolina's Research Triangle Park. The Research Triangle came into being in 1958 as a consortium of state, private, and institutional interests dedicated to the growth of a technology-based economy in North Carolina. The 7,000-acre site is situated in the center of an area bordered by the University of North Carolina at Chapel Hill, Duke University in Durham, and North Carolina State University in Raleigh. The land was assembled and developed by a nonprofit foundation. The three universities jointly incorporated the Research Triangle Institute as a separately operated research center in 1959 to provide the impetus for technological entrepreneurship in the park. The Research Triangle Institute became the nation's fourth largest nonprofit contract research organization. The North Carolina Biotechnology Center and the North Carolina Supercomputing Center were formed by the state to provide grants and support services to companies in the area. Today, more than 100 companies and research organizations employ more than 38,000 people in the Research Triangle.

The commercialization of the academy has always been a subject fraught with meaning to U.S. higher education. The institutional role in real estate development has extended that meaning to encompass localities and regions across the country. Colleges and universities are the landlords for thousands of enterprises. They have formed business collaborations with developers to build commercial projects on a land-lease basis. They are in joint ventures with private-sector partners to construct and operate institutional auxiliary facilities on their campuses. To gain control over capital costs and bonded indebtedness, institutions are outsourcing to the private sector the task of building and/or operating campus facilities for student housing, dining and recreation, guest lodging and conferences, parking, offices, and specialized research facilities. Two types of campus-sponsored development are significant in their influence on the character and economy of the local regions: campus-related research parks and mixed-use real estate projects. One of the main motivations for institutions to create research parks is to maintain a competitive edge in scientific discovery by providing the entrepreneurial climate for faculty to convert basic academic research into commercial applications. Research parks can be instrumental in cultivating corporate relationships that institutions hope will result in research grants, patents, and licenses. Most institutions undertake such ventures with the stated purpose of promoting job creation in their host localities. The institutions that undertake the development of market-rate commercial and residential projects usually do so to enliven the environment around the campus and make more livable communities. Real estate development is approached as a way for institutions to diversify sources of income and to create amenities at less cost to the institutions.

Through the development of corporate business and research parks, and various combinations of commercial, residential, and retail uses, colleges are merging their physical domains into the built environment of the towns, cities, and regions in which they are located. The character of communities beyond the campus is being redefined by the entrepreneurial initiatives of institutions that, acting in their own economic interests, are creating whole new genres of property development that mix institutional and commercial uses. Institutional real estate projects designed to spur business and technology are typically promoted by state and local economic development interests who envision the kinds of regional change that have been spurred by Stanford, Princeton, MIT, and the Research Triangle.

Higher education institutions typically approach land development with a longevity of purpose and an orientation to place that is not easily matched by conventional real estate organizations. What they build will be part of their environment for generations. Still, not all observers endorse the financial motivations behind campus-related real estate development, particularly when those motivations are tied to the commercialization of the intellectual output of academia.

In *Country of Exiles: The Destruction of Place in American Life,* William Leach disparages the growing ties between higher education and corporations. Leach concludes that in relationships with corporate interests, universities have become complicit in undermining not only their own sense of place and identity, but that of the world around them. His perspective on the growth of the university/industry connection since 1980 is that it has been "fostered by universities in quest of revenues; by governors and legislatures determined to bring new industries to their states and willing to bargain away the kitchen sink to get it; and by firms (pharmaceutical, biotech, genetic) that had shut down their own research labs and were looking to universities for ideas and knowledge."[3]

In *Universities in the Marketplace,* former Harvard President Derek Bok observes that "What made commercialization so much more prevalent in American universities after 1980 was the rapid growth of opportunities to supply education, expert advice, and scientific knowledge in return for handsome sums of money."[4]

## The New Landscape of University Science and Technology

The year 1980 marked a watershed for the involvement of higher education in for-profit research and technology enterprises, adding momentum to the development of university-related research parks. In that year, Congress enacted the Bayh-Dole Act, facilitating the ownership and patenting of scientific discoveries made by universities. Bayh-Dole enabled educational institutions, nonprofit research institutes, and small businesses to retain intellectual property rights to inventions and products developed with federal research funds. State and federal legislation subsidizing the transfer of basic academic research to marketable products gave rise to a plethora of collaborative ventures between higher education institutions and commercial technology enterprises. The impetus for the Bayh-Dole Act and other legislation easing the commercialization of basic research was to invigorate U.S. economic growth after the recessionary 1970s. Defense-driven federal support for basic science was in decline, prompting a shift toward university research that could drive the technologies of the nascent postindustrial economy. This provided powerful incentives for universities and their research faculties to work toward patenting of discoveries, through start-up companies established by faculty and affiliations with new and established technology firms. After 1980, the research-driven entrepreneurism once pioneered by Stanford and the universities making up the Research Triangle was replicated all across the United States. Twenty years after the passage of Bayh-Dole, patenting of university research discoveries had multiplied tenfold, with license fees and royalty revenues for institutions and faculties running at more than $1 billion annually.[5]

By 2004, more than 300 colleges and universities had established for-profit subsidiaries to "create, patent, publish and market not only scientific breakthroughs but also intellectual property such as library holdings, art and design images, and even syllabi, course materials, and lectures," according to a paper by the Brown University Futures Project.[6] The practice of creating for-profit subsidiaries has increased more than twelvefold since 1980. As state and federal funding for higher education becomes less reliable, the pressure to derive income from corporate and commercial endeavors will continue to grow.

A 2002 survey by the Association of University Research Parks of nearly 200 campus-related research parks in the United States and Canada found, from the 49 percent that responded, that more than 235,000 people were employed by tenant companies in the parks. The respondents accounted for more than $9 billion in capital investment in 94 million square feet of building area on 41,000 acres of land. Public funds were used to establish 70 percent of the research parks, four-fifths of which are nonprofit entities.[7]

Campus research parks and technology centers have been adopted as the center-pieces of regional development promotions throughout the country. A *biotech coast* has blossomed in the San Diego area around the University of California's San Diego campus and the dozens of companies spun off from UCSD research. In Florida, the *I-4 technology corridor* from Tampa and Orlando to the Atlantic has seen hundreds of companies started, with the University of South Florida and the University of Central Florida as the research anchors.[8] Pennsylvania's Lehigh Valley, once one of the country's most productive steel-making centers, had by 1999 become home to more than 65 technology companies providing more than 38,000 jobs.[9] Lehigh University, whose graduates have formed numerous high-tech start-ups in the region, has a research park and part of its engineering school on a mountaintop overlooking the campus in facilities donated to the university by Bethlehem Steel when the company began retrenching its operations.

Universities, on their own or in concert with public, corporate, and other non-profit organizations, have established *incubator* facilities to provide technical and financial assistance to start-up companies. Occasionally, such facilities have been sited on campus, but more often, they are in off-campus technology parks as an inducement for emerging technology companies to locate in the parks. Many institutions have located their own academic facilities in technology parks, conducting basic and applied research in the same block—sometimes the same building—where companies are conducting research and development of new products. Some developments include lodging, retail, and conference functions, even residential uses designed to make the enterprises into 24-hour communities. Indeed, many of these developments have become hybrids, merging the attributes of the campus, the technology park, and the village into a form that some refer to as a "technopolis."

One of the most dramatic examples of this trend is found at North Carolina State University, which began the development of its 1,300-acre Centennial Campus near the main campus in 1989 to house academic facilities and private-sector enterprises that have research and development links with the university. The Centennial Campus is envisaged as a multiuse community built around research for advanced materials, biotechnology, communications technologies, and education. Housing, shops, restaurants, a hotel, and recreational amenities, including an 18-hole lakeside golf course, are included in the long-range plan for the campus. An urban town center will be created as the development is built out. Currently, five of the university's colleges have 70 academic units on the site. The College of Textiles is entirely located on the Centennial Campus. More than 100 companies and agencies are housed in buildings close by the academic labs and research centers, with access to faculty expertise, specialized facilities and equipment, and student cooperative education and internship programs. The university and the companies collaborate in the development of intellectual properties and patent licenses through the North Carolina State's Office of Technology Transfer, located on the site. In 2000, the Wake County Public School System and the university jointly opened the Centennial Campus Magnet Middle School as a model for teaching science, mathematics, and technology to adolescents, with access to personnel and resources in the university and the companies located in the Centennial Campus. The Centennial Campus, in the larger context of the institutions, organizations, and enterprises that make up North Carolina's Research Triangle, is part of a regional technopolis that is fast becoming a paradigm for regional development in America's knowledge-based economy.

Because most university-based science and technology developments are undertaken with the dual purpose of advancing the research mission of the institution and stimulating the local economy, it is inevitable that the boundaries between the campus and the public domain are disappearing. Some institutions are finding ways to creatively blend the new academic technology environment into the public realm around it. Utah State University's Innovation Campus brings university-based research and high-tech companies together on a section of the campus where, until recently, the land grant institution's agricultural lands were centered. By developing the Innovation Campus in a relatively compact urban configuration (one that is uncharacteristically dense compared with the sprawling development elsewhere along the Wasatch Front), Utah State is able to preserve agricultural research fields and open lands straddling natural drainage courses as public amenities for the research campus and the communities of Logan and North Logan. The city and the university have been partners in planning the area around and including the Innovation Campus as a regional prototype for *smart growth.*

The Piedmont Triad Research Park (PTRP) in Winston-Salem, North Carolina, in the early stages of development, will be the first truly urban-based technopolis in the southeastern United States With the new second campus of Wake Forest University Health Science as its institutional anchor, PRTP will be developed by the university in partnership with the city and state. The plan differs from most of the university-based R&D parks in that it is entirely based on the redevelopment of urban industrial land, some 200 acres adjacent to downtown Winston-Salem. The development will take place in new construction on brownfield sites once occupied by railroad yards and warehouses, and in renovated structures vacated by Winston-Salem's once-thriving tobacco industry. Although most of the 5 million square feet of building area envisioned for the site is earmarked for the health science campus, buildings for other Winston-Salem colleges, biotechnology companies, urban residential, and retail uses will be located to link the complex with the downtown area. The entire project will frame a new linear park along a restored tributary of Salem Creek. If the PTRP succeeds in following its visionary plan, it will be a model for how science-based development can shape the civic environment of the twenty-first century.

On the site of the former Lowry Air Force Base near Denver, shut down by the federal government in 1994, a consortium of higher education institutions joined to develop an educational and technological complex conceived to provide work-force preparation and stimulate technological innovation in the Denver region. The Higher Education and Advanced Technology (HEAT) Center is a mainstay of an entire new community that is under construction on the old Lowry site. The HEAT Center, ultimately to be digitally connected with homes and businesses in the developing community, is located on 154 acres of land conveyed to the Colorado State Board of Community Colleges and Occupational Education in 1994, along with 1 million square feet of former Air Force building space.[10] By 2003, seven community colleges and five universities shared space in the complex, together with several businesses on and near the complex. The center houses the Colorado Electronic Community College and is a delivery site for the Web-based Western Governors University.

The center's mission to create a technological environment for teaching and learning and for business development differs from typical university research parks in fundamental ways. It was established as a public initiative with a primary goal to foster regional job creation. It aims for the benefits of collaboration at all levels of postsecondary education from the vocational focus of the member community colleges to the advanced research undertaken at the graduate level by the member universities. It is organized to facilitate learning, academic research, and business development both in place and through digital technology extending beyond Colorado's borders. It is akin to other research and technology parks, nevertheless, in forging enterprise relationships deemed beneficial to the institutions and to the local economy.

The Centennial Campus, Piedmont Triad, and HEAT Center each aim for a robust agglomeration of functions in one place, emulating the very attributes that make place-based campuses productive learning environments. The caution is that when campus functions are dispersed to new off-campus developments, the campus itself can lose some of the benefits of agglomeration, especially if the new relationship is skewed more to the interests of industry than to colleagues in the academy. The Web will be the great facilitator of relationships when scientific endeavors are dispersed, but effective transport and programmatic links will continue to be an imperative if open, collaborative relationships are to be maintained between the mother campus and its outlying research endeavors.

Much as the Stanford Research Park, the North Carolina Research Triangle, and Princeton Forrestal Center became the seedbeds of regional economic change, many of the next generation of technology-based business and mixed-use developments will have far-reaching effects on the postindustrial future of their localities. As they create new technological employment, the developments invariably generate secondary demands for new housing, roads, schools, and infrastructure that come with the new jobs. Higher education institutions have to consider the secondary impacts that such ventures will have on the quality of place in and beyond the campus because those impacts will be felt for generations.

## The Entrepreneurial Campus: Remaking the Townscape

The main message of Chapter 7 was that higher education institutions have a vested interest in the vitality of the neighborhoods and communities in which they are located. That self-interest is reflected in the urban real estate developments being promoted by colleges and universities around the country, where off-campus housing, office, hospitality, retail, and leisure uses are offered as a way to create livelier, more inviting, and stable campus neighborhoods. By those measures, real estate investment by colleges is a civic investment. At the same time, it has to make sense as an institutional investment, one that helps to make the campus a place that is attractive and functional. The institution has a fiduciary interest in the financial and strategic purposes of such developments, whether they are conceived as sources of income, as economical ways to provide services that enhance the institution, or as means of making the campus environs more appealing for recruitment of students, faculty, and staff.

The privatization initiatives that are being undertaken by the academy cover a fascinating variety of projects. Take housing, for example. Institutions develop market-rate housing for reasons that vary with local circumstances. In high-cost areas, housing is developed as an affordable off-campus living option for students and young staff families, and to alleviate the supply deficiencies in the area's housing market. In areas where the economy is less robust, campus-sponsored housing in the community is intended to revitalize the area by attracting a stable resident population. In some cases, the intent is to create community life in areas near the campus that have little or no housing. A growing number of institutions are providing student housing on and off campus by arranging for construction and operation of residential facilities by private developers in partnership with the institutions. In such arrangements, colleges typically lease campus-owned land to developers with guarantees to provide student tenants and rights of reversion of the facilities back to the institution after the projects are amortized. Approached as a way to expedite development of needed facilities at significantly lower capital costs to the institution, such projects have to be undertaken with guarantees of construction quality, maintenance, and the reliability of the operator, in order to protect the quality of the campus and community environment and the well-being of the students.

An element of the commercial residential market that has captured the interest of U.S. colleges is that of the retirement community. Chapter 5 described how alumni are drawn to retirement communities in their college towns where they can enjoy a renewed association with their alma maters. Older Americans are attracted to college towns because they typically offer cultural, educational, recreational amenities, and health services of a high caliber. The attraction is particularly high in manageable-sized campus communities where services and amenities are easy to reach.

Institutions have formed leaseholding and operating partnerships with major hotel chains to develop guest lodging and conference facilities on campus properties all across the country. Commercial hotel and conference facilities serve a multitude of functions. They provide lodging for campus visitors where few or no facilities of comparable quality are available. They can be the prime venues for conducting continuing education, executive, and extension programs, which are *profit centers* themselves. They can be de facto alumni or faculty clubs and campus social centers. Commercially operated conference centers at campuses such as Cincinnati, Penn State, Indiana University–Purdue University at Indianapolis fulfill all or most of these purposes. Michigan State, Utah State, and Northwestern are among many institutions that operate on-campus conference and lodging facilities whose main purpose is for executive and continuing education programs. Such facilities are often underwritten by nonprofit educational foundations.

The development of projects at campus edges that include shops, restaurants, and entertainment facilities is typically conceived by institutions to create more activity and amenity in the campus neighborhood. Significant economic and social benefits can accrue to the community in such ventures by adding to the local tax base and stimulating community life. Colleges are initiating developments in communities of all sizes and circumstances as illustrated as in the examples below.

In Hanover, New Hampshire, Dartmouth College built a three-story office/retail building in the town center on land adjacent to the campus, collaborating with the town's effort to construct a downtown parking structure on contiguous municipal land. By developing the college and town sites as a single parcel, Hanover was able to build a more efficient, less obtrusive parking facility, while the college was able to position the building so that it could add active storefronts to Hanover's principal downtown street.[11]

Vanderbilt University in Nashville has initiated commercial real estate developments along the urban streets at the edges of the campus for more than years. The landlocked campus has long operated under a tacit understanding with its neighbors that it would not expand its boundaries, and that it would build uses on its urban borders that are compatible with neighboring uses. The university's real estate activities are meant to comply with that understanding while, at the same time, supporting institutional needs. Vanderbilt's first project in the 1980s was a multiunit market-rate apartment complex with retail frontage across the street from the university's medical center. In the late 1990s, Vanderbilt developed a large office building and hotel complex with ground-floor stores and restaurants on West End Avenue, the main artery to nearby downtown Nashville, which had devolved from a grand avenue to a series of strip malls and drive-through establishments. The university has purchased and leased space in a number of commercial office buildings on boundary streets to house the growth of its administrative and support uses. To make room for future academic and research growth in the core campus, the university plans to decant more of its administrative and back office space on the campus and medical area to commercial buildings in business areas adjacent to the campus. The addition of Vanderbilt's working population to those areas is expected to invigorate neighborhood economic activity.

In line with the University of Pennsylvania's initiatives to help in the revitalization of its West Philadelphia neighborhood (described in "Reweaving the Town-Grown Fabric" in Chapter 7), the university has made retail development on campus property adjacent to the neighborhood a stimulus for neighborhood renewal.[12] Some 40 businesses have located on the city blocks owned by the university, making the campus part of the neighborhood's day-to-day life. The centerpiece of the development is the $100 million Sansom Commons at University Square. The project includes a Hilton Inn with a major bookstore and other specialty shops on the street level. On another block, a 24-hour grocery market, movie multiplex, and restaurants have been built. With increasing round-the-clock life, the area is safer and more appealing than it has been in decades. The main criticism, one not uncommon for such developments, is that the neighborhood has been gentrified and is economically out of reach for many who have lived in the neighborhood for years.

The University of Illinois–Chicago, isolated from the surrounding Chicago cityscape since its founding in the 1960s (see Chapter 2, "The Postwar Urban Campus"), began acquiring derelict land and properties on the southeastern edge of the campus in 2000. As the 80-acre area was assembled, UIC contracted with a development company to build University Village, a mixed-use urban community of residential, retail-commercial, and office space, as well as university dormitories and academic buildings. University Village is laid out on the city street and block grid, mainly in new buildings. The façades of several older urban structures have been preserved in the renovation of those properties. By the end of 2004, the village contained more than 700 student residences, nearly 200 private residences in townhouses and apartments, 125,000 square feet of office, shopping, and dining establishments, and new urban parks. The project has been acclaimed as a vibrant 24-hour urban neighborhood knitting UIC to Chicago, with tax-producing uses for the city in an area that was barren until the turn of the current century. One of the most contentious issues created by the development was the displacement of a venerable flea market that had cultural standing in Chicago as an affordable urban shopping enterprise.

For-profit real estate ventures at the campus-neighborhood margin invariably give rise to challenges that must be addressed in the development process. Within the institutions, people question the propriety of allocating institutional resources for commercial development, the use of campus land for nonacademic purposes, and the diversion of resources from other institutional priorities. Neighbors and municipal officials, when presented with projects that have not been properly vetted with the community beforehand, will question the impacts of land use and density changes, displacements, public service demands, and competition with private-sector businesses. Institutions are accused, sometimes with good cause, of gentrifying or "colonizing" established neighborhoods by sponsoring upscale developments. The issue of taxes on commercial projects surface early when there are no clear guidelines or agreements with the community on how for-profit activities by institutions are to be taxed. Similar issues apply to zoning, such as whether institutional zoning classifications permit for-profit real estate developments. The needs and benefits of the projects have to be clearly demonstrated if projects vary from strict zoning provisions. Public colleges and universities in some states are statutorily prevented from leasing or using campus property for real estate development by for-profit private-sector enterprises. Public institutions have long used the device of separate nonprofit foundations with independent funding for the acquisition and development of property when they are prohibited from acquiring land on their own for institutional or commercial purposes. It is critical that institutions develop legitimate, well-vetted positions on the strategic, financial, and educational merits of such projects before embarking on them. Institutions must first assess the fundamental value and capacity of the land to support the academic mission and carefully scrutinize how prospective enterprise relationships fit into that mission. The goal of creating revenue from land development must be tempered by a clear understanding of the market-attractiveness of the location, the feasibility of development, and the strategic value of the enterprise to the institution's long-range mission.

## The Shape of Things to Come: The Marketplace Metaphor and the Civic Metaphor Intertwined

The entrepreneurial campus will continue to evolve in the twenty-first century. Unquestionably, higher education's role in the development of private-sector research and technology environments will continue to grow as an institutional endeavor. Hybrid combinations of institutional and private-sector uses, on and off campus, will appear in greater numbers, blurring the distinctions between campuses and the world around them. Because they are sponsored by institutions with the staying power to take a more measured approach to development, campus real estate projects should use the land prudently and imaginatively, with deliberate attention to urban design quality, community, and sustainability. Whether the projects come about at the initiative of the institution or at the behest of the community, both parties are joined in the outcome for a very long time in what is, by definition, a civic venture. In the knowledge economy, research and technology parks are, or should be, conceived to have positive impacts on regional well-being as an institutional goal. Public and private economic development organizations are eager to make campus research and technology parks, innovation centers, and incubators key parts of their strategic economic initiatives. Communities of all sizes want them and can benefit from them if they are undertaken in conjunction with soundly conceived regional economic development strategies that build on the resources of the institutions, the public sector, and area business interests. There are probably no more than 100 research universities in America that have the scientific horsepower, funding capacity, and mission focus to support research-based development that can be transformative at a scale even close to what has happened in Silicon Valley, the Boston/Cambridge area, or North Carolina, but scores of institutions can make meaningful differences in their localities if the strategic focus is on the needs and assets of the localities.

Colleges and universities will undertake entrepreneurial real estate developments not just for their own economic purposes, but in response to the elevated expectations that states and localities will have for higher education institutions to be drivers of economic development in the global marketplace. Here is where the civic metaphor and the marketplace metaphor are fully aligned. Whether a college revitalizes an adjacent business district by developing housing and commercial properties, or builds a research and technology park that brings innovative new companies and jobs to the locality, it creates a civic connection through its entrepreneurial actions. The endeavor may be spurred by the community itself, looking for help from the institution in cleaning up an area that has fallen into neglect, or help in creating the area's next generation of good-paying, high-skilled jobs. States and communities will provide economic incentives, infrastructure, and government coordination when they see a public benefit in the entrepreneurial activities of the institutions, and they will make sure that they are heard if the development shows signs of having a deleterious impact on its surroundings.

The relationship has to proceed with the understanding that colleges and universities are going to have an impact on the community environment well beyond their boundaries when they sponsor or participate in private-sector real estate development. The Princeton and MIT stories at the beginning of this chapter illustrate how profound the impact can be when an institution uses its considerable resources to redefine the business marketplace for an entire region. Or, when the University of Illinois–Chicago, Ohio State, Marquette, or Vanderbilt determines that investment in commercial, retail, and residential development makes a better environment for the campus, the community is changed, presumably for the better, though not all will see it that way. Those who stand to be displaced, shut out, or have their lives adversely changed by congestion, traffic, and living costs must have a place at the table when campus entrepreneurism goes beyond its borders.

When institutions intervene in the local real estate marketplace, they are bound by their place in the community to approach the task as an act of regional stewardship. Unlike that of other entities, save for various levels of government, colleges are civic enterprises with deep and long-lasting ties to the future of their communities. Place-based colleges are fixed to the localities in which they are located, have been for generations, and will be for many more generations. They are obliged, for their own sakes and for the sake of their home communities, to make sure that the entrepreneurial environments that they create have lasting quality and value.

## Part Three

# The Sustainable, Authentic Campus

## An American Public Trust

American campuses have been distinguished by their openness to nature and, with few exceptions, to the life and culture of the communities in which they were founded. That distinction prevailed in successive stages of the country's development: from the scattered settlements of the colonial Eastern Seaboard to the continental expansion of a still largely rural nation to the industrial-driven urbanization that propelled the country into the twentieth century. The epic expansion in the number and the range of higher education institutions that occurred in the postwar twentieth century produced the extraordinary variety of place-based campuses that exists today. Traditional notions of campus form and character were shattered by the sheer magnitude of college growth, urban change, and the widening demands of society. Before the century was over, there was a renewed understanding of how the character of the campus environment contributes in fundamental ways to the learning experience. All the while, the rudiments of change destined to dominate in the twenty-first century were forming.

Looking at the world of the next generation of students, academicians, higher education leaders, and a society ever more reliant on the resources of higher education, we have seen that the seismic forces of the new century will affect place-based campuses more profoundly than the changes that occurred in the postwar twentieth century. Those forces will have both centrifugal and centripetal effects on America's campuses and the communities in which they are located.

*The centrifugal forces:* Rare is the campus that will be in a single place. More campuses will have functions dispersed in a multiplicity of locations, to serve an ever more diverse array of societal needs, to strengthen the fabric of the communities they are bound to, and to generate new activities and new sources of institutional revenue. More will affiliate—and possibly merge—with other institutions and enterprises to deliver a wider array of services and to realize economies in the delivery of services. More will invest in developments and technological enterprises beyond the campus, changing the economy and character of their home regions. It is impossible to imagine any campus that will not be joined with other institutions, organizations, and businesses in numerous cybernetworks to form new learning communities, to enrich the pedagogy, to streamline the transfer of information and knowledge, and to expand the capacity to produce new knowledge. Some campuses may be subsumed by regional and transnational cyber-connected institutions, becoming "academic branch offices" and, regrettably, becoming diminished as authentic local institutions.

*The centripetal forces:* To be competitive and engaged in the twenty-first century, institutions will enhance the internal character and functions of their core academic settings. They will concentrate on crafting the creative, flexible, interactive, interdisciplinary learning environment that future learners will demand. Some, in expanding their functions and their affiliations with other organizations, will bring those organizations into the boundaries of the campus. Some will fold community-oriented functions—schools, housing, day care and eldercare centers, civic and cultural facilities—into the campus environment. Some institutions, seeking to be more important players in the global academic marketplace, will make their campuses into more stimulating, urbane, festive places that will draw students and scholars from around the globe. Some, for reasons of efficiency and economy, will consolidate their campus assets, possibly offering more of their services online or sharpening their academic focus. Some institutions will distinguish themselves in the frenetic, uncertain future best by maintaining the idyllic character of their traditional campus environments.

All of these permutations in the form, organization, and dimensions of place-based campuses are happening today. All kinds of institutions in all parts of the country will continue to change in different ways and at different paces. The sense of place in tomorrow's learning community is not confined to the boundaries of the campus, because the learning institution of the twenty-first century is itself a force for change in the world beyond its campus boundaries.

The search for the twenty-first-century campus is a quest for the restoration of the fundamental attribute that distinguished the American campus as the country grew from settlements in the wilderness to a sprawling urban nation—the campus being *of* its place and *of* its environment. But now, there is an opportunity—an imperative, in fact—for higher education institutions to adopt an *ethic of place* that is built on principles of sustainability, authenticity, and community. American colleges and universities will have to prepare an informed citizenry for participation in the knowledge-based, globally connected society of the twenty-first century. A crucial part of the challenge will be for colleges to demonstrate prudent, humane ways of living, acting, seeing, and thinking in what is becoming a terribly complex and impersonal world. The demonstration must start with the environments that colleges occupy and affect.

Chapter 9 describes why the distinctive themes of place, that have shaped the American campus throughout its history, are as relevant today as they have ever been. The chapter returns to the idea put forth in the introduction to this book that the campus is itself a teacher, not just for those who learn there, but for all who depend on the ideas and resources that higher education has to offer. The case is made that colleges and universities need to collectively adopt a twenty-first century ethic of place, making the campus a living model of what the built environment in the knowledge-based society can be.

In the epilogue, I make a personal plea for America's colleges and universities to regard their campuses as a vast *public trust* showing the way to a more civil, more sustainable human environment. I offer, at the end, my thoughts on the probable forms that the twenty-first century campus will take, inviting you, the reader, to imagine for yourself what the campus of the next generation might look like.

Martin Luther King, Jr. Plaza at the University of South Florida.
(Sasaki Associates, Inc.)

# An Ethic of Place: Finding the
## Harmonic Convergence

### Reclaiming Nature and Urban Vitality in the Sunshine State

When the Tampa campus of the University of South Florida was first laid out on farmland on the outskirts of the city in 1960, the plan followed a familiar pattern. A large central lawn bordered by academic, administrative, and student service buildings was located on a slight rise in the terrain in the middle of the 1,000-acre tract. Other buildings, notably the dormitories, were located on peripheral sites beyond the central lawn enclave. In the beginning and for the next 30 years, most of the structures on the campus were no more than two stories in height and spread apart from one another in the dispersed suburban formula prevalent in much of Florida in those years. With the exception of the central lawn, large open areas separating and surrounding the buildings were filled with surface parking lots for faculty, staff, and the 90 percent of the students who commuted to USF by car.

The obvious reminder of the university's semitropical setting is the unremitting heat and humidity from May to October, punctuated by afternoon downpours. There were few acknowledgements of the Floridian environment in the design of the landscape and the architecture of the campus. Refreshing breezeways, arcades, and courtyards were designed into a handful of the first buildings. Buildings were laid out on an east-west axis with blank walls on the east and west sides to reduce morning and afternoon glare. Still, students had to navigate long distances between classroom areas under the intense sun. Many acknowledged that they drove from one part of the sprawling campus to another to get from class to class. The open expanse of the central lawn was relieved only by a few modest stands of live oaks at the edges. The campus lacked any real accommodation of the climate and ecology or encouragement of outdoor life that attracts people in the millions to the Sunshine State.

The actions needed to ameliorate these conditions emerged in the early 1990s when the university was faced with changes requiring a major planning initiative. First, the university projected an 80 percent growth in enrollment at the beginning of the twenty-first century. It decided to expand the number of resident students, creating a more traditional collegial atmosphere. Moreover, South Florida became the third public university in the state to attain the Carnegie I research designation auguring a new era of significant growth in scientific and technological research activities. The university's health science center, which includes the renowned Moffitt Cancer Center, was in line for unprecedented growth. To accommodate the impending changes, 6 to 7 million square feet of space would need to be constructed in the next two decades, more than doubling the campus building area.

The plan for the projected development was to transform the sprawling campus into a placed scaled to the human walking environment, making a more unified pattern of development. New buildings were located to fill the most glaring gaps in the campus fabric, joining with existing structures to form shaded courtyards, loggias, arbors, and pedestrian avenues. People moving across the campus would pass through a series of shaded, actively occupied spaces rather than exposed parking lots, making the walking experience measurably more pleasant. New places would promote chance encounters, giving people a sense of belonging to the campus community. Academic, social, and residential uses would be drawn together to create a more vibrant 24-hour collegial experience. Connectivity was to be enhanced by increasing the density of the campus in key academic locations. The new vocabulary of campus architecture began to shift from the bland, monochromatic forms of the 1960s and 1970s to a more exuberant design language whose shapes, colors, and textures would now express the semitropical nature and variety of the place.

As a complement to the new urban atmosphere, the university set aside a natural greenway traversing the length of the campus with the central lawn as an urban park in the center. The greenway, planned for the conservation of 125 acres of university property, provides a crucial balance to the increased building density necessary to accommodate campus growth. The greenway restores the semitropical ecosystem, making nature an authentic and functional part of the campus experience. Most important, the greenway brings an indigenous landscape back into the campus by connecting to a 750-acre regional wetland preserve adjacent to the university. The area of the greenway was calculated so that it would function as a natural storm water detention basin for future campus growth, regenerating the site's natural drainage systems. The effect is that the Floridian climate and environment have been reclaimed as integral elements of the campus.

The Dr. Martin Luther King Jr. Plaza, the main pedestrian crossroads in the central lawn, is now a lively play of shady palms and live oaks, trellis-covered walkways, and fountain squares, instituting an unprecedented sense of civic participation in a space that was once traversed only as a matter of necessity. Barbara Donerly, architect and assistant director of Facilities Planning and Construction at USF, was an early proponent of the idea of remaking the campus into a community that is highly expressive of its environment when the campus master plan was initiated in the 1990s. She enumerates, with obvious delight, the changes in the day-to-day experience of the place that have come about with the creation of the greenway: wildlife migrating back into the campus; butterflies that have not been seen on the site in anyone's memory; colors and scents of tropical plant materials such as jasmine and bougainvillea that festoon the new trellises; and more people walking and biking than ever before. She says that "the campus has a sensory quality that it never had before . . . even the fountains mitigate the heat and mask the once inescapable traffic sounds from adjacent streets." Donerly also points out that the warm colors used in the new architecture (and repainting of older structures), in contrast to the monotone buff brick of the older buildings, make for a "much more exuberant statement about the tropical environment and a much more interesting community of buildings."

The MLK Plaza is, in Donerly's words, "used for everything we hoped it would be, and more. It is more active and festive, it generates more performances and events than we ever imagined. It is a source of campus pride that we never had before."[1]

The transformation of the USF campus is still a work in progress. Parking lots remain at several locations in the area designated for the greenway and will not be removed until campus development demands more storm water management capacity, or when the cost of putting more parking in structures can be supported. More than 3 million square feet of buildings has been constructed in the last 10 years, in clusters designed to achieve a sense of interconnection that did not exist before. Donerly expects that in the future, the university will build at higher densities than were envisioned in the plan of the mid-1990s: "We want to be sure that we save land for future capacity and, of course, preserve open and tree canopy spaces, so we will need to go higher with housing, academic and research space. We are also examining how we can aggregate more disciplines under one roof rather than build separate buildings for each discipline. That will not only save land and money, but it will create a much more integrated learning environment."[2]

The USF campus has, for the first time in its young history, attained a sense of civic character and natural harmony. It has become a more collegial, more sustainable learning environment by reclaiming its sense of regional authenticity.

## The Brief for an Ethic of Place on the American Campus

The University of South Florida at Tampa is forging a new ethic for its place in the Florida sun by organizing campus growth to create an environment that is, at once, a more vibrant collegial community and a more robust expression of its natural world. In Chapter 2, we learned that Berkeley is renewing the ethic of its place, long masked by the growth that occurred in the boom decades after World War II. At Berkeley, nature's seismic power triggered the revival of the idea that civic vitality and nature can reinforce one another. Both institutions are affirming the attributes of place that have historically distinguished American campuses: the celebratory presence of nature in a setting designed to foster a lively civic community.

Chapter 1 gave an account of 300 years of campus formation in this country, reiterating the themes of nature and community that linked campuses with America's landscape and culture. Natural beauty came with the vast, diverse American territory, and it was meant to be the hallmark of every campus. From the time that Harvard College's buildings were laid out to form a three-sided space in the 1630s, campuses had an open face to the surrounding community. Campuses became more intertwined with the economic and social structure of the urbanizing nation in the nineteenth century, but they did not release nature, even if nature began to disappear in the world around them. The pragmatic, egalitarian mission of higher education in America grew with the population. Campuses took on a civic character, a kind of urbanity that was energized by people of ever more diverse backgrounds and endeavors, making complex connections between the campuses and the world beyond.

The two distinctive themes of the American campus—nature and civic engagement—will serve colleges well as they face the challenges of the twenty-first century. Institutions must be audacious in making the campus itself a learning experience for its inhabitants and an example of places that can be better for everyone. The experience of nature must now be made into a lesson for the survival of the planet. The campus—an integral part of the locality around it, but still a special place in that locality—must now be a working demonstration of how regional authenticity can be made to work in a world where authenticity is in diminishing supply. The campus, a place that has long hosted multiple forms of community, must now demonstrate how the place-based learning environment is to connect with a more fluid population of learners and a more dynamic assortment of collaborative learning organizations in the community and around the globe.

The campus of the twenty-first century must be a living, functioning demonstration of a new *ethic of place,* based on principles of sustainability, regional authenticity, and community. The ethic of place on the American campus has to permeate the experiences of those who make the campus a part of their life pilgrimage. It has to be in the minds of educational leaders with every decision that they make to improve the learning environment; to serve new constituencies; to provide new services; and to play new roles in the development of people, communities, and regions.

## The Case for the Sustainable Campus

We enter the twenty-first century staring at a planetary environmental crisis composed of a man-made witch's brew of air and water pollution, soil and resource depletion, global warming, species extinction, famine, and so on and on. The daunting fact is that the next generation, including those now in college, will have to reckon with this crisis. Sustainability as an educational imperative can no longer be tackled in the fragmentary, incremental manner currently undertaken in the country's colleges, laudable as those efforts are. Anthony Cortese, an ardent proponent of the role that higher education must play in fostering a sustainable society, reminds us that education for sustainability has to be approached as a comprehensive, interdisciplinary, culture-changing mission—one that imparts a clear understanding of the planetary effects of human activity.[3] Education in sustainability needs to identify behavioral changes necessary to slow the deleterious impacts on the planet. An essential part of the learning process is in the living, working experience of the campus environment itself. Life in a campus that imparts a more prudent, less exploitative philosophy of the built environment is a life that better understands what it takes to make a sustainable built environment. According to Dr. Cortese, built places in the United States consume 16 percent of freshwater withdrawals, 40 percent of our material and energy flows, and 70 percent of our electrical consumption.[4] Campuses that harness their own patterns of resource consumption can significantly contribute to the mission of sustainability by example and by tangible effect.

Campuses, in their design, planning, and operations, are embracing sustainable practices at a level unprecedented since the environmental movement took root in the 1970s. Sustainable practices are emerging as a cultural force on campuses all over the country. Organizations and institutions are building networks that support the development of curricula on sustainability, the formulation of institutional strategic plans that embody goals for sustainability, and practical applications that can be undertaken at the campus level.

The Association of University Leaders for a Sustainable Future brings the prestige of the world's academic leadership to the global discourse on environmental literacy as part of its mission to "make sustainability a major focus of academic disciplines, research initiatives, operations and outreach efforts of higher education institutions worldwide."[5] Surveying, chronicling, and assisting in campus conservation projects and strategies, the National Wildlife Federation's Campus Ecology Program takes a more pragmatic approach. Among its ventures, the organization produces a survey-based "National Report Card on Environmental Performance and Sustainability in Higher Education" that grades the performance of participating institutions in categories ranging from campus environmental policies to curricula and operational conservation practices. Ball State University in Muncie, Indiana, sponsors an acclaimed national conference series, the *Greening of the Campus,* at which papers from the highly theoretical to the very practical have been introduced into the national dialogue on campus conservation.[6] The Campus Consortium for Environmental Excellence and the Society for College and University Planning are prominent among organizations promulgating best campus environmental practices.

Sustainable practices reinforce the distinctiveness of a campus, strengthening the qualities that give a campus its regional integrity. The protection of native ecological systems and reintroduction of indigenous landscapes make the campus a more authentic, natural expression of its local environment. Sustainable architectural design contributes to the local character of the campus by adapting campus life to the effects of regional climate and environment. Limited land resources on the sustainable campus are organized to create compact spatial relationships, making active, healthy, and productive community settings. Continuous stewardship of facilities and grounds helps to sustain the vitality of the learning environment. Because higher education institutions have the organizational capacity to manage whole built environments in more sustainable and regionally expressive ways, they can make enormous contributions to the environmental and cultural well-being of their host localities.

Most institutions have initiated plans, policies, and management strategies for campus conservation at one level or another. Practically all institutions engage in some form of energy management, motivated by the economic and environmental benefits of energy conservation. College energy managers have a broad menu of energy conservation measures at their disposal: more efficient boilers and generators; low-wattage lighting and control systems; sensors that turn down and turn off lights, and heating and cooling systems when they are not needed; better insulation of walls, windows, and roofs; alternative energy sources and cogeneration, to name a few. Institutions are setting higher standards for energy conservation in the design and construction of campus facilities. Campuses are active in recycling; water conservation and gray water reclamation; composting; promoting alternative transportation; purchasing and installing green products; reducing the use of chemical-based fertilizers, pesticides, and herbicides; buying local products; and making more use of indigenous materials in landscape and construction. Many institutions have environmental officers and coordinators. The new Merced campus of the University of California, opened in 2005, has a director of environmental stewardship who has a pivotal role in the policy making and design of the environmental infrastructure of the campus.

The most encouraging prospects are at those institutions that are working to change the culture of the campus in fundamental ways by embedding a philosophy of sustainability into the very heartbeat of the institution. Culture change is absolutely critical in making sustainability a bedrock element in the ethic of place, and institutions are making sustainability a mainstream agenda. Ball State University, besides its sponsorship of the greening conferences, has made courses on sustainability part of the university's required core curriculum, funding faculty grant applications for campus demonstration projects.

One of the most striking examples of an institution building a collegiate culture around sustainability is Berea College in Kentucky. The 1,500-student liberal arts school has a long history of progressive policies (being the first interracial college in the South, and serving only low-income students with an endowment that covers all tuition). It is only natural that the school would set a standard for sustainable practices that can be a benchmark for colleges everywhere. A 2005 article in the *Chronicle of Higher Education* describes the philosophy of *upstream living* forged in the mid-1990s by Berea President Larry Shinn with students, faculty, and staff to prepare students to understand the "interrelationship between humans and the environment."[7] It is a philosophy that stands apart in a region whose upstream landscape is too often ravaged by indiscriminate lumbering and coal mining.

Berea has inaugurated an ambitious action program, including the construction of a student apartment complex calibrated to use only 25 percent of typical levels of energy and water consumption, and a wastewater treatment plant that converts 10,000 gallons of sewage to reusable, nonpotable water each day through the actions of fish, plants, and snails. The school has renovated 12 buildings with substantial conservation retrofits. Berea's plan is to reduce total campus energy use 40 percent by 2010. Notwithstanding these ambitious measures, Shinn acknowledges that the school is still in the early phases of developing a model for sustainable living with economic, social, and spiritual overtones that students will carry with them throughout their lives.

Academia has a moral obligation to discover, teach, and demonstrate the best, most advanced practices in sustainability. The obligation goes well beyond lessening the impacts that individual institutions impose on the environment or limiting the resources that they consume. Colleges and universities must give voice to the understanding that all built places created for the daily affairs of human beings will need to leave a lighter footprint on the planet, that sustainability has to be a moral force in American culture. It has to be a demonstrable part of the experience of every student who passes through academe and of everyone who relies on higher education to improve the quality of individual and community life. America's 4,000 campuses, with all of their branches and satellites, must be considered a great, aggregated public trust, a national resource, the stewardship and preservation of which can be a model of lasting value to the whole country.

There are a host of reasons why American higher education institutions must lead in blazing the path to the sustainable society. The most practical reason is that it is in education's economic self-interest to adopt vigorous conservation measures, to preserve the integrity of their physical assets. Smart practices in energy conservation, adaptive reuse, landscape regeneration, and growth management are the kinds of long-term investments in campus quality that colleges need to make if they are to remain competitive in an uncertain economic future. Some analysts have observed that the long-range payoff from aggressive energy-saving strategies alone can be greater than the rate of return on endowments—and far more reliable. They reason that a portion of endowment money would be better invested in energy conservation on campus than in the stock market.[8] Sustainability in the campus environment has a practical value that will accrue as resources become more scarce and as pressure mounts to reduce marginal operating costs.

Higher education has the resources to lead by example. Most campuses have an inherent advantage in being able to make substantial moves toward conservation, sustainability, and smart growth. They own and administer the land and facilities assets that they occupy. They are likely to control more extensive, organized areas of real estate, in strategic locations in their localities, than any other single entity aside from government. An institution that has 10 or 15 million square feet of buildings on 1,000 or 2,000 acres can have an undeniably positive effect on the local environment by applying more sustainable practices in the use of buildings and land. So, too, can a school with half a million square feet of buildings on a 50-acre campus. Measures to reduce campus automobile use, to control downstream storm discharges, to reduce demand on local water supplies, to design *green* buildings, or to reduce the campus contribution to the local landfill are readily felt and seen by the community.

On the sustainable campus, nature is employed to do more of the work of making buildings habitable: with natural ventilation; building orientation, overhangs, and screening systems to control seasonal solar heat gain; clearstories, skylights, and interior glazing to capture natural light in inside spaces; and landscape plantings to shade buildings and mitigate winds. The organization of functions that makes campuses work best as collegial enterprises is consonant with the most basic principles of smart, healthy, sustainable growth: a compact, walkable environment designed to foster day-to-day human interaction with shoe leather rather than 6,000 pounds of rolling steel; the mix of academic, residential, communal, and administrative functions in close, active proximity; the capacity to control vehicular use and storage; the capability to preserve nature and make it the armature upon which the built environment can be organized.

If U.S. higher education institutions were to collectively exercise the most advanced practices in the use of alternative energy, alternative transportation, conservation of energy and resources, pollution control, ecosystem protection, and growth management, the impact on this country would be staggering. As a matter of economic self-interest, institutions will have to achieve better space use; look more to the renovation and adaptive reuse of existing space; use more durable, lower-maintenance building materials; and adopt more sophisticated means of energy conservation. The real environmental effects will be significant as well. Colleges and universities occupy more than 5 billion square feet of building space, more if you add the ancillary enterprises in which they are involved. That is a small percentage of the 300 billion square feet in buildings of all sorts that exist in the country at the beginning of the third millennium,[9] but it is of potentially vast import as a demonstration of how building space can be better used, more energy efficient, and more habitable.

Given that buildings use one-third of the country's total energy and two-thirds of the electrical demand,[10] energy-conscious design, retrofitting, and operations in the collegiate building stock can have a significant national impact by demonstration and in actuality. Many institutions have been able to reduce building energy consumption by 30 percent and more. An appreciable amount of new campus building construction follows the principles of green design, with a substantial number of college buildings among the more than 500 projects that have been registered for certification under the U.S. Green Building Council's standards for Leadership in Energy and Environmental Design (LEED) as of 2003.[11] On the sustainable campus, parking will no longer be a "free good" allowed to consume disproportionate amounts of valuable campus land. By transportation management policies designed to reduce peak parking demand and by consolidation of parking spaces in structures that reduce their footprint, land is given back to higher-value academic and learning support uses and to the restoration of campus landscape.

People spend 90 percent of their time in buildings. It is critically important to higher education institutions that interior environments be designed, built, and maintained with a keener eye on human health, comfort, productivity, and enjoyment. Because academia's genetic code is wired to measure, assess, and disseminate the outcomes of everything it does, the country can gain a great deal of knowledge about sustainable building practices from the concerted efforts of America's campuses. That knowledge will be badly needed. It is estimated that the country will have to construct another 213 billion square feet of built space by the year 2030; 82 billion will be needed just to replace obsolete building space.[12]

The extent of the land resources owned by America's campuses easily exceeds 1 million acres, probably a great deal more if one takes into account holdings in real estate development, agricultural and forestry experiment stations, arboreta, and conservation areas. One million acres is 1,500 square miles—more than the area of Rhode Island, more than Grand Canyon National Park. That is the amount of land that is lost in this country every two to three years because of sprawling development, with its attendant energy consumption, air and water pollution, and habitat destruction. Nevertheless, by adopting a broadly collective ethic of place, protecting and using their millions of acres wisely, lowering their demands on the earth's resources, reducing the environmental impacts on their localities, and maintaining healthy and humane communities, America's colleges and universities can give the world a matchless demonstration of what a sustainable society can be.

## Genius Loci: Teaching the Geography of Somewhere

> Eighty percent of everything ever built in America has been built in the last fifty years, and most of it is depressing, brutal, unhealthy, and spiritually degrading—the jive-plastic commuter tract home wastelands, the Potemkin village shopping plazas with their vast parking lagoons, the Lego-block hotel complexes, the "gourmet mansardic" junk-food joints, the Orwellian office "parks" featuring buildings sheathed in the same reflective glass as the sunglasses worn by chain-gang guards, the particle-board garden apartments rising up in every meadow and cornfield, the freeway loops around every big and little city with their clusters of discount merchandise marts, the whole destructive, wasteful, toxic, agoraphobia-inducing spectacle that politicians proudly call "growth."[13]
>
> —*James Howard Kuntsler, The Geography of Nowhere*

The pattern of human settlement in the United States grows more profligate, wasteful, and undistinguished with each passing decade. Regional and local distinctions of place throughout the United States are being eclipsed by sprawling suburbs, strip developments, gated enclaves, declining older communities, and disappearing natural environments. Sprawl is undermining the integrity of natural environments in suburban and rural regions. The franchising of America is giving much of the built setting a generic, repetitive face, driving the idea of place out of the American vocabulary. Do you know where the Dunkin' Donuts Arena is? Or the Bank of America Pavilion?

We live in a transitory time and are made to feel placeless by technology, migration, consumer culture, and the pervasive imprint of the global market economy. We are in an era of cultural uncertainty exacerbated by terrorism, environmental degradation, and rising ideological conflicts pitting social change against traditional norms. It is a time to regenerate the seemingly dormant idea of the built place as a higher form of human culture, something with a vitality that transcends the uncertainties of the time and expresses our best cultural ideals. Place is shaped by our values, but it shapes our values as well.

In his article "Reality and Authenticity in the Experience Economy," Michael Benedikt wrote that we must reclaim in our cultural environment what we have been losing through:

> a disturbing shift in modern culture, namely the loss of a healthy balance between what is real in life and what is not—between what is authentic

and what is not. . . . In short, every place, every product, every service and event in the experience economy, becomes themed, as though it were part of an endless carnival.[14]

Daniel Libeskind, the architect selected to plan the rebuilding of the World Trade Center site, spoke to the idea of place as a real and living presence in a 2002 conference panel that examined the meaning of built design in post-9/11 America.[15] In Libeskind's defense of architecture's role in public culture after 9/11, his words embraced the larger responsibility of place-making as a human endeavor, of making human places into something living, something speaking a language both communicative and silent. He made a poignant analogy of what a consciously designed space should be when he reminded his audience that it is "actually something like a person, a physiognomy, a soul, a spiritual entity given to a particular locale. And that's the genius loci that we feel when we are in a place."[16]

Benedikt and Libeskind are telling us that *genius loci*—the spirit of place—must be grounded in what is living and real about the place, what, indeed, it takes to make a built place *authentic*. The campus can be—must be—an authentic American place so long as its grand mission is to be relevant, inventive, and compelling for its time and its locale. Being relevant to the locale is no longer a simple proposition—not that it ever was in the first place. The locale of influence for most institutions is now, inescapably, the globe. Still, institutions have their most fundamental meaning and relationship to the localities in which they exist, whether they are elite world universities, exclusive liberal arts colleges, or local community colleges. The brief for regional authenticity is based on the proposition that each institution's distinct sense of place and community is a unique and irreplaceable resource. Authenticity is expressed in the individuality of the campus, the vitality of its relationships with the surrounding community, and the resilience to absorb inevitable changes without destroying the history, traditions, and place character that give meaning to the institution and its constituents on and beyond the campus.

The American campus is identified with its setting: the building ensemble, the landscape, the terrain, the open vistas that make the campus a part of its larger environment. Whether the experience of the setting is rendered in a rural college in lush pastoral surroundings or in an urban university that is strung together by interstitial landscapes, the inhabitants of those campuses need to see, feel, and inhale the authentic qualities of the setting as they go about their everyday business. The authentic campus should neither be "McCampus" nor a theme park of nostalgic and borrowed collegiate icons from other times and places, although its historically significant buildings and campus districts should be protected by the wise application of historic preservation measures that can sustain the useful, authentic life of revered structures. The authentic campus is designed to reinterpret the history, culture, climate, and landscape of its locality as the University of South Florida is now doing. The authentic campus can, through architecture, landscape, and spatial order, say exactly where it is and what cultures it serves. It should be clear in its regional gestalt. It should be permeable, allowing nature to enter and thrive, absorbing the vitality and character of its locality. The campus itself should teach an authentic way of living in the built environment.

Authenticity of place is not static, nor is the brief for regional authenticity a Luddite manifesto. It is a way of thinking, a way of sustaining the conversation between the generations attending college. The living campus is one in which continuity and change constantly play off one another, where openness to fresh ideas about the place contributes to its continuing vitality. As campuses move to new ways of teaching and learning, new forms of scientific discovery and new commitments to the service of the community, their environments need to evolve as their learning communities evolve. There is no guarantee that the campus will be a better place if it subsists as an artifact, endlessly replicating traditional architectural forms and spatial patterns. However, there is a good prospect that the campus will be alive and relevant to its community through time when fresh concepts of design are sympathetically woven into the historic culture and traditions of the campus.

This is in keeping with the Olmstedian theme that the campus itself is part of the civilizing mission of higher education. There is a renewed interest in Olmsted's notion that the character of the campus as a cultural landscape is an essential part of experiential learning. Olmsted scholar David Schuyler welcomes the revival of interest in the role that the campus environment plays in the learning experience, but cautions that it must be enabled in the institutional mission:

> Welcome though this renewed attention to the campus landscape has been, it remains incomplete. Olmsted emphasized the importance of the physical landscape to the college's responsibility for refining the taste, the manners, and the habits of students. An attractive landscape today is too often thought of simply as a strategy for student admissions and retention, not as something central to the educational mission. This is dangerous because it leaves a vitally important element of the physical plant vulnerable to budget cuts in times of austerity. And it is shortsighted because it reflects a narrow view of the educational process at the very time when visual and environmental dimensions to learning are becoming increasingly important.[17]

The authentic campus—the campus that teaches an authentic way of living and seeing—responds to something basic in the human psyche. It has to do with our relationship with the land. In his paean to the lost understanding of the connections among place, environment, and culture, Wendell Berry has written an anthem of sorts for environmental authenticity:

> We have given up the understanding . . . that as we and our land are part of one another, so all that are living as neighbors here, human and plant and animal, are part of one another, and so cannot possibly flourish alone; that, therefore, our culture must be our response to our place, our culture and our places are images of one another and inseparable from each other, and so neither can be better than the other.[18]

What people seek from the college campus is not necessarily what they seek from the other built places that they experience. They seek in the campus setting a fundamental quality of authenticity that conjoins the attributes of nature and urbanity. Americans have always harbored ambivalent attitudes about the virtues of natural places versus those of urban places. A scan of twenty-first-century settlement patterns reveals that, from region to region, there is a stunning ambivalence as to what constitutes the ideal juxtaposition of rural and urban, country and city, wilderness and civilization. The effect is that the built landscape of America is an amorphous and confusing affair that is defined as much by the vagaries of the market economy as by regional geography and culture. Yet, in this transitional time, when people see the erosion of nature in their day-to-day lives and when cities are struggling to find their roles in a postindustrial world, there is a striving for better models of place that hold nature and urbanity in a more satisfying balance.

The campus is an authentic American cultural landscape that deliberately makes its natural character the setting for the civic, social, intellectual, and residential endeavors that give the campus its sense of urbanity. The landscape and open space structure of the campus is a tangible asset to be lovingly protected—for beauty, contemplation, tranquility, and psychic connection with the larger natural realm. The civic realm of the campus is an intangible asset found in the conjunction of spaces, buildings, and activities that foster interaction, encounter, community, celebration, theater, even—dare it be said—a more open, worldly perspective. It is a part of its larger cultural environment but remains a place that has its own identity. It is an ideal, an aspiration of physical place design, fitting to the role of the college campus as an environment made to impart intellectual, cultural, and social ideals.

## The Civic Imperative: Nurturing the Sense of Community

The third part of the brief for a twenty-first century ethic of place is that the campus must provide the means of nurturing community in ever-widening ways. The introduction of this book described the campus as an intentional community, created for the pursuit of the institution's learning mission in both intellectual and social terms. The intentional community is built on the needs and aspirations of individual learners who join the community to learn new skills and become whole, reasoning persons. The campus as an intentional community is a place organized to foster the complex and evolving human relationships that give substance to the learning experience, a place comprised of not one, but many, layers of community. In the twenty-first century, the communities that make up the academy come not just in layers, but in broadening orbits.

Consider the breathtaking diversity of learners who are entering the intentional community. Consider the range of needs and expectations that they bring to the academy and the dizzying pace of change in expectations that will occur in the next couple of generations. Contemplate the *modes of communication, exchange, and delivery of ideas* in real space and cyberspace that institutions will be employing to meet the needs of an expanding learning community. And consider the burgeoning links that are being forged with local and global learning communities outside campus borders. This milieu could be a recipe for the dilution of the intentional community—even the alienation of many of its participants. The ethic of place carries with it a civic imperative, which is that the campus must be the setting for civil trust and engagement that will enable the academy and its constituents to flourish in the twenty-first century.

Community starts with the intellectual foundations of the institution. Cornell President Emeritus Frank Rhodes makes an eloquent plea for restoration of community in the intellectual life of the campus when he declares that:

> Without community, knowledge becomes idiosyncratic: the lone learner, studying in isolation, is vulnerable to narrowness, dogmatism, and untested assumption, and learning misses out on being expansive and informed, contested by opposing interpretations, leavened by differing experience, and refined by alternative viewpoints. Without community, personal discovery is limited, not because the individual inquirer is being less creative or original than the group, but because his or her conclusions remain unchallenged and untested; private knowledge is knowledge lost.[19]

As we saw in Chapter 6, the stewardship of the campus and its assets must be aimed at creating a more productive learning environment. Stewardship of the learning environment is an economic and functional necessity, and, more than that, a means of transforming the ways in which people interact in the learning enterprise. Chapter 6 spoke of creating academic settings that reach across the collaborative, cross-disciplinary frontiers of learning and research that will define much of higher education in the twenty-first century. The productive learning environment is one in which teaching, research, social, and residential facilities are designed and organized to foster communities of learning in the multiplicity of forms that those communities will inevitably take in the new century.

Multiplicity is the operational term for today's campus community. Except for the most traditional or the most specialized of institutions where the sense of community is shaped by very particular institutional cultures, most of academe will build its communities on a multiplicity of cultures. Community, in the broad civic sense, becomes even more important when its constituents represent the many socioeconomic backgrounds, ethnic and national origins, genders, ages, degrees of participation, and levels of engagement that characterize today's learners. The ethic of place as a civic model for such a disparate array of constituents is, quite simply, one that shows people how to work together, how to learn from one another, how to attempt to understand one another, how to tolerate and appreciate differences in who we are. The campus is the agora of the twenty-first century, made up of the formal and informal places where people can cross paths, where people can be by themselves if they choose to be, but where no one should be made to feel alienated by the design of the place.

If the mission of American higher education is to advance the ideals of a better, more civil society, then the campus must be the living, material embodiment of those ideals. Each institution interprets those ideals as part of its educational mission and defines how those ideals should be reflected in life on the campus and in the locales that it serves. There is a discernable commonality in the way that most campuses have been designed to express authentically American values, mirroring the need to embrace nature in our lives and forming the civic setting that invites the free exchange of ideas. Though those values have become murkier in the larger culture, they persist as qualities that distinguish the campus as a civic learning environment.

The civic model of the campus can best be illustrated by an analogy taken from *The Land That Could Be,* in which William Shutkin toggles the idea of civic life with the vitality of the places in which civic life takes place:

> Civil society is the musculature of democracy. It is the schools, work places, trade unions, churches and synagogues, and associations . . . the public spaces and activities that gather citizens together, enable them to interpret

their conditions, and cultivate solidarity and civic engagement . . . the places where people can meet as equals, without regard to race, ethnicity, class, sexual orientation, or national origin. They are the places that encourage, in the words of Jane Jacobs, "casual public trust" . . . civic democracy is more than just community participation and conversation; it is rooted in a place, a physical environment conducive to collective action and community building. In a civic democracy, place and community are mutually constitutive and reinforcing.[20]

Community is a form of personal growth, burnished mainly in the informal domain of the campus. In a 1992 essay entitled "Making College a Great Place to Talk," Ray Oldenburg observed that of the three contexts of campus learning— classrooms, places of private reflection, and conversation places—it is the informal conversation environment that is not given adequate attention at most colleges. Oldenburg pleads that places for "conversation with others, especially one's peers, but also with people who are different," are nearly as important as classrooms. He advocates "great hangouts" all across campus where conversation energizes the social learning experience and enforces a kind of "democratic etiquette." Oldenburg weighs the strength and exuberance of community on campus by asking, *How good is the conversation?*[21]

The communities that make up the twenty-first-century campus will be more fluid, more dynamic than they have ever been, unconstrained by real or virtual boundaries. They will manifest themselves in new collaborations and relationships, from local and regional to global. As more institutions permeate the communities around them, their roles in nurturing—even rejuvenating—the larger sense of community will be played out in the centrifugal and centripetal patterns described in the preceding chapters. By adopting an ethic of place, they will fulfill their obligation to help in bettering the quality of community life beyond their borders and to make their campuses more magnetic, productive places enriching the civic environment.

## Preserving the "Soul" of the American Campus in the Twenty-first Century

Higher education plays a powerful role in molding the world view of those it serves. The experiences that are created by the campus setting should touch us deeply enough that they will elevate our expectations for the environments in which we conduct our lives.[22] The brief for a twenty-first-century ethic of place on the American campus recognizes that there are precious few prototypes for the man-made environment that can inform our collective consciousness about the quality and spirit of place. The college campus is—and must be—one of those prototypes.

Sustainability, authenticity, and community will take a multitude of forms, reflecting the circumstances of each institution, its environment, its cultural setting, and, most certainly, the people who are drawn to the institution by their own aspirations. Whether the campus of the next generation is one whose traditional character will change only at the margins or one reorganizing to serve whole new functions and constituencies, it will have to cultivate an ethic of place that can absorb the societal forces discussed in Part Two of this book, transcending the uncertainties of the future. American campuses will themselves be societal forces as they assume new roles and relationships in the globalizing society. They will continue to disperse certain of their functions to locations beyond the core campus to better serve their myriad constituencies. They will take on functions once provided by other institutions and enterprises, and other enterprises will take on their functions. They will combine or affiliate with other organizations to broaden their offerings, revitalize their communities, and provide the kinds of services that higher education will be asked to craft if the country is to thrive in the "flattening" world. They will simultaneously become local, national, and global institutions, offering instruction and conducting research as members of formal Web-based learning networks. They will offer larger blocks of instruction online to meet the needs of a more fluid, freelance learner population and to economize on the delivery of instruction. They will provide more extensive services within and beyond the campus domains to meet the civic and cultural needs of their communities. Some will consolidate, concentrating on curricula and services in which they have particular strengths or where the learner needs are greatest. Some will disappear. Some will change very little, relying on established reputations and specialties to draw students whose aspirations are consonant with their institutional values.

For all of the centrifugal and centripetal permutations that America's 4,000 place-based higher education institutions are undergoing in the new century, it is fair to assume that most will occupy the same ground 25 or 50 years from now as they do today. Their material shapes and forms will change to match new roles and relationships, but not their substance, which is for the place itself to be a living, energizing part of the learning experience. This book has cited the pedagogical, cultural, and civic reasons that the iconic core campus identity will persist, and that the campus will also become more borderless and intermingled with the world around it for those same reasons. That is because the learning community of the twenty-first century is made up of communities everywhere. Those who will define the future of higher education institutions will be redefining the communities and regions served by the institutions. The ethic of place for the twenty-first-century American campus—sustainability, authenticity, community—is an ethic for all places.

The collegial experience will always be shaped by the pedagogical chemistry of the institution: an inspiring faculty; a challenging, relevant curriculum; an atmosphere of intellectual excitement; and an academic environment that nourishes both individual introspection and freewheeling inquiry. Good educators and motivated students will always find ways to communicate, even in the most inhospitable settings.[23] We know, however, that the campus must be hospitable to the learning endeavor, and much more. We know that the campus itself must be the teacher, a place that gives vitality, meaning, and memory to the learning experience, not just within the confines of the institution but in the times and places beyond. I have argued that those are the fundamental attributes of the place-based institution—its *soul*, if you please—that have enabled it to persevere throughout our restless history, to continuously transform itself as it has tackled the ever-changing needs of American society.

For educational leaders, academicians, students, alumni, politicians, business leaders, citizens, planners, all of us who have a stake in navigating America's place-based higher education institutions through the waves of change in the twenty-first century, there will be many daunting challenges and many exciting opportunities. One of those challenges will have to be met with inspired, thoughtful diligence—and that is to sustain the timeless qualities that make the campus the quintessential American place that it is. If the campus is to be our society's teacher, it needs to thrive as a narrative, as an experience, as a pilgrimage, as an intentional community and as a work of art. We, as a society, must see to it that the American campus, in all of its marvelous forms, serving so many kinds of people in so many different ways in so many different locales, never loses its soul.

The University of Missouri–Columbia. (Robert Llewellyn.)

# Epilogue: In Search of an American Campus Form for the Next Generation

I approach the end of this book by acknowledging (if it wasn't already evident) that I am an unabashed "Olmstedian" in my views of the American campus. Olmsted, as you recall, contributed a fresh, distinctively American philosophy of place to his ideas for the design of the campus. He was clear in his populist vision of what the new land grant institutions needed to achieve in the expanding postbellum nation. It was Olmsted who admonished the trustees of the Massachusetts College of Agriculture in 1866 to adopt a plan that would "include arrangements designed to favorably affect the habits and inclinations of your students, and to qualify them for a wise and beneficent exercise of the rights and duties of citizens and of householders."[1] He was certain that the restorative presence of nature in the human environment would have a civilizing effect on the learning experience. He knew that a campus that was humane in its physical scale and design expression would be a place that could nurture relationships, discourses, and ideas that could be carried into other realms of civic life. He knew, in other words, that the place and the academic enterprise together would nurture an informed, practical, thoughtful citizenry. Olmsted's vision was a dynamic vision. He recognized that he was designing a world for a restless, changing population, and that to serve that population, the campus would have to adapt to change.

Those ideals are as pertinent today as they were nearly a century and a half ago. In Olmsted's time, the country was filled with an optimism buoyed by a new kind of citizen ready to take on a beckoning continent. There were no limits. Colleges were designed with that optimism at their foundation. In our time, we deal with the limits and challenges that we have largely created for ourselves during those 150 years, having metamorphosed into a very complex and competitive global society. In our time, the driving motive is determination, burnished, perhaps, with cautious optimism. But here is the good part: the campus is still, by its nature, conceived to be a seedbed of optimistic purposes. The campus is where people come to do optimistic things such as expand their minds, make their life prospects better, figure out how they and others can navigate the world's complexities and solve cosmic puzzles. Those things happen in other places too, but the campus is the one place, in the one cultural environment, that is intentionally designed for those things to happen in concert. Olmsted's conception of the campus as an integral part of the learning experience has not dimmed.

I go back farther to Thomas Jefferson, to the seminal ideas of the American campus that coalesced in his mind, and, to our good fortune, on his drawing board. He was unswerving in his determination that the academical village would be *of* its land, *of* its place, *of* a character fully expressive of the Virginia Piedmont that he so cherished. Who better than a founder of the republic and an insatiable learner himself could craft such an ensemble for the express purpose of fulfilling the cultural and intellectual ideal of the American collegial experience? I would even be so bold as to suggest that, in spite of Jefferson's diatribes on the evils of urban culture, his plan unmasked a subtle, genteel sense of urbanity that flowed into the thinking of those who would later design campuses for a more urban nation.

In my view, the conceptual leap from the academical village to Olmsted to the urbane authors of the City Beautiful campuses is not that huge. Each step held firm to the conception of the campus as a place in which a coherent sense of nature and locality was the defining paradigm. Gradually, the civic metaphor gained strength, with the proliferation of campus functions and their more complex links with the world beyond.

Neither Jefferson nor Olmsted, nor any of the others whose visions shaped the essential campus as we know it today, could have imagined the kinds of societal forces that are impinging on the character and functions of the American campus in this century. Maybe they could imagine that what they achieved in defining the *nature* of the American campus would still be valid as the setting for higher learning one, two, or more centuries later. They did, after all, apply uniquely American principles of campus place-making that they clearly intended to last well beyond their own times.

That brings us, inevitably, to how we, living inside the societal forces of the early twenty-first century, imagine the future shape of the American campus for the next generation or two. That is the future that is rising over the planning horizons of today's educational leaders. We are at a point that parallels the inception of the Morrill Act, the introduction of the German system of disciplines, and the post–World War II growth boom. The forces reshaping the campus have already made themselves clear. The "future has already happened," to paraphrase Peter Drucker, who spent a lifetime helping people understand how to manage change by continuous learning.[2] Knowing how college campuses will reshape society around them is a more daunting inquiry. The social historian Robert Heilbroner, another venerated voice, posits that we consider how imaginable it would be to affect the forces that shape the future, leaving us with "the somewhat less futile effort of inquiring into the possibilities of changing or controlling the trends of the present."[3]

If we try to picture the campus of the next generation, we know that it will be shaped by a conjunction of the forces described in Part Two of the book. We know, for example, that the learning community in America will be dynamic, multitiered, and constantly expanding if it is to maintain its critical awareness of matters driving global change—and if it is to be nimble and competitive in the "flattening" world that Thomas Friedman writes about.[4]

We need to understand that higher education will be an ever more important engine of social change and social support in its communities and in the nation. The core mission of rigorous intellectual inquiry must remain paramount, but the *service* aspect of the academic mission will drive the creation of whole new functions and relationships that will lead to heightened civic engagement and collaborations. Colleges may find themselves having to play these multiple roles with less certainty of where their financial resources will be coming from. This augurs for a future in which the learning transaction will be done more frugally and productively, where economies will be achieved by prudent stewardship, by technology, and by nontraditional collaborations with other organizations.

To this I lend my own admonition that campuses must be designed as places to heighten the learning experiences of their inhabitants, and that they need to become powerful demonstrations of what a healthy, sustainable, inspiring built environment can be. This is a public trust that our colleges must fulfill.

If those are the challenges that must be met on the college campuses of America in the next generation, what possible forms might campuses take that are different from what they are today? You recall from the examples cited in Part Two that the future forms of America's campus will mainly be extrapolations of what they are today. Remember what Drucker said about the future already having happened.

The probability is that campuses will not depart much from the essential forms that they have today, but rather in the variety of arrangements they will make to serve broader segments of the learning community more effectively. The common theme will be that institutions will be, at the same time, both more borderless and more magnetic at their cores. I believe there are at least three (somewhat idealized) futures for American campuses that we will see in greater abundance in the next few decades.

## Clicks and Mortar: Virtual Hinterlands/Vital Centers

Technology, as we are aware, will permeate the campuses of the next generation. It will be the instantaneous, economical means of delivery to a pluralistic learning population that educators mean it to be. But more than that, it will extend the virtual breadth of campuses in any direction they want to go. And even more, it will make the learning experiences within campuses more illuminating and more powerful. In the Clicks and Mortar Campus, creative, stimulating, and interactive virtual offerings are the glue that binds faculty, students, and facilitators on campus with their counterparts in an ever-changing hinterland. In this model, the mother campus is a vibrant place, featuring continuously upgraded, innovative forms of instruction in an environment abundant with opportunities for intellectual and social exchange.

The mother campus is not just the vital center of a far-reaching virtual network, but a hub of community life, a civic place that citizens look to as a source of educational, cultural, and social enrichment. The distinguishing characteristic of the Clicks and Mortar Campus is that the innovative use of technology enables the institution to allocate its resources toward a higher level of stewardship for the campus itself. The Clicks and Mortar Campus will be a more sustainable campus.

Columbia College of Missouri is a stunningly resourceful example of Clicks and Mortar. The "mortar" is provided by the historic 30-acre home campus near downtown Columbia, which hosts more than 950 students in small class settings in the Day Campus, a traditional resident academic program enlivened by cocurricular activities. The Evening Campus serves 3,000 working adult undergraduates and graduates attending five eight-week sessions each year at the Columbia location. Then, Columbia conducts accredited programs for 11,000 adult learners at its Nationwide Campus at 30 locations around the country, including 15 military bases. The "clicks" happen at Columbia's Online Campus, where 8,000 students take more than 300 online courses with 10 online degrees, many of which are the same as those taught in Columbia and the nationwide classes. To top it off, students from 25 foreign countries attend the Daytime Campus, making Columbia a global Clicks and Mortar.[5]

## The Intellectual Agora: Transformation of the Civic Metaphor

More institutions will become thoroughly intermixed with the urban fabric of their host communities. That precedent has been set by community colleges and public four-year colleges whose missions are focused on the educational and economic needs of the local populations. Public and private universities are becoming more enmeshed in the civic realm, in part to contribute to the betterment of the community, but, as well, to enhance their positions in the competitive academic marketplace. Some of the meshing will occur simply as a result of campus growth that has nowhere to go but in new locations in the city. What we will be seeing in the Intellectual Agora is a continued infusing in the urban domain of campus outreach venues, cultural facilities, recreational facilities, research institutes, medical and health facilities, off-campus residential communities, real estate developments, and nature areas.

The more that campuses take on nontraditional functions such as real estate development and urban revitalization, the more they will merge into their communities. As colleges form associations with other educational and cultural institutions, social service organizations, primary and secondary schools, and businesses, the distinctions between campus and the town will become less apparent. Institutions and cities aspiring to be players in the global marketplace are blending their cultural and creative resources to make each more attractive to the international community.

None of the moves involved in the creation of the Intellectual Agora takes away from the core campus being a vital center. Indeed, the decentralization of nontraditional functions only magnifies the value of the mother campuses. The Boston area, my home, is the archetype for the Intellectual Agora. There are more than 60 colleges in the region, each campus conveying its own distinctive identity, and all adding up to a ubiquitous presence in the urban realm with their branch campuses, academic medical centers, research parks, spin-off enterprises, and campus open spaces. Large urban districts such as the Longwood Medical Area, the Fenway, Kendall Square, and University Park near MIT are filled with institutional and related enterprise uses. If Harvard's nascent plans for expansion on the Boston side of the Charles River follow the ambitions enunciated by the university and the city, the result may be an entirely new paradigm for the integration of academic, residential, cultural, business, and community functions in the urban setting of the twenty-first century. Wouldn't it be fascinating if America's oldest college (and corporation) leads the way in creating the newest paradigm for the campus in the city?

### The Legacy Reaffirmed: Back to the Future

Finally, I offer a model of the campus of the next generation that has been the benchmark for the collegial environment through many generations of social change by staying steadfast to its core mission and by maintaining the clarity and eloquence of its campus setting. In this model, nature is embraced, human scale is preserved, and the built environment is renewed so that it remains a living resource for each generation of learners. Not a museum piece, you understand, or an artificial replication of an earlier era, but a campus whose most valued icons are restored for new cycles of life and whose newest work, fresh and transparent, is carefully and respectfully woven into the civic fabric of the place. This model, by definition, includes the traditional campuses whose very identities are associated with those essential collegiate values. It includes the campuses that are restoring distinctive heritages that were neglected during periods of unbridled growth, while judiciously building anew to refresh the sense of collegiality, intellectual vitality, and community. The Legacy Reaffirmed Campus cherishes the arts, humanities, and social sciences as much as technology and the hard sciences, affirming that the next generation of Americans are better prepared to nurture what Friedman calls a "more hopeful, life-affirming and tolerant imagination" for the world.[6]

The Legacy Reaffirmed Campus could be the vital center of the Clicks and Mortar Campus or one of the hubs of the Intellectual Agora. It could be the most technologically advanced place by its methods of offering instruction, conducting scientific research, and reaching out to learning communities outside the campus. But, still, it will be a place that recognizes the institutional value of its history, traditions, and regional heritage as the civic foundation for its ventures into the uncertain future. The examples are everywhere, from great flagship public universities such as the University of Missouri–Columbia and the University of Montana in Missoula to splendid liberal arts colleges such as Pacific University in Oregon, Sewanee (the University of the South) in Tennessee, Davidson in North Carolina, Haverford in Pennsylvania, and the diminutive public college, St. Mary's College of Maryland.

What these probable campus futures have in common is that they demonstrate the variety of ways that place and community will conjoin to provide the crucially needed lifelong learning of the twenty-first century. In the first decades of the new millennium, the inhabitants of our colleges and the larger society are no less in need of "arrangements that favorably affect their habits and inclinations" than they were when Frederick Law Olmsted worked his visions for a civilized America.

# Notes

## Foreword

1. Richard P. Dober, as quoted in Stefan Muthesius, *The Postwar University: Utopianist Campus and College* (New Haven: Yale University Press, 2000), 26.

## Acknowledgments

1. Paul V. Turner, *Campus: An American Planning Tradition* (Cambridge, MA: Architectural History Foundation/MIT Press, 1987), 305.

## Introduction

1. Frank H. T. Rhodes, "The State of the University: A Five-Year Review," *Cornell Reports,* Winter 1983, 2.
2. Frank H. T. Rhodes, *The Creation of the Future: The Role of the American University* (Ithaca, NY: Cornell University Press, 2001), 5.
3. Richard Cole, review of *The Seduction of Place,* by Joseph Rykwert, *Urban Design Quarterly* 79 (Summer 2001), 42–43.
4. Paul V. Turner, *Campus: An American Planning Tradition* (Cambridge, MA: Architectural History Foundation/MIT Press, 1987), 305.
5. Rhodes, *Creation of the Future,* 108–9.
6. Frank H. T. Rhodes, conversation with the author, 29 July 2004.

7. In *The Campus as a Work of Art* (Westport, CT: Praeger, 1991), Thomas Gaines presents a critique of the aesthetic qualities of American campuses, offering ideas on how they can be made more beautiful and more orderly.
8. Jeffrey Aper, e-mail message to author, 12 November 2004.
9. Ibid.
10. George Keller, "The Emerging Third Stage of Higher Education Planning" (paper presented at the 34th Annual Conference of the Society for College and University Planning, Atlanta, Georgia, 26 July 1999).
11. Tony Hiss, *The Experience of Place* (New York: Vintage Books, 1990), xi.
12. David Mayernik, *Timeless Cities: An Architect's Reflections on Renaissance Italy* (Boulder, CO: Westview Press, 2003), 5.
13. Frank H. T. Rhodes, conversation with the author, 29 July 2004.
14. Michel Sandel, *Democracy's Discontent: America in Search of a Public Philosophy* (Cambridge, MA: Harvard University Press, 1996), 349.

## Part One

### one

1. Nathan Schachner, *Thomas Jefferson: A Biography* (New York: Thomas Yoseloff Publishers, 1957), 1008.

2. Garry Wills, *Mr. Jefferson's University* (Washington, DC: National Geographic Directions Series, 2002), 7.
3. Paul Goldberger, "Perfect Space: University of Virginia," *Travel & Leisure,* September 1989, 128.
4. Thomas Jefferson, letter to Hugh L. White et al., 6 May 1810, *The Writings of Thomas Jefferson,* 366–88, quoted in Paul V. Turner, *Campus: An American Planning Tradition* (Cambridge, MA: Architectural History Foundation/MIT Press, 1987), 79.
5. Wills, *Mr. Jefferson's University,* 45.
6. David Mayernik, *Timeless Cities: An Architect's Reflections on Renaissance Italy* (Boulder, CO: Westview Press, 2003), 4.
7. Wills, *Mr. Jefferson's University,* 17.
8. Russell Edgerton, "Education White Paper," Pew Charitable Trust Web site, http://www.pewtrust.com/programs/edu/edwpl.cfm (accessed December 27, 1999).
9. Paul V. Turner, "Some Thoughts on History and Campus Planning," *Planning for Higher Education* 3, no. 16 (Spring 1987–88): 2.
10. Ibid.
11. Turner, *Campus,* 17.
12. Ibid., 56.
13. Wills, *Mr. Jefferson's University,* 44.
14. Turner, *Campus,* 68, footnote referencing Frederick Rudolph, the American College and University, New York, 1962.
15. Ibid.
16. Wills, *Mr. Jefferson's University,* 49.
17. Turner, *Campus,* 47.
18. Ibid., 89.
19. Clark Kerr, *The Uses of the University* (Cambridge, MA: Harvard University Press, 2003), 8.
20. Ibid., 9.
21. Ibid., 10.
22. Turner, *Campus,* 90.
23. Ibid., 101.
24. Ibid.
25. Ibid., 90.
26. Ibid., 133.
27. Edgerton, "Education White Paper."
28. Marietta Pritchard, "Root and Branch: The Land-Grant Idea at UMass," *UMass Magazine,* Summer 1999, 22.
29. Susan Rosegrant and David Lampe, *Route 128: Lessons from Boston's High Tech Community* (New York: HarperCollins/Basic Books, 1992), 32–33.
30. Pritchard, "Root and Branch," 22.
31. Ibid.
32. Ibid.
33. Ibid., 22–23.
34. David Schuyler, "Frederick Law Olmsted and the Origins of Modern Campus Design," *Planning for Higher Education* 25, no. 2 (Winter 1996–97): 1.
35. Ibid., 2.
36. Ibid., 6.
37. Ibid., 8.
38. Ibid., 10.
39. Cynthia Zaitzersky, *Frederick Law Olmsted and the Boston Park System* (Cambridge, MA: Harvard University Press, 1992), 76.
40. Ibid., 75.
41. Kerr, *Uses of the University,* 10.
42. Ibid., 11.
43. Turner, *Campus,* 164.
44. Richard Guy Wilson, "Architecture and the Representations of the Past in the American Renaissance," in *American Architectural History: A Contemporary Reader,* ed. Keith L. Eggener (London and New York: Routledge, 2004), 227.
45. Ibid., 230.
46. Turner, *Campus,* 166.
47. Mark Girovard, *Cities and People: A Social and Architectural History* (New Haven, CT: Yale University Press, 1987), 354.
48. Turner, *Campus,* 167.
49. Paul D. Spreiregen, *Urban Design: The Architecture of Towns and Cities* (New York: McGraw-Hill, 1965), 37.
50. Turner, *Campus,* 191.
51. Richard Jonas, David Neuman, and Paul V. Turner, *The Campus Guide: Stanford University* (New York: Princeton Architectural Press, 1999), 2–3.
52. Turner, *Campus,* 238.
53. Ibid., 172.
54. Edgerton, "Education White Paper."
55. George R. Boggs, "Current Issues in Community Colleges," *Facilities Management* (July–August 2003), http://www.appa.org/FacilitiesManager/articleDetail.cfm?ItemNumber+1038 (accessed August 25, 2003).

56. Edgerton, "Education White Paper."

57. Turner, *Campus,* 305.

## two

1. Historical and statistical data on Berkeley's enrollment growth provided by Steve Finacom, planning analyst, University of California–Berkeley, by e-mail message to author, 1 August 2005.

2. "Getting Ready for the Big One," *The Berkleyan,* 20 October 1999. The earthquake projection was 30 years at the time of article. Available at www.berkeley.edu/news/berkleyan/1999/1020/stability.html (accessed June 8, 2004).

3. Ibid.

4. Richard Freeland, *Academia's Golden Age: Universities in Massachusetts, 1945–1970* (New York: Oxford University Press, 1992), 74.

5. Ibid.

6. James J. Duderstadt, *A University for the 21st Century* (Ann Arbor, MI: University of Michigan Press, 2000), 110.

7. Frank H. T. Rhodes, *The Creation of the Future: The Role of the American University* (Ithaca, NY: Cornell University Press, 2001), 171.

8. Clark Kerr, "The Frantic Race to Remain Contemporary," *Deadalus,* Fall 1964, 1062.

9. Stephen S. Cohen and J. Bradford DeLong, "Shaken and Stirred," *Atlantic Monthly,* annual State of the Union issue, January–February 2005, 112.

10. Freeland, *Academia's Golden Age,* 77.

11. Ibid.

12. Ibid., 86.

13. Ibid., 87.

14. Ibid., 88.

15. Ibid.

16. Ibid., 3.

17. Ibid., 70.

18. Daniel R. Kenney, Ricardo Dumont, and Ginger Kenney, *Mission and Place: Strengthening Learning and Community through Campus Design* (Westport, CT: Praeger, 2005), 171.

19. "Talking about a Revolution: Cambridge in the '60s," *Architecture Boston,* July–August 2003, 16.

20. Paul V. Turner, *Campus: An American Planning Tradition* (Cambridge, MA: Architectural History Foundation/MIT Press, 1987), 264.

21. Ibid., 271.

22. "Campus City, Chicago," *Architectural Forum,* September 1965, 44.

23. Ibid.

24. The site was given over to campus use only after a Supreme Court ruling in 1960, overriding the original housing designation.

25. Freeland, *Academia's Golden Age,* 7.

26. Neil Levine, "Robert Venturi and the 'Return of Historicism,'" in *American Architectural History: A Contemporary Reader,* ed. Keith L. Eggener (London and New York: Routledge, 2004), 385.

27. Werner Sensbach, "Restoring the Values of Campus Architecture," *Planning for Higher Education* 20, no. 1 (Fall 1991): 8.

28. Ibid., 9.

## Part Two

1. David Pearce Snyder, "Five Meta-Trends Changing the World," *The Futurist* 38, no. 4 (July–August 2004), 22.

## three

1. Kay Mills, "Math Emporium: The Use of Technology Has Changed the Way Virginia Tech's Introductory Math Classes Are Taught," *National Crosstalk,* Winter 2005, http://www.highereducation.org/crosstalk/ct0105/news0105-virginia.shtml (accessed February 11, 2005).

2. Carol Tomlinson-Keasey, "Becoming Digital: The Challenge of Weaving Technology throughout Higher Education," in *The Future of the City of Intellect: The Changing American University,* ed. Steven G. Brint (Palo Alto, CA: Stanford University Press, 2002), 138.

3. Ibid., 147.

4. Mills, "Math Emporium."

5. Ibid.

6. Ibid.

7. Ibid.

8. "Math Emporium Wins Xcaliber Award for Courseware Technology Development," press

release, Blacksburg, Virginia, 1 April 1999, http://www.vtnews.vt.archives/1999/Mar/Math/html (accessed January 27, 2005).

9. James J. Duderstadt, *A University for the 21st Century* (Ann Arbor, MI: University of Michigan Press, 2000), 237.

10. John Seely Brown and Paul Duguid, *The Social Life of Information* (Boston: Harvard Business School Press, 2000), 227.

11. Steven G. Brint, ed., *The Future of the City of Intellect: The Changing American University* (Palo Alto, CA: Stanford University Press, 2002), xiii.

12. Ibid., xiv.

13. Brown and Duguid, *Social Life,* 121.

14. Ibid., 120.

15. Frank H. T. Rhodes, *The Creation of the Future: The Role of the American University* (Ithaca, NY: Cornell University Press, 2001), 234.

16. Brown and Duguid, *Social Life,* 226.

17. Associated Press, My Way, 27 July 2005, http://www.apnews.myway.com (accessed August 10, 2005). A survey by the Pew Internet and American Life Project found that nearly 90 percent of American youngsters between the ages of 12 and 17 had online access in 2005, compared to 66 percent of adults.

18. Barry Munitz, "Changing Landscape: From Cottage Monopoly to Competitive Industry," *Educause Review* 35, no. 1 (January–February 2000): 8.

19. David Ward, "Catching the Waves of Change in American Higher Education," *Educause Review* 35, no. 1 (January–February 2000): 26.

20. Thomas Friedman, *The World Is Flat: A Brief History of the Twenty-first Century* (New York: Farrar, Straus & Giroux, 2005), 56. Friedman cites British computer scientist Tim Berners-Lee as the creator of the first Web site.

21. John Schwartz, "A Different Course," *New York Times* Education Life supplement, 25 April 2004, 28.

22. Sloan Consortium, *Entering the Mainstream: The Quality and Extent of Online Education in the United States, 2003 and 2004* (November 2004): 5. Available at http://www.sloan-c.org/resources/entering_maintstream.pdf.

23. "A Survey Documents Growth in Distance Education in the 1990s," *Chronicle of Higher Education* 49, no. 48 (8 August 2003).

24. Society for College and University Planning, *Trends in Higher Education* (March 2005): 9. Available at www.scup.org/knowledge/ttw.html.

25. Tomlinson-Keasey, "Becoming Digital," 145.

26. David Collins, "New Business Models for Higher Education," in *The Future of the City of Intellect: The Changing American University,* ed. Steven G. Brint (Palo Alto, CA: Stanford University Press, 2002), 181.

27. Rhonda Epper and Myk Garn, "Virtual Universities: Real Possibilities," *Educause Review* 39, no. 2 (March–April 2004): 1.

28. Ibid., 6, 7.

29. Vincent Kiernan, "The Next Information Superhighway," *Chronicle of Higher Education* 50, no. 44 (9 July 2004).

30. Schwartz, "Different Course."

31. Justin Pope, "University of Phoenix to Accept Young Students," 2 August 2004, http://www.Boston.com (accessed August 9, 2004).

32. Steve Wheeler, "The Traditional University Is Dead: Long Live the Distributed University" (keynote speech delivered to the European Universities Continuing Education Committee at the University of Bergen, Norway, 4–7 May 2000), http://www.fae.plym.ac.uk/tele/longlive.html (accessed October 18, 2004).

33. Andrew Abbott, "The Disciplines and the Future," in *The Future of the City of Intellect: The Changing American University,* ed. Steven G. Brint (Palo Alto, CA: Stanford University Press, 2002), 225.

34. Matthew Battle, "Library of Babel," *Boston Globe,* 26 December 2004, D4.

35. Don Tapscott, *Growing Up Digital: The Rise of the Net Generation* (New York: McGraw-Hill, 1997). This citation refers to one of the main themes of Tapscott's book.

36. Richard Lanham, "The Audit of Virtuality," in *The Future of the City of Intellect: The Changing American University,* ed. Steven

G. Brint (Palo Alto, CA: Stanford University Press, 2002), 178.

37. Ibid., 179.

38. William Mitchell, *e-topia* (Cambridge, MA: MIT Press, 1999), 142.

39. William Mitchell, conversation with the author, 2 August 2004.

40. Mitchell, *e-topia*, 92.

41. National Academy of Sciences, *Preparing for the Revolution: Information Technology and the Future of the Research University*, quoted in Vincent Kiernan, "Technology Will Reshape Research Universities Dramatically, Science-Academy Report Predicts," *Chronicle of Higher Education* 48, no. 11 (8 November 2002).

42. William Mitchell, conversation with the author, 2 August 2004.

43. Mitchell, *e-topia*, 91.

44. Munitz, "Changing Landscape," 18.

four

1. Lewis & Clark College Web site, http://www.lclark.edu/ (accessed January 2005).

2. The statistical data and descriptive information were drawn from a program statement on Lewis & Clark's international studies program, provided to the author by the college in November 2004.

3. Ibid.

4. Lester Thurow, *Fortune Favors the Bold: What We Must Do to Build a New and Lasting Global Prosperity* (New York: HarperBusiness, 2003), 6.

5. Thomas Friedman, *The World Is Flat: A Brief History of the Twenty-first Century* (New York: Farrar, Straus & Giroux, 2005), 277.

6. David Pearce Snyder, "Five Meta-Trends Changing the World," *The Futurist* 38, no. 4 (July–August 2004), 27.

7. Thurow, *Fortune Favors the Bold*, 74.

8. Clark Kerr, *The Uses of the University* (Cambridge, MA: Harvard University Press, 2003), 115.

9. Friedman, *World Is Flat*, 2.

10. Philip Altbach, "Higher Education Crosses Borders," *Change* 36, no. 2 (March–April 2004), 18–24

11. Philip Altbach, "Globalization and the University: Myths and Realities in an Unequal World," *Tertiary Education and Management*, no. 1 (2004), Boston College Center for International Higher Education, http://www.highered@bc.edu (accessed January 26, 2005).

12. Marijk van der Wende, "The Role of U.S. Higher Education in the Global E-Learning Market" (working paper, Center for Studies in Higher Education, University of California, Berkeley, January 2002).

13. Jennifer Jacobson, "U.S. Foreign Enrollments Stagnate," *Chronicle of Higher Education* 50, no. 11 (7 November 2003): A44.

14. Ibid.

15. Altbach, "Globalization and the University," 9.

16. Michael Dobbs, "Foreign Enrollment Levels Off at U.S. Schools," *Washington Post*, 3 November 2003, A02, http://www.washingtonpost.com/wp-dyn/articles/A54978–2003Nov2.html (accessed November 7, 2003).

17. Paul Desruisseaux, "Foreign Students Continue to Flock to the U.S.," *Chronicle of Higher Education* 46, no. 16 (10 December 1999): A58.

18. Robert M. O'Neil, "Trouble at the Border: How U.S. Anti-terrorism Efforts Affect Foreign Students and Visiting Scholars," *National Crosstalk*, Fall 2004, http://www.highereducation.org/crosstalk/ct0404/voices0404-oneil.shtml (accessed November 23, 2004).

19. Institute of International Education, "Study Abroad Surging among Americans," *Open Doors 2004: American Students Studying Abroad*, 15 November 2004, http://www.opendoors.iienetwork.org/?p50138 (accessed February 2, 2005).

20. Altbach, "Globalization and the University," 8.

21. Ibid.

22. Stacy A. Teicher, "Foreign Enrollment Drops at U.S. Colleges," *Christian Science Monitor* (16 November 2004), http://www.csmonitor.com/204/1116/p11s02-legn.htm (accessed November 23, 2004).

23. O'Neil, "Trouble at the Border."

24. Ibid.

25. Ted C. Fishman, "The Chinese Century," *New York Times Magazine*, 4 July 2004.

26. Robert Weisman, "U.S. Could See Its Advantage in Technology Slip Away," *Boston Globe,* 1 February 2005, E3.

27. John Cassidy, "Winners and Losers," *New Yorker,* 2 August 2004, 30.

28. Robert Gavin, "U.S. Could Lose High Tech Edge, Study Says," *Boston Globe,* 8 August 2005.

29. Futures Project: Policy for Higher Education in a Changing World, *The Universal Impact of Competition and Globalization in Higher Education* (Providence, RI: Brown University, October 2000), 4.

30. Ibid.

31. Ibid.

32. Ibid.

33. Van der Wende, "Role of U.S. Higher Education."

34. Ibid., Citing J. S. Daniel (1996) *Mega Universities and Knowledge Media: Technology Strategies for Higher Education.* London: Kogan Page.

35. Michael Elliott, "From Davos to New York," *Time,* 4 February 2002, 72.

36. Saskid Sasser, "Globalization and the Formation of Claims," *Giving Ground: The Politics of Propinquity,* ed. Joan Copjec and Michael Sorkin (London: Verso, 1999), 102.

37. Ibid.

38. James Russell, "Do Skyscrapers Still Make Sense?" *Architectural Record Innovation* (November 2004): 31.

39. William J. Mitchell, "Where I'm @," *APA Journal* 67, no. 2 (Spring 2001): 145.

40. Ibid.

41. Richard P. Florida, *The Rise of the Creative Class: And How It's Transforming Work, Leisure, Community and Everyday Life* (New York: Basic Books, 2003), 222.

42. Ibid., 224.

43. Ibid., 227.

44. William Leach, *Country of Exiles: The Destruction of Place in American Life* (New York: Pantheon, 1999), 25–26.

45. Ibid., 134.

46. Ibid., 148.

47. Fred M. Hayward and Laura M. Siaya, *Public Experience, Attitudes and Knowledge: A Report on Two National Surveys about International Education* (Washington, DC: American Council on Education, 2001).

48. J. Michael Adams and Michael B. Sperling, "Ubiquitous Distributed Learning and Global Citizenship," *The Presidency* (Winter 2003): 31.

49. Fairleigh Dickinson University Web site, http://view.fdu.edu/default.aspx?id = 2229; also http://view.fdu.edu/default.aspx?id = 270 (accessed July 8, 2005).

50. Stephen S. Cohen and J. Bradford DeLong, "Shaken and Stirred," *Atlantic Monthly,* annual State of the Union issue, January–February 2005, 114.

51. Ibid., 116.

five

1. Richard Freeland, *Academia's Golden Age: Universities in Massachusetts, 1945–1970* (New York: Oxford University Press, 1992), 260.

2. Ibid., 265.

3. Audrey Williams June, "No Longer a Safety School," *Chronicle of Higher Education* 50, no. 33 (23 April 2004): A30.

4. Northeastern University President Richard Freeland and Vice President Larry Mucciolo, conversation with the author, 21 March 2005.

5. June, "No Longer a Safety School," A31.

6. Freeland and Mucciolo.

7. Ibid.

8. Jenna Russell, "Northeastern Allots $75 Million to Recruit 100 Professors," *Boston Globe,* 11 February 2004, A16.

9. Freeland and Mucciolo.

10. U.S. Census Bureau, "Population Projections: Final "Middle Series" Projections Consistent with the 1990 Census" (released 13 January 2000), http://www.census.gov/acsd/www/subjects.html (accessed April 2005).

11. Gordon K. Davies, "The Business We're In: When Standard Formulas Fail, the Work of Policymakers Has Got to Change," *National Crosstalk,* Winter 2004, http://www.highereducation.org/crosstalk (accessed May 20, 2004).

12. Marshall Poe, "The Other Gender Gap," *Atlantic Monthly,* January–February 2004, 137.

13. Barbara Jacoby, "What Colleges Should Do for Commuters," *Planning for Higher Education* 20, no. 3 (Spring 1992): 29.

14. Sara Hebel, "No Room in the Class," *Chronicle of Higher Education* 50, no. 43 (2 July 2004): A19.

15. Ibid.

16. Jim Taylor, "Manifest Destiny 3.0," *American Demographics* 26, no. 1 (September 2004): 29.

17. U.S. Census Bureau, Population Division, "Interim State Population Projections, 2005," http://www/census.gov (accessed April 21, 2005).

18. U.S. Department of Education, National Center for Educational Statistics, "Projections of Education Statistics to 2013," http://nces.ed.gov/programs/projections/ch3.asp (accessed June 27, 2005).

19. The term *millennial generation* was coined by Neil Howe and William Strauss in a series of books on generational cycles in America, with the *millennials* being the main topic of their 2000 book, *Millennials Rising* (New York: Vintage). Howe and Strauss see the generation as possessing a civic spirit similar to that of the GI generation.

20. The profile for the millennial generation is drawn from data and observations made in source material supporting a virtual seminar conducted by the Society for College and University Planning on 16 September 2003, entitled "How Generations X and Y (Millennials) Will Reshape Higher Education." Principal supporting articles included work by Diana Oblinger, "Boomers, Gen-Xers and Millennials: Understanding the New Students," *Educause Review* 38, no. 4 (July–August 2003): 37–47; a summary of the Higher Education Leaders Symposium: "The Next-Generation Student," Redmond, Washington, 17–18 June 2003; and Girija Kaimal, "Gen-X Meets Gen-Y," Foresight and Governance Project, Woodrow Wilson International Center for Scholars, Publication 2003–2. Material for audio seminar provided by the Society for College and University Planning, Ann Arbor, Michigan.

21. U.S. Census Bureau, "School Enrollment—Social and Economic Characteristics of Students: October 2003" (issued May 2005), http://www.census.gov/prod/2005pubs/p20-ss4.pdf (accessed June 2005).

22. James J. Duderstadt, "Navigating the American University through the Strong Seas of a Changing World" (paper presented at the National Conference of the Society for College and University Planning, Miami, Florida, 22 June 2003, 4).

23. Thomas Klein, Patsy Scott, and Joseph Clark, "A Fresh Look at Market Segments in Higher Education," *Planning for Higher Education* 30, no. 1 (Fall 2001): 5–19.

24. U. S. Census Bureau, "Current Population Survey, Annual Social and Economic Supplement Table H-3, Historical Income Tables—Household," 2005 http://www.census.gov/pubinfo.www.hotlinks.html (accessed September 27, 2005).

25. Anthony Carnevale, quoted in Blenda Wilson, "The Economic Impact of Educational Opportunity," *Connection: The Journal of the New England Board of Higher Education* 19, no. 4 (Winter 2005): 21.

26. Peter Smith, *The Quiet Crisis: How Higher Education Is Foiling America* (Bolton, VT: Anker Publishing, 2004). Quoted in Wilson, "The Economic Impact," 21.

27. Richard D. Kahlenberg, "Toward Affirmative Action for Economic Diversity," *Chronicle of Higher Education* 50, no. 28 (19 March 2004): B12.

28. Ibid.

29. Paul Simon, "A GI Bill for Today," *Chronicle of Higher Education* 50, no. 10 (31 October 2003): B16.

30. Kahlenberg, "Toward Affirmative Action," B11.

31. David P. Snyder, "Five Meta-Trends Changing the World," *Futurist,* July–August 2004, 27.

32. American Association of Community Colleges, "2004 Fast Facts," http://www.aacc.nche.edu/Content/NavigationMenu/AboutCommunityColleges/Fast_Facts (accessed September 13, 2004).

33. Ibid.

34. Ibid., summarizing from the association's "National Profile of Community Colleges Trends and Statistics, 2000."

35. Jon Travis, "The Approaching Metamorphosis of Community Colleges," *Planning for Higher Education* 25, no. 2 (Winter 1996–97): 24.

36. George R. Boggs, "Current Issues in Community Colleges," *Facilities Management* 19, no. 4 (July–August 2003), http://www.appa.org/FacilitiesManager/articleDetail.cfm?ItemNumber+1038 (accessed August 25, 2003).

37. Travis, "Approaching Metamorphosis of Community Colleges," 24.

38. George Boggs, telephone conversation with the author, 6 May 2005.

39. James J. O'Donnell, "To Youth Camp, a Long Farewell," *Educause Review* 36, no. 6 (November–December 2001): 15.

40. Ibid., 18.

41. Barbara Jacoby, "What Colleges Should Do for Commuters," 29.

42. Ibid., 20.

43. Ibid., 31.

44. Travis, "Approaching Metamorphosis of Community Colleges," 26.

six

1. Joseph Grunewald, president of Clarion University, quoted in Clare Heidler, director of Facilities Planning at Clarion University, e-mail message to the author, 26 September 2005.

2. Clara M. Lovett, "Prestige, Power, and Wealth," *Educause Review* 39, no. 6 (November–December 2004): 1.

3. Ibid., 2.

4. Robert Zemsky, "Have We Lost the 'Public' in Higher Education?" *Chronicle of Higher Education* 49, no. 38 (30 May 2003): B8.

5. Ibid.

6. National Education Association, "Average Yearly Tuition for U.S. Colleges and Universities," http://www.nea.org/neatoday/osos/images/governance02.jpg (accessed 27 June 2005).

7. National Association of Student Aid Administrators, "Overall Student Debt Has Increased Since '92, But Certain Groups Borrowed More," http://www.nasfaa.org/publications/2005/rnaceloanreport070105.html (accessed 15 August 2005).

8. U.S. Census Bureau, "Earnings by Education Level, March 2003," http://www.census.gov/acsd/wwv/subjects.html (accessed 12 April 2005).

9. Lara Couttarier, James Scurry, and Frank Newman, "Correcting Course: How We Can Restore the Ideals of Public Higher Education in a Market-driven Era," Futures Project: Policy for Higher Education in a Changing World (Providence, R.I.: Brown University Futures Project, February 2005), 1.

10. Ibid.

11. Michael Middaugh, "Understanding Education Costs," *Planning for Higher Education* 33, no. 3 (March–May 2005): 6–7.

12. Ibid., 8.

13. U.S. Department of Education, National Center for Education Statistics, http://nces.ed.gov/pubs2000/20000068.pdf (accessed June 2005).

14. "Special Report: Outlook 2005, A Year of Recovery," *Chronicle of Higher Education* 52, no. 18 (7 January 2005): A8–A14.

15. Ibid.

16. Martin van der Werf, "Colleges Turn to Debt to Finance Their Ambitions," *Chronicle of Higher Education* 45, no. 28 (19 March 1999): A38.

17. Larry R. Faulkner, "Towards Continuous Improvement: Rebuilding the Compact between Higher Education, the Public and Elected Officials," *National Crosstalk,* Spring 2005, http://www.highereducation.org/crosstalk (accessed 16 June 2005).

18. Ibid.

19. Paul Abramson, "2005 College Construction Report," *College Planning and Management* 8, no. 3 (February 2005): C3.

20. U.S. Department of Education, National Center for Education Statistics, NCES 98–015, "Digest of Education Statistics 1997, Table 171. Historical Summary of Faculty, Students, Degrees, and Finances in Institutions of Higher Education: 1869–70 to 1994–95," Washington, D.C., 1998.

21. Karen M. Kroll, "Taking the Long View on Facilities," 1996, http://www.facilitiesnet.com (accessed 8 March 2001).

22. Sean Rush and Sandra Johnson, *The Decaying American Campus: A Ticking Time Bomb* (Alexandria, Va.: Association of Physical Plant Administrators of Universities and Colleges, 1989), 12.

23. William Mitchell, conversation with the author, 2 August 2004.

24. Robert Campbell, "Dizzying Heights," *Boston Globe,* 25 April 2004.

25. David Ward, "Catching the Waves of Change in American Higher Education," *Educause Review* 35, no. 1 (January–February 2000): 30.

26. Marcia Baxter Magolda and Patrick Teerenzin, in consultation with Pat Hutchings, "Learning and Teaching in the Twenty-first Century: Trends and Implications for Practice," in *ACPA—Higher Education Trends for the Next Century,* http://www.acpa.nche.edu (accessed 26 March 2002).

27. Ibid.

## seven

1. Martin van der Werf, "Urban Universities Try New Ways to Reach Out to Their Communities," *Chronicle of Higher Education* 45, no. 34 (30 April 1999): A38.

2. Audrey Williams June, "As It Seeks More Room, Columbia Treads Carefully," *Chronicle of Higher Education* 51, no. 6 (1 October 2004): A2a.

3. Daniel R. Kenney, Ricardo Dumont, and Ginger Kenney, *Mission and Place: Strengthening Learning and Community through Campus Design* (Westport, CT: Praeger, 2005), 169.

4. David Maurrasse, *Beyond the Campus: How Colleges and Universities Form Partnerships*

*with Their Communities* (New York: Routledge, 2001), 23–25.

5. Ibid., 24.

6. Richard Levin, "The University as Urban Citizen," *Boston Globe,* 13 June 1997.

7. Kathy Witowski, "Ambitious Agenda: Michael Crow Has Brought an Entrepreneurial Spirit to Arizona State University," *National Crosstalk,* Winter 2004, http://www.highereducation.org/crosstalk/ct0104/news0104-ambitious.shtml (accessed May 20, 2004).

8. Robert Campbell, "Universities Are the New City Planners," *Boston Globe,* 20 March 2005.

9. Ira Harkavy and John Puckett, "Universities and the Inner Cities," *Planning for Higher Education* 20, no. 4 (Summer 1992): 29.

10. Ibid.

11. James J. Duderstadt, *A University for the 21st Century* (Ann Arbor, MI: University of Michigan Press, 2000), 132.

12. Ibid., 135.

13. Campus Compact, "Record Numbers of Colleges and Universities Are Making Community Service a Top Priority," http://www.compact.org/newscc/highlights.html (accessed August 15, 2005).

14. Judith Rodin, "Common Cause: Investing in the Community," *The Presidency* 4, no. 2 (Spring 2001): 28–35.

15. Ibid.

16. Ibid., 34.

17. Akiko Busch, "A Good Neighbor by Design," *Metropolis,* February 2003, 121.

18. Ibid.

19. Case example adapted from synopsis prepared 15 June 2004 for the author by Judith Steinkamp, then director of Space Management at the University of Massachusetts–Amherst.

20. Ibid.

21. Ibid.

22. John Sexton, "The Common Enterprise University," (keynote address, North Atlantic Regional Conference of the Society for College and University Planning, New York University, New York, 17 March 2005).

23. Charles Schroeder, "Collaboration and Partnerships," in *ACPA—Higher Education*

*Trends for the Next Century,* www.acpa.
nche.edu/ (accessed March 26, 2002).

**e i g h t**

1. Robert Wolfe, general manager of Princeton
   Forrestal Center, telephone conversation
   with the author, 19 August 2005.
2. Forest City Web site, http://www.
   forestcity.net/projects_detail_mixed.asp?id
   = 380 (accessed November 4, 2004).
3. William Leach, *Country of Exiles: The
   Destruction of Place in American Life* (New
   York: Pantheon, 1999), 129–30.
4. Derek Bok, *Universities in the Marketplace:
   The Commercialization of Higher Education*
   (Princeton, NJ: Princeton University Press,
   2004), 10.
5. Ibid., 12.
6. Lara Couttarier, James Scurry, and Frank
   Newman, "Correcting Course: How We Can
   Restore the Ideals of Public Higher Education
   in a Market-driven Era," Futures Project:
   Policy for Higher Education in a Changing
   World (Providence, R.I.: Brown University
   Research Project, February 2005), 4–5.
7. Association of University Research Parks,
   *Research Park Statistics,* January 2003,
   http://www.aurp.net/about/statistics (accessed August 28, 2005).
8. Carey Goldberg, "Across the U.S.,
   Universities Are Fueling High-tech Booms,"
   *New York Times,* 8 October 1999, A20.
9. Claudia Deutsch, "Lehigh Phoenix Rises
   from Big Steel's Ashes," *New York Times,* 7
   October 1999, 1.
10. George H. Copa and William Ammentorp,
    "Site Background," *Benchmarking New
    Designs for the Two-year Institution of
    Higher Education,* MDS-1108 (research
    paper for the National Center for Research
    in Vocational Education, January 1998,
    47), http://www.vocserve.berkeley.edu/
    Summaries/1108sum.html (accessed
    November 30, 2004).
11. Charles Tseckares and Christopher Hill,
    "When Gown Builds Town," *College
    Planning and Management* 6, no. 11
    (November 2003): 16–17.
12. Elizabeth Crane, "Revitalizing the Campus
    through Retail," *University Business,* http://
    www.universitybusiness.com/pageprint.
    cfm?p = 657 (accessed November 23, 2004).

**P a r t   T h r e e**

**n i n e**

1. Barbara Donerly, telephone conversation
   with the author, 3 May 2005.
2. Ibid.
3. Anthony Cortese, "Making Sustainability
   'Second Nature' in the Education of Design
   and Planning Professionals" (Second Nature:
   Education for Sustainability working paper,
   Boston, Massachusetts), http://www.sec-
   ondnature.org (accessed May 20, 2005).
4. Anthony Cortese, "Why Sustainability and
   Why Now?" (presentation at Green Day
   event, Sasaki Associates, Inc., Watertown,
   Massachusetts, 20 May 2005).
5. Statement of purpose in the regular issues
   of the association's journal, *The Declaration.*
   The association is a program of the Center
   for Respect of Life and the Environment in
   Washington, D.C.
6. I first presented the ideas in this book in a
   paper at the 1997 conference at Ball State,
   postulating that the greening of the campus
   was a national social imperative.
7. Malcolm Scully, "Berea College's 'Ecological
   About-Face,'" *Chronicle of Higher Education*
   51, no. 23 (11 February 2005): B11.
8. William Moomaw, "Aligning Values for
   Effective Sustainability Planning," *Planning
   for Higher Education* 31, no. 3 (March–May
   2003): 163.
9. Arthur C. Nielson, "Toward a New
   Metropolis: The Opportunity to Rebuild
   America" (discussion paper, Brookings
   Institution Metropolitan Policy Program,
   Washington, D.C., December 2004,
   Executive Summary, v).
10. Paul Hawken, Amory Lovins, and L. Hunter
    Lovins, *Natural Capitalism* (Boston: Little,
    Brown/Back Bay Press, 2000), 85.
11. William D. Browning, "Successful
    Strategies for Planning a Green Building,"

*Planning for Higher Education* 31, no. 3 (March–May 2003): 116.

12. Nielson, "Toward a New Metropolis."

13. James Howard Kuntsler, *The Geography of Nowhere: The Rise and Decline of America's Man-made Landscape* (New York: Simon & Schuster, 1993), 10.

14. Michael Benedikt, "Reality and Authenticity in the Experience Economy," *Architectural Record* (November 2001): 84–86.

15. James S. Russell, "Where Are We Now? Architecture's Place in an Era of Evolving Values," *Architectural Record* (March 2003): 91.

16. Ibid., 92.

17. David Schuyler, "Frederick Law Olmsted and the Origins of Modern Campus Design," *Planning for Higher Education* 25, no. 2 (Winter 1996–97): 10.

18. Wendell Berry, *The Unsettling of America: Culture and Agriculture* (San Francisco: Sierra Club Books, 1986), 22.

19. Frank H. T. Rhodes, *The Creation of the Future: The Role of the American University* (Ithaca, NY: Cornell University Press, 2001), 45.

20. William Shutkin, *The Land That Could Be* (Cambridge, Mass.: The MIT Press, 2000), 30.

21. Ray Oldenburg, "Making College a Great Place to Talk," *Planning for Higher Education* 20, no. 4 (Summer 1992): 59–63.

22. M. Perry Chapman, "The Campus at the Millennium: A Plea for Community and Place," *Planning for Higher Education* 27, no. 4 (Summer 1999): 31.

23. Ibid.

## Epilogue

1. Paul V. Turner, *Campus: An American Planning Tradition* (Cambridge, MA: Architectural History Foundation/MIT Press, 1987), 142.

2. Peter Drucker, with Joseph Maciariello, *The Daily Drucker* (New York: HarperCollins, 2004), entry for January 2, 2004.

3. Robert L. Heilbroner, *Visions of the Future: The Distant Past, Yesterday, Today and Tomorrow* (New York: Oxford University Press, 1995), 95.

4. Thomas Friedman, *The World Is Flat: A Brief History of the Twenty-first Century* (New York: Farrar, Straus & Giroux, 2005). Friedman's thesis is that technology, globalization, and the entry of countries such as China and India into the technology-driven free market system have leveled the economic playing field in which the United States must compete. He argues that education and innovation will be America's most important natural resource in the flat world.

5. Columbia College of Missouri Web site, http://www.ccis.edu (accessed September 9, 2005).

6. Friedman, *World Is Flat,* 447.

# Index

219

Rhode Island, Providence, 148
Rhode Island School of Design, 148–49
Rhodes, Frank, 193
Rice University, 49, 131
Richardson, Henry Hobson, 21
Rochester Institute of Technology, 46
Rockefeller, John D., 161
Rockefeller Center (NY), 161
Rodin, Judith, 147–48
Rogers, James Gamble, 22
Roosevelt, Franklin, 33
Roosevelt University, 150
Rostbelt, 101, 108
Rudolph, Paul, 41
Rural Italian style (also Tuscan vernacular), 22

Saarinen, Eero, 41
Sansom Commons (University of Pennsylvania), 170
Sasser, Saskid, 88
Schachner, Richard, 3
Schuyler, David, 15, 16, 191
Sensbach, Werner, 49, 50
Sert, Josep Luis, 41
Sestric, Michael, 79
Sexton, John, 152
Shinn, Larry, 185
Shutkin, William, 194
Skidmore, Owings and Merrill, 44, 45
Sloan Consortium, 66
Smith, Peter, 104
Snyder, David, 106
Society for College and University Planning, 184
South, 24, 101, 146
South Carolina, Columbia, 9
Southeast Asia, 86
Southern Africa, 86
South Korea, 80
Soviet Union (former), 32, 80
Sperling, Michael, 91
Sputnik (1957), 31, 32, 80
Stanford, Leland, 21
Stanford Research Park (originally Stanford Industrial Park), 161–62, 168
Stanford University, 21, 22, 161, 163
Stata Center, MIT, 129
Stein, Gertrude, 65
Stern, Robert, 49
Stone, Edward Durrell, 41
Student costs, 120

"Sublime nature," 12
Sunbelt, 101, 108, 145
Sustainability, the sustainable campus, 177, 183–88, 196

Tapscott, Don, 96
Tennessee, Nashville, 170
Texas, 101
Thurow, Lester, 80, 81
Tomlinson-Keasey, Carol, 59
Tougaloo College, 44
Traditional and nontraditional students, 99–100, 102–3
Trinity College, 144, 149, 150, 152
Turner, Jonathan Baldwin, 13
Turner, Paul Venable, 8, 10, 12, 17, 22, 24, 42, 44

Union College, 10, 11, 17, 131
University Center (Columbia College, DePaul University, Roosevelt University), 150–51
University of Alabama–Birmingham, 145
University of Berlin, 11
University of California–Berkeley, 15, 19, 20, 27–31, 182
University of California–Merced, 185
University of California–Monterey Bay, 104
University of California–Santa Cruz, 44, 45
University of California system growth after World War II, 34
University of Chicago, 23, 68, 88, 140
University of Cincinnati, 169
University of Colorado–Boulder, 122
University of Illinois–Chicago, 45, 140, 171
University of Illinois–Urbana-Champaign, 20
University of Maine (also Maine College of Agriculture and Mechanic Arts), 15
University of Maryland, 110
University of Massachusetts (also Massachusetts Agricultural College), 14, 15, 199
University of Massachusetts–Boston, 45, 46
University of Michigan, 11, 105
University of Minnesota–Twin Cities, 20
University of Missouri–Columbia, 34, 204
University of Montana–Missoula, 204
University of North Carolina–Chapel Hill, 9, 162
University of North Texas at Dallas, 101
University of Pennsylvania, 10, 11, 17, 119, 145, 147–48, 149–50, 170
University of Phoenix, 67, 86

## About the Author

M. PERRY CHAPMAN is a professional planner and principal at Sasaki Associates, Inc., where he specializes in college campus design. He also directed the firm's environmental plans for the 1980 Lake Placid Winter Olympics and the 1984 Los Angeles Olympics. He has lectured at several colleges, presented numerous conference papers, and has written articles on campus design for journals and publications such as *Architecture* and the *Architectural Record Review*. He was a finalist in the 1982 Mitchell Prize international competition for essays on the sustainable society and a 1984 Practitioner Fellow at the Lincoln Institute of Land Policy in Cambridge, MA.

*(continued from front flap)*

bridge between institutional traditions and the societal changes that higher education institutions must address in the new century if they are to maintain their currency as important American places. The campus setting binds the memories of generations, giving it the perceived attribute of timelessness. *American Places* is a plea: that 21$^{st}$-century American campuses will collectively adopt an ethic of place supported by principles of sustainability, authenticity, and community.

---

**M. PERRY CHAPMAN** is a professional planner and principal at Sasaki Associates, Inc., where he specializes in college campus design. He directed the firm's environmental plans for the 1980 Lake Placid Winter Olympics and the 1984 Los Angeles Olympics, and has written articles on campus design for journals and publications such as *Architecture* and the *Architectural Record Review*.